STUDY GUIDE
Tracy Tuten
Longwood University

PRINCIPLES OF MARKETING
13th edition

Philip Kotler
Gary Armstrong

Prentice Hall

New York Boston San Francisco
London Toronto Sydney Tokyo Singapore Madrid
Mexico City Munich Paris Cape Town Hong Kong Montreal

Editorial Director: Sally Yagan
AVP/Executive Editor: Melissa Sabella
Editorial Project Manager: Melissa Pellerano
Production Editor: Kerri Tomasso
Operations Specialist: Arnold Vila

Pearson Prentice Hall™ is a trademark of Pearson Education, Inc.
Pearson® is a registered trademark of Pearson plc
Prentice Hall® is a registered trademark of Pearson Education, Inc.

Pearson Education Ltd., London
Pearson Education Singapore, Pte. Ltd
Pearson Education, Canada, Inc.
Pearson Education–Japan
Pearson Education Australia PTY, Limited

Pearson Education North Asia, Ltd., Hong Kong
Pearson Educación de Mexico, S.A. de C.V.
Pearson Education Malaysia, Pte. Ltd
Pearson Education Upper Saddle River, New Jersey

Prentice Hall
is an imprint of

www.pearsonhighered.com

10 9 8 7 6 5 4 3 2 1

ISBN-13: 978-0-13-608075-6
ISBN-10: 0-13-608075-8

CONTENTS

Preface

Congratulations! You have chosen to experience a journey of creativity critical thinking, strategic challenges, and most importantly, fun! This journey is called the world of marketing and the discipline of marketing is an amazing combination of the best of the business disciplines, a melting pot of finance, advertising, business administration, management, leadership, and even a dash of psychology.

This Study Guide has been specifically designed for students using Kotler/Armstrong's *Principles of Marketing*, 13th edition text. Covering all twenty chapters, this Study Guide provides you with an in-depth review of chapter material and the ability to apply the concepts you are learning to the "real world." Use this Study Guide as a valuable resource to support your marketing learning experience. The features of the Guide are described below.

LEARNING OBJECTIVES

Each chapter of the Study Guide contains a list of important learning objectives. Starting off each chapter, these objectives introduce the material to you and provide a checklist of all concepts that will be covered. The fundamental understanding of marketing begins with the real comprehension of terms, and there are many of them.

CHAPTER OVERVIEW

The Chapter Overview summarizes the information contained in each chapter. It will reinforce the main concepts of the chapter and will be helpful when you review the material. It often helps to read the Chapter Overview first.

CHAPTER OUTLINE

This is a thorough outline of the text material, using actual phrases and definitions from the textbook. You may find it helpful to peruse this outline prior to class discussions in order to strengthen your familiarity with the material. After reading the textbook chapter, you may find it useful to again refer to this outline, reviewing important concepts and reflecting on the material. Use a highlighter to reinforce the key concepts and terms.

STUDENT EXERCISES

The nature of marketing is very similar to the role of film director. The marketplace is a fluid stage and you, the marking manager, must respond, choreograph and give stage directions for a successful "show." Each exercise is based on a key term from the chapter and a specific scenario, industry trend or competitive fact that you, as a marketing manager, would react to as the situation arises. Suggested answers can be found at the end of the Study Guide.

MARKETING ADVENTURE EXERCISES

This section of the Study Guide provides a number of specific challenges in the form of exercises to use in conjunction with a bank of advertisements that are available at www.prenhall.com/adventure. For all of the exercises, the category is provided and specific ads noted, around which to develop your response. Suggested answers can be found at the end of the Study Guide.

SUGGESTED ANSWERS

This section offers suggested answers to the STUDENT EXERCISES and MARKETING ADVENTURE EXERCISES offered in each chapter of the Study Guide.

Chapter 1
Marketing: Creating and Capturing Customer Value

Learning Objectives

1. Define marketing and outline the steps in the marketing process.
2. Explain the importance of understanding customers and the marketplace, and identify the five core marketplace concepts.
3. Identify the key elements of a customer-drive marketing strategy and discuss the marketing management orientations that guide marketing strategy.
4. Discuss customer relationship management, and identify strategies for creating value *for* customers and capturing value *from* customers in return.
5. Describe the major trends and forces that are changing the marketing landscape in this age of relationships.

Chapter Overview

In this chapter, we introduce the basic concepts of marketing. It starts with the question, "What is marketing?" Simply put, marketing is managing profitable customer relationships. The aim of marketing is to create value *for* customers and to capture value *from* customers in return. Next is discussed the five steps in the marketing process – from understanding customer needs, to designing customer-driven marketing strategies and programs, to building customer relationships and capturing value for the firm. Finally is discussed the major trends and forces affecting marketing in this age of customer relationships.

Chapter Outline

1. INTRODUCTION

Procter & Gamble (the makers of Tide) is a great marketing organization. Tide controls 43 percent of the detergent market. To keep Tide competitive in the market it became important to determine how Tide "speaks" to customers. Tide was viewed as getting clothes clean, but also as being an "arrogant, masculine" brand. P&G was successful in repositioning the product as being more relevant in the day-to-day existence of its largely female clientele. Today's successful companies have one thing in common: they are strongly customer focused and heavily committed to marketing.

Opening Vignette Questions

1. Why was Tide perceived in consumers' minds as being an "arrogant, masculine" brand?
2. Who is the main market for Tide?

3. What did P&G do to effectively reposition this powerhouse brand?

2. WHAT IS MARKETING?

A simple definition of marketing is *managing profitable customer relationships*. Marketing must both attract new customers and grow the current customers. Every organization must perform marketing functions, not just for-profit companies. Non-profits (colleges, hospitals, churches, etc.) also must also perform marketing.

2.1 Marketing Defined

Most people think of marketing as selling and/or advertising—"telling and selling." Marketing must focus on satisfying customer needs.

We define marketing as the process by which companies create value for customers and build strong customer relationships in order to capture value from customers in return.

2.2 The Marketing Process

Figure 1-1 shows the five-step marketing process.
- Understand the marketplace and customer needs and wants.
- Design a customer-driven marketing strategy.
- Construct a marketing program that delivers superior value.
- Build profitable relationships and create customer delight.
- Capture value from customers to create profits and customer quality.

In the first four steps, companies work to understand consumers, create customer value, and build strong customer relationships.

In the final step, companies reap the rewards of creating superior customer value. By creating value *for* consumers, they in turn capture value *from* consumers in the form of sales, profits, and long-term customer equity.

3.0 UNDERSTANDING THE MARKETPLACE AND CUSTOMER NEEDS

Five core customer and marketplace concepts are critical: (1) needs, wants, and demands; (2) marketing offers (products, services, and experiences); (3) value and satisfaction; (4) exchanges and relationships; and (5) markets.
3.1 Customer Needs, Wants, and Demands

The most basic concept underlying marketing is that of human needs. Human needs are states of felt deprivation. They include *physical, social, and individuals* needs. These needs were not created by marketers; they are a basic part of the human makeup. Wants are the form human needs take as they are shaped by culture and individual personality. An American *needs* food but *wants* a Big Mac.

When backed by buying power, wants become demands. The best marketing companies go to great lengths to learn and understand their customers' needs, wants, and demands.

3.2 Market Offerings—Products, Services, and Experiences

Needs and wants are fulfilled through market offerings—some combination of products, services, information, or experiences offered to a market to satisfy a need or want.

Market offerings include *products* and *services*—activities or benefits offered for sale that are essentially intangible and do not result in the ownership of anything.

Marketing myopia occurs when a company becomes so taken with their own products that they lose sight of underlying customer needs.

3.3 Customer Value and Satisfaction

Customers form expectations about the value and satisfaction that various market offerings will deliver and buy accordingly.

Satisfied customers buy again and tell others about their good experiences.

Dissatisfied customers switch to competitors and disparage the product to others.

Customer value and customer satisfaction are key building blocks for developing and managing customer relationships.

3.4 Exchanges and Relationships

Exchange is the act of obtaining a desired object from someone by offering something in return.

Marketing consists of actions taken to build and maintain desirable exchange *relationships* with target audiences.

3.5 Markets

A market is the set of actual and potential buyers of a product. Marketing means managing markets to bring about profitable customer relationships. Figure 1.2 shows the main elements in a modern marketing system.

4.0 DESIGNING A CUSTOMER-DRIVEN MARKETING STRATEGY

Marketing management is defined as the art and science of choosing target markets and building profitable relationships with them.

The marketing manager must answer two important questions:
1. What customers will we serve (what's our target market)?
2. How can we serve these customers best (what's our value proposition)?

4.1 Selecting Customers to Serve

A company must decide *who* it will serve. It does this by dividing the market into segments of customers (*market segmentation*) and selecting which segments it will go after (*target marketing*). Marketing managers know they cannot serve all customers. By trying to do so, they end up not serving any well.

Demarketing is the act of purposefully reducing the number of customers or to shift their demand temporarily or permanently.

Marketing management is *customer management* and *demand management*.

4.2 Choosing a Value Proposition

A company's *value proposition* is the set of benefits or values it promises to deliver to consumers to satisfy their needs. Such value propositions *differentiate* one brand from another.

4.3 Marketing Management Orientations

Marketing management wants to design strategies that will build profitable relationships with target consumers. But what *philosophy* should guide these marketing strategies? There are five alternative concepts under which organizations design and carry out their marketing strategies:

1) The Production Concept

The production concept holds that consumers will favor products that are available and highly affordable. Management should focus on improving production and distribution efficiency.

2) The Product Concept

The product concept holds that consumers will favor products that offer the most in quality, performance, and innovative features. Under this concept, marketing strategy focuses on making continuous product improvements.

3) The Selling Concept

The selling concept holds that consumers will not buy enough of the firm's products unless it undertakes a large-scale selling and promotion effort. The concept is typically practiced with unsought goods—those that buyers do not normally think of buying, such as insurance or blood donations. These industries must be good at tracking down prospects and selling them on product benefits.

4) The Marketing Concept

The marketing concept holds that achieving organizational goals depends on knowing the needs and wants of target markets and delivering the desired satisfactions better than competitors do. Under the marketing concept, customer focus and value are the *paths* to sales and profits. It views marketing not as "hunting," but as "gardening." The job is not to find the right customers for your product but to find the right products for your customers. *Customer-driven* companies research current customers deeply to learn about their desires, gather new product and service ideas, and test proposed product improvements.

5) The Societal Marketing Concept

The societal marketing concept questions whether the pure marketing concept overlooks possible conflicts between consumer *short-run wants* and consumer *long-run welfare*. The societal marketing concept holds that marketing strategy should deliver value to customers in a way that maintains or improves both the consumer's *and the society's* well-being.

5.0 PREPARING AN INTEGRATED MARKETING PLAN AND PROGRAM

The company's marketing strategy outlines which customers the company will serve and how it will create value for these customers. Next, the marketer develops an integrated marketing program that will actually deliver the intended value to target customers. The marketing program consists of the firm's *marketing mix*, the set of marketing tools the firm uses to implement its marketing strategy.

The marketing mix tools are classified into the *four Ps* of marketing: product, price, place, and promotion. The firm blends all of these marketing mix tools into a comprehensive *integrated marketing program* that communicates and delivers the intended value to chosen customers.

6.0 BUILDING CUSTOMER RELATIONSHIPS

6.1 Customer Relationship Management

Customer relationship management is the most important concept of modern marketing. Customer relationship management is the overall process of building and maintaining profitable customer relationships by delivering superior customer value and satisfaction.

6.2 Relationship Building Blocks: Customer Value and Satisfaction

The key to building lasting customer relationships is to create superior customer value and satisfaction.

Customer Value. This is the customer's evaluation of the difference between all the benefits and all the costs of a market offering relative to those of competing offers. Customers often do not judge values and costs "accurately" or "objectively." Customers act on customer perceived value.

Customer Satisfaction. Customer satisfaction depends on the product's perceived performance relative to a buyer's expectations. If the product's performance falls short of expectations, the customer is dissatisfied. If performance matches expectations, the customer is satisfied. If performance exceeds expectations, the customer is highly satisfied or delighted.

Although the customer-centered firm seeks to deliver high customer satisfaction relative to competitors, it does not attempt to *maximize* customer satisfaction. A company can always increase customer satisfaction by lowering its price or increasing its services. But this may result in lower profits.

The purpose of marketing is to generate customer value profitably.

6.3 Customer Relationship Levels and Tools

Companies can build customer relationships at many levels. At one extreme, a company with many low-margin customers may seek to develop *basic relationships* with them. At the other extreme, in markets with few customers and high margins, sellers want to create *full partnerships* with customers. Many companies offer *frequency marketing programs* that reward customers who buy frequently or in large amounts.

6.4 The Changing Nature of Customer Relationships

Yesterday's big companies focused on mass marketing to all customers at arm's length. Today's companies are building deeper, more direct, and more lasting relationships with carefully selected customers.

6.5 Relating with More Carefully Selected Customers

Called *selective relationship management*, many companies now use customer profitability analysis to weed out losing customers and to target winning ones for pampering.

6.6 Relating More Deeply and Interactively

Today's marketers are incorporating interactive approaches that help build targeted, two-way customer relationships. Increasingly, marketers are using new communications approaches in building closer customer relationships. Consumers have more information about brands than ever before.

Companies can no longer rely on marketing by *intrusion*. Companies must practice marketing by *attraction*—creating market offerings and messages that involve consumers rather than interrupt them.

Consumer-generated marketing has become a significant marketing force.

6.7 Partner Relationship Management

    6.7.1 Partners Inside the Company

    Every employee must be customer focused. Today, firms are linking all departments in the cause of creating customer value. Rather than assigning only sales and marketing people to customers, they are forming cross-functional customer teams.

    6.7.2 Marketing Partners Outside the Firm

    Marketing channels consist of distributors, retailers, and others who connect the company to its buyers.

The *supply chain* describes a longer channel, stretching from raw materials to components to final products that are carried to final buyers.

Through *supply chain management*, many companies today are strengthening their connections with partners all along the supply chain.

7.0 CAPTURING VALUE FROM CUSTOMERS

The first four steps in the marketing process involve building customer relationships. The final step involves capturing value in return. By creating superior customer value, the firm creates highly satisfied customers who stay loyal and buy more.

7.1 Creating Customer Loyalty and Retention

The aim of customer relationship management is to create not just customer satisfaction, but customer delight. This means that companies must aim high in building customer relationships. Customer delight creates an emotional relationship with a product or service, not just a rational preference. Companies are realizing that losing a customer means losing more than a single sale. It means losing customer lifetime value.

7.2 Growing Share of Customer

Share of customer is defined as the share the company gets of customers purchasing in their product categories. (Thus, banks want to increase "share of wallet.")

7.3 Building Customer Equity

Companies want not only to create profitable customers, but to "own" them for life, capture their customer lifetime value, and earn a greater share of their purchases.

What Is Customer Equity?

Customer equity is the total combined customer lifetime values of all of the company's current and potential customers. Clearly, the more loyal the firm's profitable customers, the higher the firm's customer equity. Customer equity may be a better measure of a firm's performance than current sales or market share.

7.4 Building the Right Relationships with the Right Customers

Not all customers, not even all loyal customers, are good investments. Figure 1.5 classifies customers into one of four relationship groups, according to their profitability and projected loyalty. "Strangers" show low potential profitability and little projected loyalty. The relationship management strategy for these customers is simple: Don't invest anything in them. "Butterflies" are potentially profitable but not loyal. The company should use promotional blitzes to attract them, create satisfying and profitable transactions with them, and then cease investing in them until the next time around. "True friends" are both profitable and loyal. There is a strong fit between their needs and the company's offerings. The firm wants to make continuous relationship investments to delight these customers and retain and grow them. "Barnacles" are highly loyal but not very profitable. There is a limited fit between their needs and the company's offerings. The goal is to build the *right relationships* with the *right customers*.

8.0 THE CHANGING MARKETING LANDSCAPE

This section looks at four major developments: the new digital age, rapid globalization, the call for more ethics and social responsibility, and the growth in not-for-profit marketing.

8.1 The Digital Age

The recent technology boom has created a digital age. The most dramatic new technology is the Internet. Beyond competing in traditional market*places*, companies now have access to exciting new market*spaces*. The Internet has now become a global phenomenon. The number of Internet users worldwide now stands at almost 1.2 billion and will reach an estimated 3.4 billion by 2015. Online marketing is now the fastest growing form of marketing. In addition to the "click-only" dot-coms, most traditional "brick-and-mortar" companies have now become "click-and-mortar" companies.

8.2 Rapid Globalization

Marketers are now connected *globally* with their customers and marketing partners. Almost every company, large or small, is touched in some way by global competition. American firms have been challenged at home by the skillful marketing of European and Asian multinationals. McDonald's now serves 52 million customers daily in 31,600 restaurants worldwide—some 65 percent of its revenues come from outside the United States. Today, companies are buying more supplies and components abroad.

8.3 The Call for More Ethics and Social Responsibility

Marketers are being called upon to take greater responsibility for the social and environmental impact of their actions. Corporate ethics and social responsibility have become hot topics for almost every business. Forward-looking companies view socially responsible actions as an opportunity to do well by doing good.

8.4 The Growth of Not-for-Profit Marketing

The nation's nonprofits face stiff competition for support and membership. Sound marketing can help them to attract membership and support.

9.0 SO, WHAT IS MARKETING? PULLING IT ALL TOGETHER

Marketing is the process of building profitable customer relationships by creating value for customers and capturing value in return. The first four steps in the marketing process create value *for* customers. The final step in the process allows the company to capture value *from* customers.

After the marketing strategy is defined, the marketing program is developed, which consists of the four Ps. When building value for customers, companies must utilize marketing technology, go global in both selling and sourcing, and act in an ethical and socially responsible way. Figure 1.6 shows a model of the marketing process.

Student Exercises

1.   Key Term: Marketing

The two-fold goal of marketing is to attract new customers by promising superior value and keep and grow current customers by keeping them happy. Take a look at Apple Computers (www.apple.com) and the American Cancer Society (www.cancer.org). How would you say these companies use marketing?

2.   Key Term: Market Offering

According to the chapter, a market offering is some combination of products, services, information, or experiences offered to a market to satisfy a need or want. Bank of America (www.bankofamerica.com) sponsored an open forum concerned with identifying the challenges and opportunities in providing residents of communities with healthy food options that traditionally have little or no access to grocery stores and quality, nutritious food choices. What is the market offering, in this instance?

3.   Key Term: Marketing Myopia

Paying undue attention to the specific products offered and not enough attention to the benefits and experiences created by those products is classic marketing myopia. Examine the current battle between Blu-ray DVD technology (http://www.blu-ray.com/) and HD-DVD technology (http://www.thelookandsoundofperfect.com) in the race to replace the current DVD format. Point out possible instances of marketing myopia based on their promotional materials.

4.   Key Term: Market Segmentation

Firms decide who to serve (partly) through the process of market segmentation. Visit the websites of Starbucks coffee (www.starbucks.com) and Caribou Coffee (www.cariboucoffee.com). What major market segments are being targeted by each of these coffee companies?

5.   Key Term: Societal Marketing Concept

The societal marketing concept is concerned with the long-term welfare of the consumer and society. However, at times this viewpoint may be seen as contradictory with the products a company may offer. How do you believe (or, do you believe) tobacco makers are employing this concept in the marketing of cigarettes? You may want to visit the websites of Phillip Morris (www.philipmorrisusa.com), R.J. Reynolds (www.rjrt.com), and Lorillard (http://www.lorillard.com).

6.   Key Term: Customer Relationship Management

The overall process of building and maintaining profitable customer relationships—the acquiring, keeping, and growing of customers is known as Customer Relationship Management (CRM). Examine your college/university. How are they implementing CRM?

7.   Key Term: Partner Relationship Management

Sometimes, to bring greater value to customers, even competitors have been known to work together and/or join forces. Time Warner and CBS, highlighted in the chapter, is one good example. What are some other high profile examples of competitors joining forces for the overall good of the consumer?

8.   Key Term: Customer Equity

Maintaining loyal, profitable customers is the key to high customer equity. Dell Computers (www.dell.com), L.L. Bean (www.llbean.com), and Lexus (www.lexus.com) are all great examples. Look for examples in your local community of companies you consider holding high levels of customer equity. Why?

9.   Key Term: Globalization

Even the smallest company today is impacted by the global community, whether it is sparing with competitors halfway across the globe or receiving internet orders for products to ship to another country. How has this globalization impacted you directly? Do you believe this globalization has benefited you or do you think it has created more headaches than good?

10.   Key Term: Social Responsibility

The social responsibility movement will place ever-stricter demands on companies in the future. Some companies resist this movement, adapting only when forced. Others, however, embrace their social responsibility to their customers and the world around them. What are some examples of companies you believe have this forward-looking view of social responsibility? Also, what are some examples of companies you do not believe place much emphasis on this view?

Marketing ADventure Exercises

1.   Ad Interpretation Challenge: New Marketing Frontiers
        Ad: Apparel—Levis New Collection

Market offerings change over time. For a company to remain current and relevant, they must. What is this ad saying about the Levi Jean Company and it current market offering?

2.   Ad Interpretation Challenge: Insightful Segmentation
        Ad: Electronics—Compaq

Careful segmentation of the markets to serve is one of the challenges facing every marketer. Consider the featured ad. What market segment do you believe Compaq is attempting to reach with this ad? Do you believe this ad effectively reaches this segment?

3.   Ad Interpretation Challenge: The Production Concept
        Ad: Student Choice

One of the oldest marketing management orientations is the production concept, which states that consumers favor products that are available and highly affordable.

4.   Ad Interpretation Challenge: The Marketing Concept
        Ad: Travel and Tourism—Leisure Entertainment—Bali

The "outside-in" perspective is the key to the marketing concept. This concept focuses on what the consumer wants and needs and then seeks to develop a market offering to satisfy those needs and wants. Take a look at this ad. How is this ad employing the marketing concept?

5.   Ad Interpretation Challenge: The Marketing Concept
        Ad: Student Choice

Based on your work in the previous ADventure, find another ad of your selection that prominently displays the marketing concept and explain it. Remember, the marketing concept is a *customer*-driven concept.

6.   Ad Interpretation Challenge: What's Good for Society
        Ad: Auto—Hyundai Avante

The social marketing concept is a principle of enlightened marketing that considers, among other things, what is in the long-run best interest of society. However, nothing says that this has to be contradictory to what is good for the marketer. How does this particular ad fulfill both requirements—doing what is best for society AND what is best for the company?

7.   Ad Interpretation Challenge: Value
        Ad: General Retail—World's Biggest

The customer will buy from the firm that offers the highest perceived value. Perceived value is the difference between all of the benefits and all of the costs of a market offering relative to those of competing offers. How does this ad for World's Biggest Bookstore show value for the customer?

8.   Ad Interpretation Challenge: Making the Customer Happy
        Ad: Auto—Volvo S60

Providing superior customer satisfaction is the ultimate goal of all customer-oriented companies. Higher levels of customer satisfaction lead to greater customer loyalty that leads to greater company performance. How does this ad show customer loyalty? Select another ad of your choice, which also overtly displays customer loyalty.

9.   Ad Interpretation Challenge: Club Marketing Program
        Ad: Student Choice

One of the great ways to build customer loyalty is for the marketer to create programs that offer members special benefits and create member communities. Such programs have the potential to assist in long-term customer retention. For the ADventure, select an ad that you believe displays this concept of club marketing.

10.   Ad Interpretation Challenge: Increasing Lifetime Value and Customer Equity
Ad: Auto—Jaguar

Whereas sales and market share reflect the past, customer equity suggests the future. Building that long-term relationship with the customer is the key to creating customer equity. Clearly, the more loyal a firm's profitable customers, the greater the firm's customer equity. How do the two ads for Jaguar relate to lifetime value and customer equity?

Chapter 2
Company and Marketing Strategy:
Partnering to Build Customer Relationships

Learning Objectives

1. Explain companywide strategic planning and its four steps.
2. Discuss how to design business portfolios and develop growth strategies.
3. Explain marketing's role under strategic planning and how marketing works with its partners to create and deliver customer value.
4. Describe the elements of a customer-driven marketing strategy and mix, and the forces that influence it.
5. List the marketing management functions, including the elements of a marketing plan, and discuss the importance of measuring and managing return on marketing.

Chapter Overview

In the first chapter, we explored the marketing process by which companies create value for consumer in order to capture value in return. In this chapter, we look at designing customer-driven marketing strategies and constructing marketing programs. First we look at the organization's overall strategic planning, which guides marketing strategy and planning. Next, we discuss how marketing partners closely with others inside and outside the firm to create value for customers. We then examine marketing strategy and planning – how marketers choose target markets, position their market offering, develop a marketing mix, and manage their marketing programs. Lastly, we will look at the step of measuring and managing return on marketing investment.

Chapter Outline

1. INTRODUCTION

NASCAR is a great marketing organization. It is the second highest-rated regular season sport on television (only the NFL has more viewers). It has a single-minded focus: creating lasting customer relationships. A big part of the NASCAR experience is the feeling that the sport itself is personally accessible. Because of this, NASCAR has attracted more than 250 big-name sponsors. Today's successful companies have one thing in common: they are strongly customer focused and heavily committed to marketing.

1. What are some of the many media that NASCAR uses to reach its audience?
2. Why do you believe NASCAR has been able to attract so many big-name sponsors?

2. COMPANYWIDE STRATEGIC PLANNING: DEFINING MARKETING'S ROLE

The hard task of selecting an overall company strategy for long-run survival and growth is called strategic planning. Strategic planning is the process of developing and maintaining a strategic fit between the organization's goals and capabilities and its changing market opportunities. Strategic planning sets the stage for the rest of the planning in the firm. Companies typically prepare annual plans, long-range plans, and strategic plans.

2.1 Defining a Market-Oriented Mission

Many organizations develop formal mission statements. A mission statement is a statement of the organization's purpose – what it wants to accomplish in the larger environment. A clear mission statement acts as an "invisible hand" that guides people in the organization. A market-oriented mission statement defines the business in terms of satisfying basic customer needs. Management should avoid making its mission too narrow or too broad. Missions should be realistic, specific, fit the market environment, based on the company's distinctive competencies, and motivating.

2.2 Setting Company Objectives and Goals

The company's mission needs to be turned into detailed supporting objectives for each level of management. The mission leads to a hierarchy of objectives, including business objectives and marketing objectives. Marketing strategies and programs must be developed to support these marketing objectives.

2.3 Designing the Business Portfolio

A business portfolio is the collection of businesses and products that make up the company. The best portfolio is the one that best fits the company's strengths and weaknesses to opportunities in the environment. The major activity in strategic planning is business portfolio analysis, whereby management evaluates the products and businesses making up the company.

A strategic business unit (SBU) is a unit of the company that has a separate mission and objectives and that can be planned independently from other company businesses. The next step in business portfolio analysis calls for management to assess the attractiveness of its various SBUs and decide how much support each deserves. Most standard portfolio-analysis methods evaluate SBUs on two important dimensions – the attractiveness of the SBU's market or industry and the strength of the SBU's position in that market or industry.

2.3.1   The Boston Consulting Group Approach

The best-known portfolio-planning method was developed by the Boston Consulting Group.

This matrix defines four types of SBUs:
- Stars: High-growth market, high-share product;
- Cash cows: Low-growth market, high-share product;
- Question marks: Low-share product, high-growth market;
- Dogs: Low-share product, low-growth market.

Once it has classified its SBUs, the company must determine what role each will play in the future.

The company can invest more in the business unit in order to grow its share. It can invest just enough to hold the SBU's share at the current level. It can harvest the SBU, milking its short-term cash flow regardless of the long-term effect. Or it can divest the SBU by selling it or phasing it out

2.3.2   Problems with matrix approaches

Portfolio-analysis approaches have limitations.
- They can be difficult, time-consuming, and costly to implement.
- Management may find it difficult to define SBUs and measure market share and growth.
- These approaches focus on classifying current businesses but provide little advice for future planning.

Because of such problems, many companies have dropped formal matrix methods in favor of more customized approaches that are better suited to their specific situations.

2.3.3 Developing Strategies for Growth and Downsizing

Designing the business portfolio involves finding businesses and products the company should consider in the future. Marketing has the main responsibility for achieving profitable growth for the company.

Marketing must identify, evaluate, and select market opportunities and lay down strategies for capturing them.

The product/market expansion grid is shown in Figure 2.3.

- Market penetration involves making more sales to current customers without changing its products.
- Market development involves identifying and developing new markets for its current products.
- Product development is offering modified or new products to current markets.
- Diversification is where a company starts up or buys businesses outside of its current products and markets. Companies must also develop strategies for downsizing their businesses.

3. PLANNING MARKETING: PARTNERING TO BUILD CUSTOMER RELATIONSHIPS

Within each business unit, more detailed planning takes place. The major functional departments in each unit must work together to accomplish strategic objectives. Marketing provides a guiding philosophy—the marketing concept—that suggests that company strategy should revolve around building profitable relationships with important customer groups. Marketing provides inputs to strategic planners by helping to identify attractive market opportunities and by assessing the firm's potential to take advantage of them. Marketing designs strategies for reaching the unit's objectives.

3.1 Partnering with Other Company Departments

Each company department can be thought of as a link in the company's value chain. Value chain is the series of departments that carry out value-creating activities to design, produce, market, deliver, and support the firm's products. A company's value chain is only as strong as its weakest link. Success depends on how well each department performs its work of adding customer value and on how well the activities of various departments are coordinated. In practice, departmental relations are full of conflicts and misunderstandings.

3.2 Partnering with Others in the Marketing System

The firm needs to look beyond its own value chain and into the value chains of its suppliers, distributors, and ultimately, customers. More companies today are partnering with other members of the supply chain to improve the performance of the customer value-delivery network. Increasingly, today's competition no longer takes place between individual competitors. Rather, it takes place between the entire value-delivery networks created by these competitors.

4. MARKETING STRATEGY AND THE MARKETING MIX

Marketing's role and activities are show in Figure 2.4; it summarizes the major activities involved in managing marketing strategy and the marketing mix. Marketing strategy is the marketing logic by which the company hopes to achieve these profitable relationships.

4.1 Customer-Driven marketing Strategy

Companies know that they cannot profitably serve all consumers in a given market – at least not all consumers in the same way. The process of dividing a market into distinct groups of buyers with different needs, characteristics, or behavior who might require separate products or marketing programs is called market segmentation.

A market segment consists of consumers who respond in a similar way to a given set of marketing efforts. Market targeting involves evaluating each market segment's attractiveness and selecting one or more segments to enter. A company should target segments in which it can profitably generate the greatest customer value and sustain it over time.

4.2 Market Differentiation and Positioning

A product's position is the place the product occupies relative to competitors in consumers' minds. Marketers want to develop unique market positions for their products. Market positioning is arranging for a product to occupy a clear, distinctive, and desirable place relative to competing products in the minds of target customers. Positioning establishes differentiation. To gain competitive advantage, the company must offer value to target consumers. This is accomplished through product differentiation – actually differentiating the company's market offering so that it gives consumers more value.

4.3 Developing an Integrated Marketing Mix

The marketing mix is the set of controllable, tactical marketing tools that the firm blends to produce the response it wants in the target market. This is described in Figure 2.5.

Product means the goods-and-services combination the company offers to the target market.
Price is the amount of money customers pay to obtain the product.
Place includes company activities that make the product available to target consumers.
Promotion means activities that communicate the merits of the product and persuade target customers to buy it.

An effective marketing program blends all of the marketing mix elements into a coordinated program designed to achieve the company's marketing objectives by delivering value to consumers. Some critics feel that the 4 Ps may omit or underemphasize certain important activities. From the buyer's viewpoint, in this age of customer relationships, the 4 Ps might be better described as the 4 Cs:
- Customer solution,
- Customer cost,
- Convenience,
- Communication.

5. MANAGING THE MARKETING EFFORT

Managing the marketing process requires the four marketing management functions shown in Figure 2.6.
- Analysis,
- Planning,
- Implementation,
- Control.

5.1 Marketing Analysis

Managing the marketing function begins with a complete analysis of the company's situation. The company must analyze its markets and marketing environment to find attractive opportunities and avoid environmental threats. The marketer should conduct a SWOT analysis, by which it evaluates the company's overall strengths, weaknesses, opportunities, and threats.

5.2 Marketing Planning

Marketing planning involves deciding on marketing strategies that will help the company attain its overall strategic objectives. A detailed marketing plan is needed for each business, product, or brand. Table 2.2 outlines the major sections of a typical product or brand plan. A marketing strategy consists of specific strategies: target markets, positioning, the marketing mix, and marketing expenditure levels.

5.3 Marketing Implementation

Marketing implementation is the process that turns marketing plans into marketing actions in order to accomplish strategic marketing objectives. Implementation involves day-to-day, month-to-month activities that effectively put the marketing plan to work. Implementation addresses the *who, where, when*, and *how.* In an increasingly connected world, people at all levels of the marketing system must work together to implement marketing strategies and plans. Successful marketing implementation depends on how well the company blends its people, organizational structure, decision and reward systems, and company culture into a cohesive action program that supports its strategies. Finally, to be successfully implemented, the firm's marketing strategies must fit with its company culture – the system of values and beliefs shared by people in the organization.

5.4 Marketing Department Organization

The company must design a marketing organization that can carry out marketing strategies and plans. The most common form of marketing organization is the *functional organization.* Under this organization functional specialists head the various marketing activities. A company that sells across the country or internationally often uses a geographic organization.

Companies with many very different products or brands often create a product management organization. A product manager develops and implements a complete strategy and marketing program for a specific product or brand. For companies that sell one product line to many different types of markets and customers that have different needs and preferences, a market or customer management organization might be best. A market management organization is similar to the product management organization.

Market managers are responsible for developing marketing strategies and plans for their specific markets or customers. Large companies that produce many different products flowing into many different geographic and customer markets usually employ some combination of the functional, geographic, product, and market organization forms. Many companies are finding that today's marketing environment calls for less focus on products, brands, and territories and more focus on customers and customer relationships. More and more companies are shifting their brand management focus toward customer management.

5.5 Marketing Control

Marketing control involves evaluating the results of marketing strategies and plans and taking corrective action to ensure that objectives are attained. Operating control involves checking ongoing performance against the annual plan and taking corrective action when necessary. Its purpose is to ensure that the company achieves the sales, profits, and other goals set out in its annual plan. Strategic control involves looking at whether the company's basic strategies are well matched to its opportunities. A major tool for such strategic control is a marketing audit. This is a comprehensive, systematic, independent, and periodic examination of a company's environment, objectives, strategies, and activities to determine problem areas and opportunities.

5.6 Measuring and Managing Return on Marketing Investment

Marketing managers must ensure that their marketing dollars are being well spent. Many companies now view marketing as an investment rather than an expense. Marketers are developing better measures of return on marketing investment (Marketing ROI) – the net return from a marketing investment divided by the costs of the marketing environment. A company can assess return on marketing in terms of standard marketing performance measures, such as brand awareness, sales, or market share. Some companies are combining such measures into marketing dashboards – useful sets of marketing performance measures in a single display. Increasingly marketers are using customer-centered measures of marketing impact, such as customer acquisition, customer retention, and customer lifetime value.

<u>Student Exercises</u>

1.   Key Term: Strategic Planning

For long-term survival, every company must engage in effective strategic planning—the process of developing and maintaining a strategic fit between the organization's goals and capabilities and its marketing opportunities. Consider the competitive U.S. automobile market. How would you describe the strategic planning of Ford Motor Company (www.ford.com)?

2.   Key Term: Mission Statement

A mission statement is a statement of the organization's purpose—what it wants to accomplish in the larger environment. Take a look at the mission statements of Starbucks coffee (www.starbucks.com), IBM (www.ibm.com), and John Deere (www.deere.com). Look for similarities and differences. Are any better than others?

3.   Key Term: Business Portfolio

The collection of businesses and products that make up a company is known as its *business portfolio*. Visit the home page of Ford Motor Company (www.ford.com) and make a list of the products and/or businesses that comprise this company.

4.   Key Term: Market Penetration

Market penetration—a strategy for company growth by increasing sales of current products to current market segments without changing the product—is only one possible strategy for growth. Find a company whose strategy you believe follows market penetration.

5.   Key Term: Diversification

Another strategy for company growth is diversification, which is growing through the acquisition or starting of businesses outside of a company's current products and markets. Find a company whose strategy you believe typifies diversification.

6.   Key Term: Downsizing

Business unit growth is not always the desirable or achievable option. Downsizing involves reducing the business portfolio by eliminating products or business units that are not profitable or no longer fit the company's overall corporate strategy. What are two companies you believe have employed downsizing in past few years?

7.   Key Term: Market Segment

A market segment is a group of consumers who respond in a similar way to a given set of marketing efforts. Take a look at Rolls Royce (www.rolls-roycemotorcars.com) and Chery Automobile Company (www.cheryglobal.com). Describe the basic market segments these two companies are attempting to reach.

8.   Key Term: Positioning

Positioning is arranging for a product to occupy a clear, distinctive, and desirable place relative to competing products in the minds of target consumers. How is your favorite local restaurant attempting to position itself, relative to its competition? Is it working?

9.   Key Term: Marketing Mix

The marketing mix is the set of controllable, tactical marketing tools the firm blends to product the responses it wants from the target market. These marketing tools can all be collected into four sets of variables known as the "4 Ps." Consider Southwest Airlines (www.southwest.com). Briefly describe the "4 Ps" employed by Southwest.

10.   Key Term: SWOT Analysis

A complete analysis of the company situation is a key component in managing the marketing function. A SWOT analysis is central to this evaluation process. Think about your school. What do you consider to be the primary strengths, weaknesses, opportunities, and threats it is facing?

Marketing ADventure Exercises

1.   Ad Interpretation Challenge: The Mission Statement
      Ad: Apparel—Polartec

The mission statement is the core of what a company is all about. Take a look at this Polartec ad. How would you interpret the company's mission statement, based on this ad?

2.   Ad Interpretation Challenge: Distinctive Competencies
      Ad: Apparel—Umbro

A company should base its mission statement on its distinctive competencies—those things it does extremely well. What distinctive competency is being displayed by these two Umbro ads?

3.   Ad Interpretation Challenge: Business Portfolio
      Ad: Food and Beverage—Pizza World

A business portfolio is the collection of businesses or products that make up the company. How does this Pizza World ad give the consumer insight into the products of the company?

4.   Ad Interpretation Challenge: Stars
      Ad: Student Choice

"Stars" are defined as being high-growth, high-share businesses or products. Find an ad that you believe is promoting a "star."

5.   Ad Interpretation Challenge: Market Penetration
      Ad: General Retail—Drugmart

The idea of market penetration is to increase sales of your current products to your current market segments. How does this ad for Drugmart seek to accomplish this?

6.   Ad Interpretation Challenge: Market Development
      Ad: Travel and Tourism—Turkish Airlines

A company undertakes a strategy of product development when it decides to offer new or modified products to its current market segments. Examine this ad for Turkish Airlines. How does it epitomize the strategy of product development?

7.   Ad Interpretation Challenge: Value Chain
      Ad: Exhibits and Entertainment—D-Day (Melting Pot)

A firm's success depends not only on how well each department performs its work but also on how well the activities of various departments are coordinated. Consider this advertisement for the National D-Day Museum in New Orleans. What does this ad say about value chains?

8.   Ad Interpretation Challenge: The Value-Delivery Network
      Ad: Internet—Shopnow

A value-delivery network is a network made up of the company, suppliers, distributors, and the customer who "partner" with each other to improve the performance of the system and, therefore, provide greater value to the customer. How does Shopnow accomplish this?

9. Ad Interpretation Challenge: Product Positioning
   Ad: Auto—Lincoln

Successfully positioning a product involves clearly and distinctively placing the product as superior to competing products in the mind of the consumer. How has Lincoln achieved this in the featured ad?

10. Ad Interpretation Challenge: The Product
    Ad: Student Choice

All successful ads make certain you know what the product is they are highlighting, otherwise they have accomplished nothing. Sometimes, however, they may do this very subtly. Find an ad when the product is evident, but not "in your face."

Chapter 3
Analyzing the Marketing Environment

Learning Objectives

1. Describe the environmental forces that affect the company's ability to serve its customers.
2. Explain how changes in the demographic and economic environments affect marketing decisions.
3. Identify the major trends in the firm's natural and technological environments.
4. Explain the key changes in the political and cultural environments.
5. Discuss how companies can react to the marketing environment.

Chapter Overview

This chapter shows that marketing does not operate in a vacuum but rather in a complex and changing environment. Other *actors* in this environment—suppliers, intermediaries, customers, competitors, publics, and others—may work with or against the company. Major environmental *forces*—demographic, economic, natural, technological, political, and cultural—shape marketing opportunities, pose threats, and affect the company's ability to serve customers and develop lasting relationships with them. To understand marketing, and to develop effective marketing strategies, you must first understand the environment in which marketing operates.

Chapter Outline

1. INTRODUCTION

Xerox introduced the first plain-paper copier almost 50 years ago. For years, the company that invented photocopying dominated the field. In 1998, Xerox's profits were growing at 20 percent a year. Then everything went wrong. In only 18 months, Xerox lost $38 billion in market value. The company was on the brink of bankruptcy. The world had quickly gone digital and Xerox had not kept up. While Xerox was busy perfecting copy machines, customers were looking for more sophisticated document management solutions. Since those dark days, Xerox has rethought, redefined and reinvented itself. The new Xerox mission is to "help companies and people be smarter about their documents." The message is clear. Even the most dominant companies can be vulnerable to changing marketing environments.

More than any other group in the company, marketers must be the trend trackers and opportunity seekers. A company's marketing environment consists of the actors and forces outside marketing that affect marketing management's ability to build and maintain successful relationships with target customers. The microenvironment consists of the actors close to the company that affect its ability to service its customers. The macroenvironment consists of larger societal forces that affect the microenvironment.

Opening Vignette Questions

1. How did Xerox get caught unaware?
2. What actions did they take to "save" the company?
3. Do you believe Xerox is once again the dominant powerhouse it once was?

2. THE COMPANY'S MICROENVIRONMENT

Marketing management's job is to build relationships with customers by creating customer value and satisfaction.

2.1 The Company

All the interrelated groups form the internal environment. All groups should work in harmony to provide superior customer value and relationships.

2.2 The Suppliers

Suppliers provide the resources needed by the company to produce its goods and services. Marketing managers must watch supply availability—supply shortages or delays, labor strikes, and other events can cost sales in the short run and damage customer satisfaction in the long run. Marketing managers monitor the price trends of their key inputs.

2.3 Marketing Intermediaries

Marketing intermediaries help the company to promote, sell, and distribute its products to final buyers.
- *Resellers* are distribution channel firms that help the company find customers or make sales to them. These include wholesalers and retailers.
- *Physical distribution firms* help the company to stock and move goods from their points of origin to their destinations.
- *Marketing services agencies* are the marketing research firms, advertising agencies, media firms, and marketing consulting firms that help the company target and promote its products to the right markets.
- *Financial intermediaries* include banks, credit companies, insurance companies, and other businesses that help finance transactions or insure against the risks associated with the buying and selling of goods.

Marketers recognize the importance of working with their intermediaries as partners rather than simply as channels through which they sell their products.

2.4 Competitors

Marketers must gain strategic advantage by positioning their offerings strongly against competitors' offerings in the minds of consumers. No single competitive marketing strategy is best for all companies.

2.5 Publics

A public is any group that has an actual or potential interest in or impact on an organization's ability to achieve its objectives.

- *Financial publics* influence the company's ability to obtain funds.
- *Media publics* carry news, features, and editorial opinion.
- *Government publics*. Management must take government developments into account.
- *Citizen-action publics*. A company's marketing decisions may be questioned by consumer organizations, environmental groups, etc.
- *Local publics* include neighborhood residents and community organizations.
- *General public*. The general public's image of the company affects its buying.
- *Internal publics* include workers, managers, volunteers, and the board of directors.

2.5 Customers

Five types of customer markets. The company may target any or all of these five markets.

1. *Consumer markets:* individuals and households that buy goods and services for personal consumption.
2. *Business markets:* buy goods and services for further processing or for use in their production process.
3. *Reseller markets:* buy goods and services to resell at a profit.
4. *Government markets:* made up of government agencies that buy goods and services to produce public services.
5. *International markets:* buyers in other countries, including consumers, producers, resellers, and governments.

3. THE COMPANY'S MACROENVIRONMENT

3.1 Demographic Environment

Demography is the study of human populations in terms of size, density, location, age, gender, race, occupation, and other statistics. Changes in the world demographic environment have major implications for business. Thus, marketers keep close track of demographic trends and developments in their markets, both at home and abroad.

3.1.1 Changing Age Structure of the Population

The U.S. population stood at over 302 million in 2007 and may reach almost 364 million by the year 2030. The single most important demographic trend in the United States is the changing age structure of the population.

Baby Boomers

The post-World War II baby boom produced 78 million **baby boomers**, born between 1946 and 1964. Baby boomers account for nearly 30 percent of the population, spend about $2.3 trillion annually, and hold three-quarters of the nation's financial assets. The youngest boomers are now in their early-to-mid forties; the oldest are entering their sixties. Boomers are spending $30 billion a year on *anti*aging products and services.

Generation X

The baby boom was followed by a "birth dearth," creating another generation of 49 million people born between 1965 and 1976. Author Douglas Coupland calls them Generation X. Others call them the "baby busters." Increasing parental divorce rates and higher employment for their mothers made them the first generation of latchkey kids. They developed a more cautious economic outlook. The GenXers are a more skeptical bunch.

Millennials (also called Generation Y or the echo boomers)

Born between 1977 and 2000, these children of the baby boomers number 83 million. This group includes several age cohorts:
- *tweens* (aged 8-12),
- *teens* (13-18); and
- *young adults* (the twenty-somethings).

3.1.2 The Changing American Family

The "traditional household" consists of a husband, wife, and children (and sometimes grandparents).
In the U.S.:
- Married couples with children make up 23 percent of the households;
- Married couples without children make up 29 percent;
- Single parents comprise 16 percent.
- Nonfamily households make up 32 percent.

Both husband and wife work in 57 percent of all married-couple families.

3.1.3 Geographic Shifts in Population

About 14 percent of all U.S. residents move each year. The U.S. population has shifted toward the Sunbelt states. Americans have been moving from rural to metropolitan areas.

3.1.4 A Better-Educated, More White-Collar, More Professional Population

The U.S. population is becoming better educated. In 2004, 86 percent of the U.S. population over age 25 had completed high school. Between 2006 and 2016 the number of professional workers is expected to increase 23 percent and manufacturing is expected to decline 10 percent.

3.1.5 Increasing Diversity

The United States has become more of a "salad bowl" in which various groups have mixed together but have maintained their diversity by retaining important ethnic and cultural differences. The U.S. population is about 66 percent white, 15 percent Hispanics and 13 percent African Americans. The Asian American population now totals about 5 percent of the population. By 2050, whites will comprise and estimated 47 percent of the population, while Hispanics will grow to just under one-third, and African Americans will remain at about 13 percent. Many companies have begun to target gay and lesbian consumers. They are twice as likely as the general population to have a household income over $250,000. Another attractive segment is the nearly 54 million adults with disabilities.

3.2 Economic Environment

The economic environment consists of factors that affect consumer purchasing power and spending patterns.
Subsistence economies – consume most of their own agricultural and industrial output.
Industrial economies – constitute rich markets for many different kinds of goods.

3.2.1 Changes in Income

In recent years, American consumers fell into a consumption frenzy. Consumers now face repaying debts acquired during earlier spending splurges.
Value marketing—just the right combination of product quality and service at a fair price. *Income distribution* in the United States is very skewed. The rich has gotten richer, the middle class has shrunk, and the poor have stayed poor.

3.2.2 Changing Consumer Spending Patterns

Food, housing, and transportation use up the most household income. Engel's law states that as family income rises, the percentage spent on food declines. Changes in major economic variables have a large impact on the marketplace.

3.3 Natural Environment

The natural environment involves the natural resources that are needed as inputs by marketers or that are affected by marketing activities.

Trends in the natural environment:
1. Shortages of raw materials.
2. Increased pollution.
3. Increased government intervention.

3.4 Technological Environment

The technological environment is perhaps the most dramatic force now shaping our destiny. Technology has released such wonders as antibiotics, robotic surgery, miniaturized electronics, laptop computers, and the Internet. The United States leads the world in research and development spending.

3.5 Political and Social Environment

Governments develop *public policy* to guide commerce.

3.5.1 Increasing Legislation

Legislation affecting business around the world has increased steadily over the years. Business legislation has been enacted for a number of reasons.

1. To *protect companies* from each other.
2. To *protect consumers* from unfair business practices.
3. To *protect the interests of society* against unrestrained business behavior.

3.5.2 Changing Government Agency Enforcement

Because government agencies have discretion in enforcing laws, they can have an impact on a company's marketing performance.

3.5.3 Increased Emphasis on Ethics and Socially Responsible Actions

1) Socially Responsible Behavior
2) Cause-Related Marketing

3.6 Cultural Environment

The cultural environment is made up of institutions and other forces that affect a society's basic values, perceptions, preferences, and behaviors.

3.6.1 Persistence of Cultural Values

Core beliefs and values are passed on from parents to children and are reinforced by schools, churches, business, and government. *Secondary* beliefs and values are more open to change.

3.6.2 Shifts in Secondary Cultural Values

Marketers want to predict cultural shifts in order to spot new opportunities or threats.

3.6.2.1 People's Views of Themselves

3.6.2.2 People's Views of Others

3.6.2.3 People's Views of Organizations

3.6.2.4 People's Views of Society

3.6.2.5 People's Views of Nature

3.6.2.6 People's Views of the Universe

4. RESPONDING TO THE MARKETING ENVIRONMENT

Many companies think the marketing environment is an uncontrollable element to which they have to adapt. Other companies take an *environmental management perspective* to affect the publics and forces in their environment. Marketing managers should take a *proactive* rather than *reactive* approach to the marketing environment.

Student Exercises

1.   Key Term: Microenvironment

The marketing environment is made up of both a macroenvironment and a microenvironment. The microenvironment consists of the actors close to a company that affect its ability to serve its customers. Take a look at your school. What elements comprise its microenvironment?

2.   Key Term: Marketing Intermediaries

Marketing intermediaries are firms that help the company promote, sell, and distribute its goods to the final buyers. Take a look at the websites for Amazon.com (www.amazon.com) and Bebe (www.bebe.com). From an examination of their websites and other materials, what marketing intermediaries are assisting either of these two very different companies?

3.   Key Term: Publics

A "public" is any group that has an actual or potential interest in or impact on an organization's ability to achieve its objectives. Once again, consider your university. What are the publics that your college administrators must be cognizant of?

4.   Key Term: Baby Boomers

The Baby Boomers are those individuals born during the post-World War II euphoria of 1946 to 1964. They number almost 78 million Americans and account for over 27 percent of the U.S. population. The aging of this group has opened numerous opportunities for marketers. Find two companies that appear to be targeting this group.

5.   Key Term: Generation Y

If you were born between the years 1977 and 2000, you are a member of Generation Y. This "echo boom" amounts to over 75 million people—much larger than Generation X and almost as large as the Baby Boomers. Take a look at Scion (www.scion.com), the new brand that Toyota created strictly to appeal to this group. Do you think the Scion holds attraction to members of Generation Y?

6.   Key Term: Traditional Family

The "traditional American household" typically consists of a husband, wife, and kids. However, today, that once idealistic view of the American family seems to be covering a smaller and smaller portion of the American population. Currently, only about 23 percent of households are made up of mom, dad, and kids. Find two companies that seem to be targeting this group.

7.   Key Term: Diversity

Countries vary in their ethnic and racial makeup. According to your text, we find Japan at one extreme, where pretty much everyone is Japanese. At the other end, we have the United States, where we have people from everywhere. Companies have to be careful in their promotions to faithfully and responsibly depict their customer markets as they really are. Take a look at Abercrombie and Fitch (www.abercrombie.com). Do you believe they have reasonably represented their target markets?

8.   Key Term: Engel's Law

According to Engel's Law, consumers at different income levels have different spending patterns. Percent of spending on transportation remains relatively flat across all income categories. How can you explain Jaguar and BMW's decisions to offer lower-priced luxury models to appeal to a new group of consumers?

9.   Key Term: Technological Environment

Technology continues to evolve at an astounding pace. It is difficult to predict where technology will lead us next. The technological environment is perhaps the most dramatic force now shaping the future. Impressive technological achievements continue to occur with remarkable speed. Make a list of four new accomplishments that would not have been possible without technology.

10.   Key Term: Political Environment

Every company must operate within the existing political environment and be able to anticipate changes to that environment. Mounting legislation has increasing impacted many U.S. businesses over the years. One of the most controversial, yet increasingly invoked pieces of legislation has been the implementation of smoking bans in public facilities, including outdoor sporting arenas, and indoor restaurants and bars. What do you feel about this? Is this serving the public good or is it unfairly targeting a legal product (tobacco)?

Marketing ADventure Exercises

1.   Ad Interpretation Challenge: The Macroenvironment
        Ad: Auto—Hyundai Avante

The macroenvironment is composed of the larger societal forces that impact a company, such as demographic, economic, natural, environmental, political, and cultural forces. Take a look at this ad. How is this ad appealing to the larger macroenvironment?

2.   Ad Interpretation Challenge: The Macroenvironment
        Ad: Food and Beverage—McDonald's

Again, consider what makes up the macroenvironment in which a company must operate. Consider the McDonald's ads pertaining to the Sydney Olympics. What factor(s) of the macroenvironment is(are) these ads targeting?

3.   Ad Interpretation Challenge: Marketing Intermediaries
        Ad: Student Choice

Marketing intermediaries are firms that help the company promote, sell, or distribute its goods or services to the final users. Many types of companies are included here, such as physical distribution firms, financial intermediaries, and resellers. Find an ad that highlights a marketing intermediary.

4.   Ad Interpretation Challenge: Competition
      Ad: Student Choice

Everybody has competitors. To be successful, a company must provide greater customer value and satisfaction than its competitors. Locate an ad that is attempting to show consumers that the company provides better value than does its competitors.

5.   Ad Interpretation Challenge: Publics
      Ad: Auto—Cadillac Escalade

A company's marketing environment also includes various publics. Publics are any group that has an interest or impact (actual or potential) on an organization. What potential publics might Cadillac want to consider due to this ad?

6.   Ad Interpretation Challenge: Demography
      Ad: Travel and Tourism—Leisure Entertainment

Demography is the study of human populations in terms of size, density, location, age, occupation, and other statistics. How does the featured ad show a foundation in the study of demography?

7.   Ad Interpretation Challenge: Baby Boomers
      Ad: Student Choice

Baby boomers spend over $2 trillion annually and will soon control over 40 percent of this nation's disposable income. Baby boomers are those 78 million people born after World War II and up until 1964. Find an ad that is clearly targeted to this generation of people.

8.   Ad Interpretation Challenge: Generation Y
      Ad: Apparel—Levis New Collection

Levi's is an apparel company that was late in joining the newest fashion craze touting $100 jeans. But they are attempting to rapidly catch up with the Levi's New Collection of jeans. Why would this ad appeal to those of Generation Y?

9.   Ad Interpretation Challenge: The "Traditional Family"
      Ad: Auto—Toyota

The traditional American family (mom, dad, and children) seems to have lost a bit of its luster as a smaller and smaller percentage of households are comprised of this once American ideal. Today, only around 23 percent of households are made up of married couples with children. How would you say this Toyota ad appeals to this group?

10.   Ad Interpretation Challenge: Diversity
       Ad: Nonprofit Corporate Images—Nike

Increasing diversity in the American landscape is an everyday fact of life. As Americans, we are not all alike. Diversity is not just ethnic heritage, but also includes the 60 million people with disabilities in the United States. How is Nike seeking to recognize this group and bring them more into the mainstream?

Chapter 4
Managing Marketing Information to Gain Customer Insights

Learning Objectives

1. Explain the importance of information in gaining insights about the marketplace and customers
2. Define the marketing information system and discuss its parts
3. Outline the steps in the marketing research process
4. Explain how companies analyze and use marketing information
5. Discuss the special issues some marketing researchers face, including public policy and ethics issues.

Chapter Overview

This chapter looks at how companies develop and manage information about important marketplace elements. This chapter is an examination of marketing information systems designed to assess the firm's marketing information needs, develop the needed information, and help managers to use the information to gain actionable customer and market insights.

Chapter Outline

1. INTRODUCTION

ZIBA is a new-product design consultancy. It digs in and really gets to know consumers. At the heart of ZIBA's success is its Consumer Insights and Trends Group. ZIBA teaches its clients that successful new products don't begin in their R&D labs. They begin with a deep understanding of customers and their emotional connections to the products they buy and use. Marketers must *use* the information to gain powerful *customer and market insights*.

Opening Vignette Questions

1. How is ZIBA's approach to marketing research different than that of a traditional marketing research company?
2. What approach did ZIBA take for Sirius to design the hit Stiletto radio product?
3. ZIBA states that successful new products do not begin in the R&D labs. Where do they begin?

2. MARKETING INFORMATION AND CUSTOMER INSIGHTS

Companies use such customer insights to develop competitive advantage. To gain good customer insights, marketers must effectively manage marketing information from a wide range of sources. The real value of marketing research and marketing information lies in how it is used—in the customer insights that it provides. Customer insights group collect customer and market information from a wide variety of sources. A marketing information system (MIS) consists of people and procedures for assessing information needs, developing the needed information, and helping decision makers to use the information to generate and validate actionable customer and market insights.

3. ASSESSING MARKETING INFORMATION NEEDS

A good marketing information system balances the information users would *like* to have against what they really *need* and what is *feasible* to offer. Sometimes the company cannot provide the needed information, either because it is not available or because of MIS limitations. By itself, information has no worth; its value comes from its *use*.

4. DEVELOPING MARKETING INFORMATION

4.1 Internal Data

Internal databases are electronic collections of consumer and market information obtained from data sources within the company network. Information in the database can come from many sources.

Problems with internal data:
* It may be incomplete or in the wrong form for making marketing decisions.
* Keeping the database current requires a major effort, because data ages quickly.
* All the data must be well integrated and readily accessible.

4.2 Marketing Intelligence

Marketing intelligence is the systematic collection and analysis of publicly available information about consumers, competitors, and developments in the marketplace. Marketing intelligence gathering has grown dramatically. Firms use competitive intelligence to gain early warnings of competitor moves and strategies. Much competitor intelligence can be collected from people inside the company. Competitors often reveal intelligence information through their annual reports, business publications, trade show exhibits, press releases, advertisements, and Web pages. Most companies are now taking steps to protect their own information.

5. MARKETING RESEARCH

Marketing research is the systematic design, collection, analysis, and reporting of data relevant to a specific marketing situation facing an organization.

The marketing research process has *four steps* (see Figure 4.2):

5.1. Defining the Problem and Research Objectives

Defining the problem and research objectives is often the hardest step in the research process. A marketing research project might have one of three types of objectives.

Exploratory research: to gather preliminary information that will help define the problem and suggest hypotheses.

Descriptive research: to describe things, such as the market potential for a product.

Causal research: to test hypotheses about cause-and-effect relationships.
Start with exploratory research and later follow with descriptive or causal research.

5.2 Developing the Research Plan

The research plan outlines sources of existing data and spells out the specific research approaches, contact methods, sampling plans, and instruments that researchers will use to gather new data. Research objectives must be translated into specific information needs. The research plan should be presented in a *written proposal*. Secondary data consist of information that already exists somewhere, having been collected for another purpose. Primary data consist of information collected for the specific purpose at hand.

5.2.1 Gathering Secondary Data

Researchers usually start by gathering secondary data. Using commercial online databases, marketing researchers can conduct their own searches of secondary data sources. Can usually be obtained more quickly and at a lower cost than primary data. Can provide data an individual company cannot collect on its own.

Secondary data can present problems.
- The needed information may not exist.
- The data might not be very usable.
  - *relevant* (fits research project needs), *accurate* (reliably collected and reported),
  - *current* (up-to-date enough for current decisions), and
  - *impartial* (objectively collected and reported).

5.2.2 Primary Data Collection

Observational Research involves gathering primary data by observing relevant people, actions, and situations. Observational research can obtain information that people are unwilling or unable to provide.

Ethnographic research involves sending trained observers to watch and interact with consumers in their "natural habitat." Ethnographic research often yields the kinds of details that just don't emerge from traditional research questionnaires or focus groups.

Survey research, the most widely used method for primary data collection, is the approach best suited for gathering descriptive information. The major advantage of survey research is its flexibility.

Experimental Research is best suited for gathering causal information.

5.2.3 Contact Methods

Mail, Telephone, and Personal Interviewing

Mail questionnaires can be used to collect large amounts of information at a low cost per respondent. Respondents give more honest answers to more personal questions. No interviewer is involved to bias the respondent's answers.

Telephone interviewing is the one of the best methods for gathering information quickly, and it provides greater flexibility than mail questionnaires. Interviewers can explain difficult questions. Response rates are higher than with mail questionnaires.

Personal interviewing takes two forms—individual and group interviewing.
- *Individual interviewing* involves talking with people one-on-one.
- *Group interviewing* (focus group interviewing) consists of inviting six to ten people to meet with a trained moderator to talk about a product, service, or organization.

5.2.3.1 Online Marketing Research

Increasingly, researchers are collecting primary data through online marketing research. Global marketing research spending reached an estimated $4.4 billion in 2008, triple the amount spent in 2005. It is estimated that up to one-third of all research will be conducted online by 2010. The Internet is well suited to *quantitative* research, but researchers are also adopting *qualitative* approaches. Online research usually costs much less than research conducted through mail, phone, or personal interviews. The primary qualitative Web-based research approach is online focus groups.

5.2.4 Sampling Plan

A sample is a segment of the population selected for marketing research to represent the population as a whole.

Designing the sample requires three decisions.
Who is to be surveyed (what *sampling unit*)?
How many people should be surveyed (what *sample size*)?
How should the people in the sample be *chosen* (what *sampling procedure*)?

The two types of samples are:
- *Probability samples*
- *Nonprobability samples*

5.2.5 Research Instruments

The questionnaire is the most common data collection instrument. Closed-end questions include all the possible answers, and subjects make choices among them. Open-end questions allow respondents to answer in their own words. Care should be given to the wording and ordering of questions. Researchers also use mechanical instruments to monitor consumer behavior. People meters and checkout scanners are examples.

5.3 Implementing the Research Plan

The data collection phase of the marketing research process is generally the most expensive and the most subject to error. Researchers must process and analyze the collected data to isolate important information and findings.

5.4 Interpreting and Reporting the Findings

Researchers should present important findings and insights that are useful in the major decisions faced by management.

6. ANALYZING AND USING MARKETING INFORMATION

6.1 Customer Relationship Management (CRM)

Companies capture information at every possible customer *touch point.*
Customer relationship management (CRM) is used to manage detailed information about individual customers and carefully manage customer touch points in order to maximize customer loyalty. CRM integrates everything that a company knows about individual customers to provide a 360-degree view of the customer relationship. A *data warehouse* is a companywide electronic database of finely detailed customer information that needs to be sifted through for gems. *Data mining* is the use of high-powered techniques to sift through the mounds of data and dig out interesting findings about customers.
CRM is just one part of an effective overall *customer relationship management strategy.*

6.2 Distributing and Using Marketing Information

The marketing information system must make the information available to managers and others who make marketing decisions or deal with customers. Many companies use an *intranet* to facilitate information distribution. The intranet provides ready access to data, stored reports, and so forth. Companies are increasingly allowing key customers and value-network members to access account and product information, along with other information. The systems that do this are called *extranets*.

7. OTHER MARKETING INFORMATION CONSIDERATIONS

7.1 Marketing Research in Small Businesses and Nonprofit Organizations

Managers of small businesses and nonprofit organizations can obtain marketing insights by *observing* things around them. Managers can conduct *informal surveys* using small convenience samples. Managers can glean a wealth of competitive data and information by turning to the Internet.

7.2 International Marketing Research

International marketing researchers follow the same steps as domestic researchers. The international researcher may have a difficult time finding good secondary data. International researchers often must collect their own primary data. Reaching respondents is often not easy in other parts of the world. Cultural differences from country to country cause additional problems for international researchers. Language is the most obvious obstacle. Even when respondents are *willing* to respond, they may not be *able* to because of high functional illiteracy rates.

7.3 Public Policy and Ethics in Marketing Research

7.3.1 Intrusions on Consumer Privacy

Many consumers strongly resent or even mistrust marketing research. Increasing consumer resentment has led to lower survey response rates in recent years. The best approach is for researchers to ask only for the information they need, to use it responsibly to provide customer value, and to avoid sharing information without the customer's permission.

7.3.2 Misuse of Research Findings

Many research studies appear to be little more than vehicles for pitching the sponsor's products. Several associations have developed codes of research ethics and standards of conduct.

Student Exercises

1.   Key Term: Internal Database

Internal databases are electronic collections of consumer and market information obtained from data sources within the company. In today's highly competitive environment, colleges and universities are continually striving to provide better service and be more responsive to the various publics it serves. How does your school use internal databases in its effort to provide better quality customer service to students?

2.   Key Term: Marketing Research

Take a look at Domino's Pizza (www.dominos.com). If you were in charge of marketing research for this company, what are the two types of information you would be interested in having available to you? Remember that marketing research is the systematic design, collection, analysis, and reporting of data relevant to a specific marketing situation facing an organization.

3.   Key Term: Secondary Data

Secondary data is information that already exists somewhere, having been collected for another purpose. Review the website media kit for the new magazine, *Beach Blvd* (www.beachblvd.bz). What secondary data do you see displayed?

4.   Key Term: Secondary Data—External Information Sources

You know what secondary data is now. Many possible sources exist that a company can turn to in an effort to secure needed secondary information. Among government data sources available for use are the U.S. Census (www.census.gov). Take a look. What types of information can you find from an examination of the U.S. Census?

5.   Key Term: Survey

Survey research is the most popular method for primary data collection. It is the approach best suited for gathering descriptive information. Many online data collection company now exist to facilitate the gathering of survey research. One of the most popular is called Zoomerang (www.zoomerang.com). Log on to Zoomerang, take the self guided tour of its capabilities, and then design your own survey.

6.   Key Term: Focus Groups

Group interviewing consists of inviting a small number of people (usually six to ten) to meet with a trained moderator to talk about a product, service, or organization. It is the moderator's job to keep the conversation "focused" on the relevant issues. Focus groups allow marketers access and insights into consumer thoughts and feelings. If you were in charge of marketing for CiCi's Pizza (www.cicispizza.com), how might you employ a focus group to learn more about your market?

7.   Key Term: The Sample

You can't survey everyone. Due to this, marketers typically draw conclusions about the market as a whole by studying a small sample of the total consumer population. A sample is a segment of the population selected to represent the population as a whole. Imagine that your school is contemplating becoming an only online provider of education. You have been asked to design a plan to sample the relevant individuals about there feelings regarding this. What factors must you consider as you determine who to sample, how many people to sample, and how you would choose the sample?

8.   Key Term: The Questionnaire

The questionnaire is by far the most popular data collection instrument—whether administered in person, online, or by phone. Find two examples of online questionnaires.

9.   Key Term: Data Mining

Data mining is the process of sifting through mounds of data to dig out interesting findings about customers. These findings can then be used as the basis of future marketing endeavors. How might Harrah's Entertainment (www.harrahs.com), the world's largest casino operator, use data mining?

10.   Key Term: Small Business Marketing Research

Even small businesses need the benefits of marketing research. To make long-term strategic decisions without the benefits of research is potentially disastrous. However, small businesses many times can not afford the large formalized marketing research programs of the larger organizations. A friend of yours is contemplating opening a new coffee shop close to school and has turned to you for insight on conducting marketing research. How would you advise your friend?

Marketing ADventure Exercises

1.   Ad Interpretation Challenge: Marketing Information System
       Ad: Services and B2B—24 Hour Fitness

A marketing information system is the people, equipment, and procedures used to gather, sort, analyze, evaluate, and distribute needed, timely, and accurate information to marketing decision makers. The effective use of a marketing information system can provide the marketer with a wealth of competitively useful information. Consider 24 Hour Fitness. How could the effective use of a marketing information system have led to the creation of this company?

2.	Ad Interpretation Challenge: Internal Data
	Ad: Apparel—Puma

Internal data is that information obtained from data sources within a company's network. It is information based on current customers. This information may include anything from their purchases over the past year to attitudinal data on likes and dislikes. Look at this ad for Puma. How might a review of Puma's internal data have led to the creation of this ad?

3.	Ad Interpretation Challenge: Internal Data
	Ad: Services and B2B—University of Toronto

Internal data can provide a company with incredibly valuable information about its current (or past) customers. Skillfully used, this information may be used as the basis of a campaign designed to bring more customers into the company fold. Review the ads for the University of Toronto. How do you believe these ads could be the product of the artful use of internal data?

4.	Ad Interpretation Challenge: Causal Research
	Ad: Student Choice

The basic objective of causal research is to test hypotheses about cause-and-effect. For example, if I were to raise my prices by 10 percent, what would happen to sales? Find an ad that highlights the basic premise of cause-and-effect.

5.	Ad Interpretation Challenge: Secondary Data
	Ad: Auto—Cadillac Escalade

Take a look at this ad for the Cadillac Escalade. The information presented in this ad is based on secondary data sources. Secondary data is information that already exists somewhere. You did not create this information. What information is this ad presenting from a secondary data source?

6.	Ad Interpretation Challenge: Primary Data
	Ad: Autos—Dunlop

Primary data is data that is collected specifically for the purpose at hand. Review this ad for Dunlop tires. What is the primary data finding this ad is presenting?

7.	Ad Interpretation Challenge: Ethnographic Research
	Ad: Student Choice

Ethnographic research is a form of observational research that involves sending trained observers to watch and interact with consumers in their "natural habitat." Find an ad that you believe may have been based on ethnographic research.

8.   Ad Interpretation Challenge: Contact Methods—Personal
        Ad: Financial—Alliance

There are many different ways to collect information—by mail, telephone, online, and personal interview. Each method has its own advantages and disadvantages. How does this ad for Alliance Financial Services make use of the personal interview method to get its informational point across?

9.   Ad Interpretation Challenge: Data Mining
        Ad: Internet—EPage

Data mining is a great technique to sift through the mounds of data and dig out interesting and useful bits of information about your customers. Look at the EPage ad. How does this company propose to use data mining to the benefit of its customers?

10.   Ad Interpretation Challenge: Public Policy
        Ad: Nonprofit Corporate Images—Labatt

Companies must always be cognizant of the publics within which they operate and must at all times be good corporate citizens. Public policy issues that have an impact on the company should be addressed and incorporated into the company framework. Labatt, a well-known Canadian brewery, is acknowledging a public policy issue in this ad. What is it?

Chapter 5
Consumer Markets and Consumer Buyer Behavior

Learning Objectives

1. Define the consumer market and construct a simple model of consumer buyer behavior.
2. Name the four major factors that influence consumer buyer behavior.
3. List and define the major types of buying decision behavior and stages in the buyer decision process.
4. Describe the adoption and diffusion process for new products.

Chapter Overview

In this chapter, we continue our marketing journey with a closer look at the most important element of the marketplace—customers. The goal of marketing is to affect how customers think about and behave toward the organization and its market offerings. But to affect the *whats, whens,* and *hows* of buying behavior, marketers must first understand the *whys*. We look first at *final consumer* buying influences and processes and then at the buying behavior of *business customers*.

Chapter Outline

1. INTRODUCTION

Buyers of Harley-Davidson motorcycles are intensely loyal and devoted to the brand. Because of this, Harley-Davidson is at the top of the heavyweight motorcycle market. Harley-Davidson's marketing managers spend a lot of time studying their buyers—they want to know who their customers are, what they think, how they feel, and why they buy a Harley rather than another brand. Who rides a Harley? They are just a likely to be CEOs and investment bankers as they are to be the stereotype outlaw bad-boy. Harley owners are buying more than just a good quality machine. They are buying self-expression and a lifestyle statement. As they ad states, "Things are different on a Harley."

Opening Vignette Questions

1. "I'd rather push a Harley than drive a Honda." What does this statement say about the typical Harley owner?
2. "A Harley renews your spirits and announces your independence." Analyze this statement.
3. What are Harley buyers really buying when they buy a Harley?

Consumer buyer behavior refers to the buying behavior of final consumers—individuals and households who buy goods and services for personal consumption. All of these consumers combine to make up the consumer market. The American consumer market consists of more than 300 million people.

2. MODEL OF CONSUMER BEHAVIOR

The central question for marketers is: How do consumers respond to various marketing efforts the company might use? The starting point is the stimulus-response model of buyer behavior shown in Figure 5.1. Marketing stimuli consist of the Four Ps: product, price, place, promotion. Other stimuli include major forces and events in the buyer's environment: economic, technological, political, and cultural. The marketer wants to understand how the stimuli are changed into responses inside the consumer's black box, which has two parts.

1. The buyer's characteristics influence how he or she perceives and reacts to the stimuli.
2. The buyer's decision process itself affects the buyer's behavior.

3. CHARACTERISTICS AFFECTING CONSUMER BEHAVIOR

3.1 Cultural Factors

Culture is the most basic cause of a person's wants and behavior. Marketers are always trying to spot *cultural shifts*.

Subcultures are groups of people with shared value systems based on common life experiences and situations.

Social classes are society's relatively permanent and ordered divisions whose members share similar values, interests, and behaviors. Social class is not determined by a single factor, but is measured as a combination of occupation, income, education, wealth, and other variables.

3.2 Social Factors

> 3.2.1 Groups and Social Networks: A person's behavior is influenced by many small groups. Opinion leaders are people within a reference group who, because of special skills, knowledge, personality, or other characteristics, exert social influence on others. These 10 percent of Americans are called the *influentials* or *leading adopters*. Marketers use *buzz marketing* to spread the word about their brands. Online social networks are online spaces where people socialize or exchange information and opinions. Family is the most important consumer buying organization in society.

3.2.2   Roles and Status: A role consists of the activities people are expected to perform. Each role carries a status reflecting the general esteem given to it by society.

3.3 Personal Factors

- Age and Life-Cycle Stage
- Occupation
- Economic Situation
- Lifestyle (activities, interests, and opinions)
- Personality and Self-Concept

Personality refers to the unique psychological characteristics that lead to relatively consistent and lasting responses to one's own environment.

A *brand personality* is the specific mix of human traits that may be attributed to a particular brand. One researcher identified five brand personality traits:
- Sincerity (down-to-earth, honest, wholesome, and cheerful)
- Excitement (daring, spirited, imaginative, and up-to-date)
- Competence (reliable, intelligent, and successful)
- Sophistication (upper class and charming)
- Ruggedness (outdoorsy and tough)

The basic *self-concept* premise is that people's possessions contribute to and reflect their identities; that is, "we are what we have."

3.4 Psychological Factors

3.4.1 Motivation

- A motive (or drive) is a need that is sufficiently pressing to direct the person to seek satisfaction.
- Perception is the process by which people select, organize, and interpret information to form a meaningful picture of the world.
  - *Selective attention* is the tendency for people to screen out most of the information to which they are exposed.
  - *Selective distortion* describes the tendency of people to interpret information in a way that will support what they already believe.
  - *Selective retention* is the retaining of information that supports their attitudes and beliefs.
  - *Subliminal advertising* refers to marketing messages received without consumers knowing it. Studies find no link between subliminal messages and consumer behavior.
- Learning describes changes in an individual's behavior arising from experience.
  - A *drive* is a strong internal stimulus that calls for action.

o   A drive becomes a motive when it is directed toward a particular *stimulus object.*

o   *Cues* are minor stimuli that determine when, where, and how the person responds.

3.4.2 Beliefs and Attitudes

- A *belief* is a descriptive thought that a person has about something.
- *Attitude* describes a person's relatively consistent evaluations, feelings, and tendencies toward an object or idea.

4. TYPES OF BUYING DECISION BEHAVIOR

Figure 5.5 shows types of consumer buying behavior based on the degree of buyer involvement and the degree of differences among brands.

4.1 Complex Buying Behavior

Consumers undertake complex buying behavior when they are highly involved in a purchase and perceive significant differences among brands. Consumers may be highly involved when the product is expensive, risky, purchased infrequently, and highly self-expressive. Typically, the consumer has much to learn about the product category. Marketers of high-involvement products must understand the information-gathering and evaluation behavior of high-involvement consumers.

4.2 Dissonance-Reducing Buying Behavior

Dissonance-reducing buying behavior occurs when consumers are highly involved with an expensive, infrequent, or risky purchase, but see little difference among brands. After the purchase, consumers might experience postpurchase dissonance (after-sale discomfort) when they notice certain disadvantages of the purchased brand or hear favorable things about brands not purchased. To counter such dissonance, the marketer's after-sale communications should provide evidence and support to help consumers feel good about their brand choices.

4.3 Habitual Buying Behavior

Habitual buying behavior occurs under conditions of low consumer involvement and little significant brand difference. Consumer behavior does not pass through the usual belief-attitude-behavior sequence. Consumers do not search extensively for information about the brands, evaluate brand characteristics, and make weighty decisions about which brands to buy. They passively receive information as they watch television or read magazines. Because buyers are not highly committed to any brands, marketers of low-involvement products with few brand differences often use price and sales promotions to stimulate product trial.

4.4 Variety-Seeking Buying Behavior

Consumers undertake variety-seeking buying behavior in situations characterized by low consumer involvement but significant perceived brand differences. In such cases, consumers often do a lot of brand switching and marketing in particular. After presenting the concepts of consumer behavior, have the students discuss the concepts in terms of their own buying habits, their backgrounds, and how they differ from others in the class.

5. THE BUYER DECISION PROCESS

The buyer decision process consists of five stages:
1. *need recognition*,
2. *information search*,
3. *evaluation of alternatives*,
4. *purchase decision*, and
5. *postpurchase behavior*.

5.2 Need Recognition
5.2
The buyer recognizes a problem or need. The need can be triggered by either an *internal stimuli* or *external stimuli*.

5.2 Information Search

Information search may or may not occur. Consumers can obtain information from any of several sources.

- *Personal sources* (family, friends, neighbors, acquaintances),
- *Commercial sources* (advertising, salespeople, Web sites dealers, packaging, displays),
- *Public sources* (mass media, consumer-rating organizations, Internet searches), and
- *Experiential sources* (handling, examining, using the product).

5.3 Evaluation of Alternatives

Alternative evaluation: how the consumer processes information to arrive at brand choices. How consumers go about evaluating purchase alternatives depends on the individual consumer and the specific buying situation. In some cases, consumers use careful calculations and logical thinking. At other times, the same consumers do little or no evaluating; instead they buy on impulse and rely on intuition.

5.2 Purchase Decision

In the evaluation stage, the consumer ranks brands and forms purchase intentions. Generally, the consumer's purchase decision will be to buy the most preferred brand, but two factors can come between the purchase intention and the purchase decision. The first factor is the attitudes of others. The second factor is unexpected situational factors.

5.5 Postpurchase Behavior

The difference between the consumer's expectations and the perceived performance of the good purchased determines how satisfied the consumer is. If the product falls short of expectations, the consumer is disappointed; if it meets expectations, the consumer is satisfied; if it exceeds expectations, the consumer is said to be delighted. Cognitive dissonance, or discomfort caused by postpurchase conflict, occurs in most major purchases.

6. THE BUYER DECISION PROCESS FOR NEW PRODUCTS

A new product is a good, service, or idea that is perceived by some potential customers as new. The adoption process is the mental process through which an individual passes from first learning about an innovation to final adoption. *Adoption* is the decision by an individual to become a regular user of the product.

6.1 Stages in the Adoption Process

Consumers go through five stages in the process of adopting a new product:
- *Awareness:* The consumer becomes aware of the new product, but lacks information about it.
- *Interest:* The consumer seeks information about the new product.
- *Evaluation:* The consumer considers whether trying the new product makes sense.
- *Trial:* The consumer tries the new product on a small scale to improve his or her estimate of its value.
- *Adoption:* The consumer decides to make full and regular use of the new product.

6.2 Individual Differences in Innovativeness

People differ greatly in their readiness to try new products. People can be classified into the adopter categories shown in Figure 5.7.

The five adopter groups have differing values.
- *Innovators* are venturesome—they try new ideas at some risk.
- *Early adopters* are guided by respect—they are opinion leaders in their communities and adopt new ideas early but carefully.
- The *early majority* are deliberate—although they rarely are leaders, they adopt new ideas before the average person.
- The *late majority* are skeptical—they adopt an innovation only after a majority of people have tried it.
- *Laggards* are tradition bound—they are suspicious of changes and adopt the innovation only when it has become something of a tradition itself.

51

6.3 Influence of Product Characteristics on Rate of Adoption

Five characteristics are important in influencing an innovation's rate of adoption.
- *Relative advantage*: the degree to which the innovation appears superior to existing products.
- *Compatibility*: the degree to which the innovation fits the values and experiences of potential consumers.
- *Complexity*: the degree to which the innovation is difficult to understand or use.
- *Divisibility*: the degree to which the innovation may be tried on a limited basis.
- *Communicability*: the degree to which the results of using the innovation can be observed or described to others.

Student Exercises

1.   Key Term: Cultural Shifts

Culture is not a static phenomenon. It is constantly changing and evolving. This results in cultural shifts—the shifting of culture to incorporate these changes. Companies have to pay attention and adapt to these shifts if they are to remain viable businesses. The cigarette industry is a great example. Take a look at RJR Tobacco Company (www.rjrt.com). How are they adapting as the U.S. culture shifts towards non-smoking?

2.   Key Term: Subculture

Every culture contains subcultures. Subcultures are groups of people with shared value systems based on common life experiences and situations. Many subcultures make up important markets and marketers design products and programs tailored to their specific needs. Think about how your school is attempting to reach important subcultures.

3.   Key Term: Hispanic Market

The Hispanic market now contains more than 41 million consumers. It is the fastest growing U.S. subsegment. Hispanic consumers tend to buy more branded, higher-quality products. They tend to make shopping a family affair. How is Chevrolet (www.chevrolet.com) catering to this important subsegment of the U.S. population?

4.   Key Term: Mature Consumers

The U.S. population is getting older. Due to this, mature consumers are becoming a very attractive market segment. Currently, over 37 million Americans are over the age of 65, and the number is growing rapidly. Mature consumers are typically better off financially than their under counterparts. What is one company that caters exclusively to this market?

5.   Key Term: Social Groups

Pretty much every society has some form of social class structure. Social classes are a society's relatively permanent and ordered divisions whose members share similar values, interests, and behaviors. Go to Bentley Motorcars (www.bentleymotors.com). To what social class do you believe this company caters?

6.   Key Term: Opinion Leader

People within a reference group who, because of special skills, knowledge, personality, or other characteristic, exert social influence on others are known as opinion leaders. These people are also called the "influentials" or "leading adopters." They are a very important group to marketers as they influence those who adopt a product after them. Take a look at the homepage for Scion (a marquee of Toyota Motors) (www.scion.com). How would you say Scion has used opinion leaders to get the word out about their cars?

7.   Key Term: Family

The American family isn't what it used to be. Cultural shifts have caused changes in family structure and functions. Undoubtedly, the family is the most important consumer buying organization in our society. Many companies focus on the family with their products and promotions. In many cases, children also have a strong influence on family buying decisions. Find examples of companies that promote to children in hopes of reaching the parents.

8.   Key Term: Lifestyle

A lifestyle is a person's pattern of living as expressed in his/her psychographics. It is based around their AIO dimensions—activities (work, school, hobbies, shopping, etc.), interests (fashion, recreation, food, etc.), and opinions (about themselves, the community, business, anything). What is your lifestyle and what does it say about you?

9.   Key Term: Motive

A motive (or a drive) is a need that is sufficiently pressing to direct the person to seek satisfaction. It is believed that motivation drives us to satisfy lower level needs before we can reach attempt to satisfy higher level need. (You may want to review Maslow's hierarchy of needs.) Find a company whose purpose it is to satisfy our lower level needs.

10.   Key Term: Cognitive Dissonance

Almost all major purchases result in some form of cognitive dissonance. Cognitive dissonance is buyer discomfort caused by post-purchase conflict. There is a tendency for consumers to feel some level of post-purchase dissonance (or discomfort) for every purchase. Companies want to do what they can to help lessen this post-purchase anxiety.

Take a look at L.L. Bean (www.llbean.com). What does this company do to help its customers do away with cognitive dissonance and remain happy, satisfied customers?

Marketing ADventure Exercises

1. Ad Interpretation Challenge: Cultural Shifts
   Ad: Apparel—Levi's New Collection

Culture is constantly changing and evolving. It is not a static phenomenon. This results in cultural shifts—the shifting of culture to incorporate these changes. Companies have to pay attention and adapt to these shifts if they are to remain viable businesses. Often, companies miss out on these shifts and face the real risk of becoming marginalized by their competition. Take a look at this ad for Levi's New Collection. What does this ad say about their response to this phenomenon?

2. Ad Interpretation Challenge: Subcultures
   Ad: Autos—Chevy S10 Truck

Each culture contains multiple subcultures—those groups of people with shared value systems based on common life experiences and situations. The U.S. Hispanic market is one such subculture. The Hispanic market is the fastest growing submarket in the United States today. Soon, this group will make up almost 25 percent of the U.S. population. No wonder businesses are starting to pay attention. How does this ad for the S10 truck appeal to this important subculture?

3. Ad Interpretation Challenge: Mature Consumers
   Ad: Student Choice

Mature consumers are becoming increasingly important to American business. Currently, more than 68 million consumers are considered part of this market. Generally, mature consumers have more time and money than other age groups. Find an ad for a product that you believe appeals to this market segment.

4. Ad Interpretation Challenge: Social Class
   Ad: Autos—Jaguar

Social classes are society's relatively permanent and ordered divisions whose members share similar values, interests, and behaviors. Products are designed to appeal to members of particular social classes. Look at the Jaguar ads. To which social class would you say Jaguar is attempting to appeal?

5.　　Ad Interpretation Challenge: Opinion Leader
　　　　Ad: Internet—Leaping Salmon

Manufacturers of products or services subjected to strong group influence must figure out how to reach the opinion leaders. Opinion leaders are those people within a particular reference group who exert social influence on others within the group. How might Leaping Salmon use opinion leaders to encourage adoption of its products?

6.　　Ad Interpretation Challenge: Family
　　　　Ad: Food and Beverage—McDonald's Happy Meal

Family is the most important consumer buying organization in society. All family members can have a strong influence on buyer behavior. Recognizing the importance of family, many companies target this group. Look at this ad for McDonald's. Who, within the family, does this ad target?

7.　　Ad Interpretation Challenge: Life-Cycle
　　　　Ad: Financial—MasterCard Home Alone

People change the products and services they buy over the course of their lifetimes. Tastes in food, clothes, transportation, and recreation are often age related. Find an ad that is targeted to a specific stage of the life-cycle. To whom do you believe this ad it targeted? How might this ad be changed to target a different stage?

8.　　Ad Interpretation Challenge: Brand Personality
　　　　Ad: Student Choice

Brand personality is the specific mix of human traits that may be attributed to a particular brand. Researchers have identified five brand personality traits. Find an ad that personifies the brand personality trait of "sophistication."

9.　　Ad Interpretation Challenge: Selective Attention
　　　　Ad: Cosmetics and Pharmaceuticals—Schick

Selective attention is the tendency for people to screen out most of the information to which they are exposed. Because of this, marketers have to work especially hard to attract the consumer's attention to where they really want it. Look quickly at this ad for Lady Schick. What features within this ad did you initially notice? Now, go back and review this ad again in detail. What other information do you notice? This exemplifies the issues facing marketers—to get you to notice all the information contained in an ad in the initial review.

10. Ad Interpretation Challenge: Information Search
    Ad: Student Choice

Information search is the stage of the buyer decision process in which the consumer is aroused to search for more information. At this time, the person may simply have heightened attention or may go into an active information search. Find an ad that provides the reader with a quantity of information with which to make comparisons between alternatives.

Chapter 6
Business Markets and Business Buyer Behavior

Learning Objectives

1. Define the business market and explain how business markets differ from consumer markets.
2. Identify the major factors that influence business buyer behavior.
3. List and define the steps in the business buying-decision process.
4. Compare the institutional and government markets and explain how institutional and government buyers make their buying decisions.

Chapter Overview

This chapter examines business customers – those that buy goods and services for use in producing their own products and services or for resale to others. As with firms selling to final buyers, firms marketing to business customers must build profitable relationships with business customers by creating superior customer value.

Chapter Outline

1. INTRODUCTION

Less than one-third of GE's annual sales come from consumer products. The vast majority of sales for GE come from commercial and industrial customers across a wide range of industries. GE locomotives might not seem glamorous, but they provide big dollars to the bottom line. The challenge is to win buyers' business by building day-in, day-out, year-in, year-out partnerships with them based on superior products and close collaboration. Locomotive performance is only part of the buying equation. GE wins contracts by partnering with business customers to help them translate that performance into moving their passengers and freight more efficiently and reliably. Business customer buying decisions are made within the framework of a strategic, problem-solving partnership. Says GE chairman and CEO Immelt, "We are viewed as a technical partner by customers around the world."

Opening Vignette Questions

1. Where does GE earn most of its revenue?
2. What is GE doing when it "partners" with an industrial customer?
3. Why does GE have to go to such lengths to help their customers succeed?

Business buyer behavior refers to the buying behavior of the organizations that buy goods and services for use in the production of other products and services that are sold, rented, or supplied to others. It also includes the behavior of retailing and wholesaling firms that acquire goods for the purpose of reselling or renting them to others at a profit. In the business buying process, business buyers determine which products and services their organizations need to purchase, and then find, evaluate, and choose among alternative suppliers and brands. *Business-to-business (B2) marketers* must do their best to understand business markets and business buyer behavior.

2. BUSINESS MARKETS

The business market is huge. In fact, business markets involve far more dollars and items than do consumer markets. The main differences between consumer and business markets are in *market structure* and *demand*, the *nature of the buying unit,* and the *types of decisions and the decision process* involved. (See Table 6.1)

2.1 Market Structure and Demand

The business marketer normally deals with far fewer but far larger buyers than the consumer marketer does. Business markets are more geographically concentrated.

Business demand is **derived demand**—it ultimately derives from the demand of consumer goods.

B2B marketers sometimes promote their products directly to final consumers to increase business demand. Many business markets have *inelastic demand*; that is, total demand for many business products is not affected much by price changes, especially in the short run. Business markets have more *fluctuating demand*. The demand for many business goods and services tends to change more—and more quickly—than the demand for consumer goods and services does.

2.2 Nature of the Buying Unit

Compared with consumer purchases, a business purchase usually involves *more decision participants* and a *more professional purchasing effort.* Often, business buying is done by trained purchasing agents who spend their working lives learning how to buy better. The more complex the purchase, the more likely that several people will participate in the decision-making process.

2.3 Types of Decisions and The Decision Process

Business buyers usually face *more complex* buying decisions than do consumer buyers. Purchases often involve large sums of money, complex technical and economic considerations, and interactions among many people at many levels of the buyer's organization. The business buying process also tends to be *more formalized* than the consumer buying process. In the business buying process, buyer and seller are often much more dependent on each other. Many customer companies are now practicing supplier development, systematically developing networks of supplier-partners to ensure an appropriate and dependable supply of products and materials that they will use in making their own products or reselling to others.

3. BUSINESS BUYER BEHAVIOR

At the most basic level, marketers want to know how business buyers will respond to various marketing stimuli. Within the organization, buying activity consists of two major parts: the buying center and the buying decision process.

3.1 Major Types of Buying Situations

There are three major types of buying situations. In a *straight rebuy*, the buyer reorders something without any modifications. It is usually handled on a routine basis by the purchasing department. In a *modified rebuy*, the buyer wants to modify the product specifications, prices, terms, or suppliers. A company buying a product or service for the first time faces a *new task* situation. In such cases, the greater the cost or risk, the larger the number of decision participants and the greater their efforts to collect information will be. Many business buyers prefer to buy a packaged solution to a problem from a single seller. Instead of buying and putting all the components together, the buyer may ask sellers to supply the components and assemble the package or system. Thus, *systems selling* is often a key business marketing strategy for winning and holding accounts.

3.2 Participants in the Business Buying Process

The decision-making unit of a buying organization is called its buying center: all the individuals and units that participate in the business decision-making process. The buying center includes all members of the organization who play any of five roles in the purchase decision process.

- **Users** are members of the organization who will use the product or service.
- **Influencers** often help define specifications and also provide information for evaluating alternatives.
- **Buyers** have formal authority to select the supplier and arrange terms of purchase.
- **Deciders** have formal or informal power to select or approve the final suppliers.
- **Gatekeepers** control the flow of information to others.

The buying center is not a fixed and formally identified unit within the buying organization. It is a set of buying roles assumed by different people for different purchases. Within the organization, the size and makeup of the buying center will vary for different products and for different buying situations. The buying center concept presents a major marketing challenge. The business marketer must learn who participates in the decision, each participant's relative influence, and what evaluation criteria each decision participant uses. The buying center usually includes some obvious participants who are involved formally in the buying process. It may also involve less obvious, informal participants, some of whom may actually make or strongly affect the buying decision. Sometimes, even the people in the buying center are not aware of all the buying participants.

3.3 Major Influencers on Business Buyers

Business buyers are subject to many influences when they make their buying decisions. Business buyers respond to both economic and personal factors. Business buyers are heavily influenced by factors in the current and expected *economic environment*, such as the level of primary demand, the economic outlook, and the cost of money. An increasingly important environmental factor is *shortages* in key materials. Business buyers also are affected by technological, political, and competitive developments in the environment. *Culture* and *customs* can strongly influence business buyer reactions to the marketer's behavior and strategies, especially in the international marketing environment.

Each buying organization has its own objectives, policies, procedures, structure, and systems, and the business marketer must understand those factors as well. The buying center usually includes many participants who influence each other; so *interpersonal factors* also influence the business buying process. It is often difficult to assess such interpersonal factors and group dynamics. Each participant in the business buying-decision process brings in personal motives, perceptions, and preferences. These individual factors are affected by personal characteristics such as age, income, education, professional identification, personality, and attitudes toward risk.

3.4 The Business Buying Process

Buyers who face a new-task buying situation usually go through all stages of the buying process. Buyers making modified or straight rebuys may skip some of the stages.

3.4.1 Problem Recognition

Problem recognition can result from internal or external stimuli. *Internally*, the company may decide to launch a new product that requires new production equipment and materials. *Externally*, the buyer may get some new ideas at a trade show, see an ad, or receive a call from a salesperson who offers a better product or a lower price.

3.4.2 General Need Description

The buyer next prepares a general need description that describes the characteristics and quantity of the needed item. For standard items, this process presents few problems. For complex items, however, the buyer may have to work with others—engineers, users, consultants—to define the item.

3.4.3 Product Specification

The buying organization next develops the item's technical product specifications, often with the help of a value analysis engineering team. *Product value analysis* is an approach to cost reduction in which components are studied carefully to determine if they can be redesigned, standardized, or made by less costly methods of production. The team decides on the best product characteristics and specifies them accordingly.

3.4.4 Supplier Search

The buyer now conducts a supplier search to find the best vendors. The buyer can compile a small list of qualified suppliers by reviewing trade directories, doing a computer search, or phoning other companies for recommendations. The newer the buying task, the more complex and costly the item, and the greater the amount of time the buyer will spend searching for suppliers.

3.4.5 Proposal Solicitation

In the proposal solicitation stage of the business buying process, the buyer invites qualified suppliers to submit proposals. When the item is complex or expensive, the buyer will usually require detailed written proposals or formal presentations from each potential supplier.

3.5.5 Supplier Selection

During supplier selection, the buying center often will draw up a list of the desired supplier attributes and their relative importance. Buyers may attempt to negotiate with preferred suppliers for better prices and terms before making the final selections. In the end, they may select a single supplier or a few suppliers.

3.5.6 Order Routine Specification

The buyer now prepares an order-routine specification. It includes the final order with the chosen supplier or suppliers and lists items such as technical specifications, quantity needed, expected time of delivery, return policies, and warranties. In the case of maintenance, repair, and operating items, buyers may use blanket contracts rather than periodic purchase orders. A blanket contract creates a long-term relationship in which the supplier promises to resupply the buyer as needed at agreed prices for a set time period.

3.5.7 Performance Review

The performance review may lead the buyer to continue, modify, or drop the arrangement. The eight-stage model provides a simple view of the business buying-decision process. The actual process is usually much more complex.

3.6 E-Procurement: Buying on the Internet

E-procurement gives buyers access to new suppliers and lower purchasing costs, and hastens order processing and delivery. In turn, business marketers can connect with customers online to share marketing information, sell products and services, provide customer support services, and maintain ongoing customer relationships. Companies can conduct *reverse auctions* or engage in online *trading exchanges*. Companies can also conduct e-procurement by setting up their own *company buying sites* or by setting up *extranet links* with key suppliers.

E-procurement reduces the time between order and delivery. Time savings are particularly dramatic for companies with many overseas suppliers. Beyond the cost and time savings, e-procurement frees purchasing people to focus on more strategic issues.

4. INSTITUIONAL AND GOVERNMENT MARKETS

Much of this discussion also applies to the buying practices of institutional and government organizations. However, these two non-business markets have additional characteristics and needs.

4.1 Institutional Markets

The institutional market consists of schools, hospitals, nursing homes, prisons, and other institutions that provide goods and services to people in their care. Institutions differ from one another in their sponsors and in their objectives. Many institutional markets are characterized by low budgets and captive patrons. Many marketers set up separate divisions to meet the special characteristics and needs of institutional buyers.

4.2 Government Market

In the United States alone, federal, state, and local governments contain more than 82,000 buying units. Government organizations typically require suppliers to submit bids, and normally they award the contract to the lowest bidder. In some cases, the government unit will make allowance for the supplier's superior quality or reputation for completing contracts on time. Government buyers are affected by environmental, organizational, interpersonal, and individual factors.

Most governments provide would-be suppliers with detailed guides describing how to sell to the government. Non-economic criteria also play a growing role in government buying.

Several companies have established separate government marketing departments. These companies anticipate government needs and projects, participate in the product specification phase, gather competitive intelligence, prepare bids carefully, and produce stronger communications to describe and enhance their companies' reputations.

Student Exercises

1.   Key Term: B2B Marketers

In essence, B2B marketers are those organizations that sell to other organizations. This includes companies as diverse as Boeing, Caterpillar, General Mills, and Procter and Gamble. Take a look at the Folgers Coffee (a product of P&G) website (www.folgers.com). From this review, why would you say Folgers (and P&G) operates as a B2B marketer?

2.   Key Term: Derived Demand

Derived demand is demand that originates from the consumer and their purchase of consumer goods. Your text uses the example of Intel. HP, Dell, and other computer manufacturers buy Intel chips because consumers buy PCs. If consumer demand for personal computers slows, so will the demand for computer chips. Log on to American Bolt and Screw's website (www.absfasteners.com) and take a look at the products they offer. How is their business a function of derived demand?

3.   Key Term: Supplier Development

The systematic development of networks of supplier-partners to ensure an organization appropriate and dependable supplies of products and materials that will be used in the making of their own products or in resell to others is known as supplier development. This is the result of shifts in the relationship between customers and suppliers from somewhat adversarial to close alliances. Find two companies that promote this supplier-partner relationship (other than listed in your chapter).

4.   Key Term: Straight Rebuy

There are only three major types of buying situations, one of which is the straight rebuy. A straight rebuy occurs when a buyer reorders something without any modification. Think about your favorite restaurant in town. What would be examples of a straight rebuy your restaurant might place?

5.   Key Term: Systems Selling

When a vendor provides a packaged solution to a problem, thus alleviating a company from having to make all of the separate decisions involved in a complex buying situation, they are engaging in "systems selling." Systems selling is a key marketing strategy for winning and holding accounts. Find a company that engages in systems selling.

6.   Key Term: The Buying Center

The buying center of an organization is made up of all the individuals and units that play a role in the purchase decision-making process. To bring the buying center to a more personal level, think about your family. Describe your family in "buying center" terms for the purchase of a new automobile.

7.   Key Term: Environmental Factors

Business buyers are heavily influenced by factors in the current and expected economic environment—factors such as supply conditions, technological change, and political and regulatory developments. Consider R.J. Reynolds (www.rjrt.com), the manufacturer of one out of three cigarettes sold in the U.S. How may have environmental factors impacted the buyers within this company?

8.   Key Term: Proposal Solicitation

The stage of the business buying process in which the buyer invites qualified suppliers to submit a proposal is known as the proposal solicitation stage. Locate a company that is currently seeking proposals from qualified suppliers.

9.   Key Term: E-Procurement

Online purchasing is growing at a very rapid pace, thanks to advances in information technology. B2B marketers help customers who wish to purchase online by providing them with easy-to-use websites. Take a look at e-procurement site for Office Depot (https://bsd.officedepot.com/). How are they making it easier for organization to take advantage of online purchasing?

10.   Key Term: Institutional Markets

Institutional markets are different from other markets. In many cases, the lowest price is not the primary objective. Take a look at your school's cafeterias. Why would you characterize them as an institutional market?

Marketing ADventure Exercises

1.   Ad Interpretation Challenge: Business Markets
        Ad: Service and B2B—SpeedStart

As your text points out, the business market is huge—far larger than the consumer market. The business market is made up of goods and services for use in the production of other products and services that are sold to others. This ad for SpeedStart is just one of many examples of advertisements directed to a business market. From this ad, what lets you know that SpeedStart is a B2B company?

2.   Ad Interpretation Challenge: Derived Demand
      Ad: Electronics—Axiom

Derived demand is business demand that ultimately comes from the demand for consumer goods or services. How does Axiom provide an example of derived demand?

3.   Ad Interpretation Challenge: Inelastic Demand
      Ad: Autos—Dunlop

Many business markets have inelastic demand—meaning that total demand for many business products is affected very little by price changes, at least in the short run. Think about this ad for Dunlop tires. What business products, used by Dunlop in the production of these tires, may display inelastic demand?

4.   Ad Interpretation Challenge: Straight Rebuy
      Ad: Services and B2B—EMS

A straight rebuy situation occurs when the business routinely reorders something without any modification. They use the same product or service over and over. Check out this ad for EMS. Think of a situation in which EMS services become a straight rebuy for a company.

5.   Ad Interpretation Challenge: Systems Selling
      Ad: Services and B2B—Springbow

Many business buyers prefer to buy a packaged solution to a problem from a single supplier. This keeps the company from having to buy the separate components and create the package solution themselves. This is systems selling. How is Springbow engaging in systems selling?

6.   Ad Interpretation Challenge: Environmental Factors
      Ad: Services and B2B—Posta

Business buyers are heavily influenced by factors in the current and anticipated economic environment. Business buyers are also impacted by technological, political, and competitive developments in the environment. Additionally, culture and customs can play a significant role in buyer behavior. What environmental factors may be at play in this ad for the Italian Postal System?

7.   Ad Interpretation Challenge: Problem Recognition
      Ad: Services and B2B—Varig

The first stage of the business buying process is when someone in the company recognizes a problem or need that can be met by acquiring a good or a service. Sometimes, marketers can facilitate this problem recognition by providing information to buying centers that may assist them is recognizing a problem. Think about this ad for Varig cargo services. How might this ad be useful in helping a member of the buying center realize a problem exists?

8.   Ad Interpretation Challenge: E-Procurement
        Ad: Student Choice

During the past several years, technology has made it much easier to accomplish online purchasing (e-procurement). This advance is changing the face of the B2B marketing process. Find an ad for a company that you believe could have their product or services purchased through an e-procurement system.

9.   Ad Interpretation Challenge: Institutional Markets
        Ad: Student Choice

The institutional market consists of schools, hospitals, prisons, and other institutions that provide goods and services to people in their care. Many institutional markets are characterized by captive patrons. Find an ad for an institutional marketer.

10.   Ad Interpretation Challenge: Government Markets
        Ad: Electronics—Energizer

In most countries, government organizations are major buyers of goods and services. Although government buying and business buying are alike in many ways, differences do exist. Government organizations typically award contracts to the lowest bidder, but not always. How could Energizer hope to persuade a government organization to accept their bid for batteries, even though it was not the lowest?

Chapter 7
Customer-Driven Marketing Strategy:
Creating Value for Target Customers

Learning Objectives

1. Define the four major steps in designing a customer-driven marketing strategy: market segmentation, market targeting, differentiation, and positioning
2. List and discuss the major bases for segmenting consumer and business markets
3. Explain how companies identify attractive market segments and choose a market targeting strategy
4. Discuss how companies differentiate and position their products for maximum competitive advantage in the marketplace.

Chapter Overview

This chapter looks further into key customer-driven marketing strategy decisions—how to divide up markets into meaningful customer groups (*segmentation*), choose which customer groups to serve (*targeting*), create market offerings that best serve targeted customers (*differentiation*), and positioning the offerings in the minds of consumers (*positioning*). Then, the chapters that follow explore the tactical marketing tools—the Four Ps—by which marketers bring these strategies to life.

Chapter Outline

1. INTRODUCTION

One of Procter & Gamble's fastest-growing brands, odor fighter Febreze, is not targeting a new lifestyle segment: college students. The brand recently kicked off "What Stinks," an online and viral campaign for its fabric-refresher spray aimed at this sometimes hard to reach, fickle segment. For most of the brand's existence, it has been directed toward working adults and soccer moms, positioning itself as a "Breath of Fresh Air." However, P&G realized that this targeting was leaving out an entire group of customers – Millennials, which includes college students. Why is Febreze a natural for college students? "Washing is not a convenient part of the lifestyle at college," says Martin Hertich, North American marketing direction for Febreze. In recent years, P&G has launched a movement to help students find ways to rewear unwashed clothes. For example, it recently introduced a new Swash line of dewrinkling sprays, stain-removing pens, and odor-removing sprays. Febreze is a natural extension.

A traditional, mainstream marketing approach would probably fail to reach this college student-segment. So, Febreze opted for an online and viral approach, built around an interactive website, www.WhatStinks.com, linked directly through Facebook. The student-targeted Febreze What Stinks campaign, along with P&G's other skillful targeting and positioning efforts for the brand, have helped make Febreze the world's leading fabric freshener and deodorizer. It's also one of P&G's fastest growing brands.

Opening Vignette Questions

1. Why did P&G decide to change the marketing of Febreze? After all, it was already a successful product within their company.
2. How does P&G promote the Febreze brand?
3. When P&G made the decision to reposition the product, why did it feel it had to market Febreze differently to reach this new target market?

Most companies have moved away from mass marketing and toward *target marketing*—identifying market segments, selecting one or more of them, and developing products and marketing programs tailored to each.

Figure 7.1 shows the four major steps in designing a customer-driven marketing strategy.

- Market segmentation involves dividing a market into smaller groups of buyers with distinct needs, characteristics, or behaviors that might require separate marketing strategies or mixes.
- Market targeting (or targeting) consists of evaluating each market segment's attractiveness and selecting one or more market segments to enter.
- Differentiation involves actually differentiating the firm's market offering to create superior customer value.
- Positioning consists of arranging for a market offering to occupy a clear, distinctive, and desirable place relative to competing products in the minds of target consumers.

2. MARKET SEGMENTATION

Through market segmentation, companies divide large, heterogeneous markets into smaller segments that can be reached more efficiently and effectively with products and services that match their unique needs.

2.1 Consumer Markets

Table 7.1 outlines the major variables that might be used in segmenting consumer markets.

2.1.1 Geographic Segmentation

Geographic segmentation calls for dividing the market into different geographical units such as nations, regions, states, counties, cities, or even neighborhoods.

2.1.2 Demographic Segmentation

Demographic segmentation divides the market into groups based on variables such as age, gender, family size, family life cycle, income, occupation, education, religion, race, generation, and nationality. Demographic factors are the most popular bases for segmenting customer groups. Age and Life-Cycle Stage is offering different products or using different marketing approaches for different age and life-cycle groups. Gender segmentation has long been used in clothing, cosmetics, toiletries, and magazines. Income segmentation has long been used by the marketers of products and services such as automobiles, clothing, cosmetics, financial services, and travel.

2.1.3 Psychographic Segmentation

Psychographic segmentation divides buyers into different groups based on social class, lifestyle, or personality characteristics. Marketers use *personality* variables to segment markets.

2.1.4 Behavioral Segmentation

Behavioral segmentation divides buyers into groups based on their knowledge, attitudes, uses, or responses to a product.

- Occasion segmentation is grouping buyers according to occasions when they get the idea to buy, actually make their purchase, or use the purchased item.
- Benefit segmentation is grouping buyers according to the different *benefits* that they seek from the product.
- User Status is segmenting markets into nonusers, ex-users, potential users, first-time users, and regular users of a product.
- Usage Rate is grouping markets into light, medium, and heavy product users.
- Loyalty Status is dividing buyers into groups according to their degree of loyalty.

2.1.5 Using Multiple Segmentation Bases

Marketers rarely limit their segmentation analysis to only one or a few variables. PRIZM NE (one of the leading segmentation systems) classifies every American household based on a host of demographic factors.

2.2 Business Markets

Consumer and business marketers use many of the same variables to segment their markets. Business marketers also use some additional variables, such as customer *operating characteristics*, *purchasing approaches*, *situational factors*, and *personal characteristics*. Many marketers believe that *buying behavior* and *benefits* provide the best basis for segmenting business markets.

2.3 Segmenting International Markets

Companies can segment international markets using one or a combination of several variables.

- *Geographic factors:* Nations close to one another will have many common traits and behaviors.
- *Economic factors:* Countries may be grouped by population income levels or by their overall level of economic development.
- *Political and legal factors:* Type and stability of government, receptivity to foreign firms, monetary regulations, and the amount of bureaucracy.
- *Cultural factors:* Grouping markets according to common languages, religions, values and attitudes, customs, and behavioral patterns.

Intermarket segmentation is segmenting of consumers who have similar needs and buying behavior even though they are located in different countries.

2.4 Requirements for Effective Segmentation

To be useful, market segments must be:

- Measurable: The size, purchasing power, and profiles of the segments can be measured.
- Accessible: The market segments can be effectively reached and served.
- Substantial: The market segments are large or profitable enough to serve.
- Differentiable: The segments are conceptually distinguishable and respond differently to different marketing mix elements and programs.
- Actionable: Effective programs can be designed for attracting and serving the segments

3. MARKET TARGETING

3.1 Evaluating Market Segments

In evaluating different market segments, a firm must look at three factors:

- Segment size and growth,
- Segment structural attractiveness, and
- Company objectives and resources.

The largest, fastest-growing segments are not always the most attractive ones for every company. The company also needs to examine major structural factors that affect long-run segment attractiveness.

- A segment is less attractive if it already contains many strong and aggressive *competitors*.
- The existence of many actual or potential *substitute products* may limit prices and the profits.
- The relative *power of buyers* also affects segment attractiveness.

70

- A segment may be less attractive if it contains ***powerful suppliers*** who can control prices.

3.2 Selecting Target Market Segments

A target market consists of a set of buyers who share common needs or characteristics that the company decides to serve. (Figure 7.2)

3.2.1 Undifferentiated Marketing

Using an undifferentiated marketing (or mass-marketing) strategy, a firm might decide to ignore market segment differences and target the whole market with one offer. This mass-marketing strategy focuses on what is *common* in the needs of consumers rather than on what is *different*.

3.2.2 Differentiated Marketing

Using a differentiated marketing (or segmented marketing) strategy, a firm decides to target several market segments and designs separate offers for each.

3.2.3 Concentrated Marketing

Using a concentrated marketing (or niche marketing) strategy, instead of going after a small share of a large market, the firm goes after a large share of one or a few smaller segments or niches. It can market more *effectively* by fine-tuning its products, prices, and programs to the needs of carefully defined segments. It can market more *efficiently*, targeting its products or services, channels, and communications programs toward only consumers that it can serve best and most profitably.

3.2.4 Micromarketing

Micromarketing is the practice of tailoring products and marketing programs to suit the tastes of specific individuals and locations. Micromarketing includes *local marketing* and *individual marketing*. Local marketing involves tailoring brands and promotions to the needs and wants of local customer groups—cities, neighborhoods, and even specific stores. Individual marketing is the tailoring of products and marketing programs to the needs and preferences of individual customers. Individual marketing has also been labeled *one-to-one marketing*, *mass customization,* and *markets-of-one marketing*.

3.3 Choosing a Targeting Strategy

Which strategy is best depends on company resources, product variability, product life cycle stage, market variability and competitor marketing strategy.

3.4 Socially Responsible Target Marketing

Target marketing sometimes generates controversy and concern. Issues usually involve the targeting of vulnerable or disadvantaged consumers with controversial or potentially harmful products. Problems arise when marketing adult products to kids, whether intentionally or unintentionally. The growth of the Internet and other carefully targeted direct media has raised concerns about potential targeting abuses. The issue is not so much who is targeted, but how and for what. Controversies arise when marketers attempt to profit when they unfairly target vulnerable segments or target them with questionable products or tactics. Socially responsible marketing calls for segmentation and targeting that serve not just the interests of the company, but also the interests of those targeted.

4. DIFFERENTIATION AND POSITIONING

Value proposition: How a company will create differentiated value for targeted segments and what positions it wants to occupy in those segments. A product's position is the way the product is *defined by consumers* on important attributes.

4.1 Positioning Maps

Perceptual positioning map show consumer perceptions of their brands versus competing products on important buying dimensions.

4.2 Choosing a Differentiation and Positioning Strategy

The differentiation and positioning task consists of three steps:

- Identifying a set of differentiating competitive advantages upon which to build a position,
- Choosing the right competitive advantages, and
- Selecting an overall positioning strategy.

4.2.1 Identifying Possible Value Differences and Competitive Advantages

To the extent that a company can differentiate and position itself as providing superior customer value, it gains competitive advantage. It can differentiate along the lines of *product, services, channels, people,* or *image*.

4.2.2 Choosing the Right Competitive Advantages

4.3 How Many Differences to Promote

Ad man Rosser Reeves believes a company should develop a *unique selling proposition* (USP) for each brand and stick to it. Other marketers think that companies should position themselves on more than one differentiator.

4.4 Which Differences to Promote

A difference is worth establishing to the extent that it satisfies the following criteria:

- Important: *The difference delivers a highly valued benefit to target buyers.*
- Distinctive: *Competitors do not offer the difference, or the company can offer it in a more distinctive way.*
- Superior: *The difference is superior to other ways that customers might obtain the same benefit.*
- Communicable: *The difference is communicable and visible to buyers.*
- Preemptive: *Competitors cannot easily copy the difference.*
- Affordable: *Buyers can afford to pay for the difference.*
- Profitable: *The company can introduce the difference profitably*

4.4.1 Selecting an Overall Positioning Strategy

The full positioning of a brand is called the brand's value proposition. **More for More** positioning involves providing the most upscale product or service and charging a higher price to cover the higher costs. **More for the Same** positioning involves introducing a brand offering comparable quality but at a lower price. **The Same for Less positioning** can be a powerful value proposition—everyone likes a good deal. **Less for Much Less positioning is offering** products that offer less and therefore cost less. "Less-for-much-less" positioning involves meeting consumers' lower performance or quality requirements at a much lower price. **More for Less positioning is the winning** value proposition. In the long run, companies will find it very difficult to sustain such best-of-both positioning.

4.4.2 Developing a Positioning Statement

Company and brand positioning should be summed up in a positioning statement. The statement should follow the form: *To (target segment and need) our (brand) is (concept) that (point of difference).*

4.5 Communicating and Delivering the Chosen Position

Once it has chosen a position, the company must take strong steps to deliver and communicate the desired position to target consumers. All the company's marketing mix efforts must support the positioning strategy.

Student Exercises

1.   Key Term: Market Segmentation

In designing a customer-driven marketing strategy, the company must first decide which customers it will serve. Market segmentation is dividing a market into smaller groups with distinct needs, characteristics, or behaviors who might require separate products or marketing mixes. Take a look at Bebe (www.bebe.com). Bebe has done a nice job of segmenting the overall women's clothing market. They do not attempt to service everyone. How has Bebe segmented this market?

2.   Key Term: Geographic Segmentation

There are many ways to segment a consumer market. Geographic segmentation is but one. Geographic segmentation is dividing a market into different geographical units such as nations, regions of a country, states, or even neighborhoods. Go to Polaris Industries website (www.polarisindustries.com) and take a look at their product offering. Polaris is best known for two products: snowmobiles and all-terrain vehicles (ATVs). Talk about the geographic segmentation you would employ to reach customers most interested in both of these products.

3.   Key Term: Gender Segmentation

Gender segmentation has long been used to effectively market some product categories, such as clothing, cosmetics, and magazines. Your text talks about the efforts Nike has made to better service the female segment of its market, like overhauling its women's apparel line to make it more appealing. Take a look at Clinique cosmetics (www.clinique.com). What are they doing in an effort to reach male customers?

4.   Key Term: Psychographic Segmentation

Psychographic segmentation divides buyers into different groups based on social class, lifestyle, or personality characteristics. Just because you are in the same demographic group as someone else does not mean you share the same psychographic makeup. Pottery Barn (www.potterybarn.com), mentioned in your text, has done an excellent job of using psychographic segmentation to effectively segment the market it serves. Review the Pottery Barn website. How would you say they use psychographic segmentation?

5.   Key Term: Occasion Segmentation

Buyers can be segmented on the basis of when they get the idea to buy, actually buy, or consume a purchased product. For example, flowers are mostly commonly purchased for Mother's Day or Valentine's Day. Fruit juices are most likely consumed in the morning. There is always a spike in Champaign sales around New Year's. What are two other types of products whose increase in consumption can be predicted by the occasion?

6.   Key Term: Loyalty Status

A company's customers can be completely loyal, somewhat loyal, or not loyal at all. Obviously, companies would prefer their customers to be completely loyal customers. As such, they buy one brand all of the time. They do not generally take the time to consider the marketing efforts of competing companies. Companies spend considerable time, effort, and expense, in catering to these loyal customers, in an effort to keep them loyal and to keep them coming back time after time. Look at Wyndham Hotels (www.wyndham.com). What are they doing to keep loyal customers loyal?

7.   Key Term: International Markets

The world seems to be becoming a smaller and smaller place. As such, more and more companies are operating in the international arena, to one degree or the other. Few companies have the resources to operate in all corners of the globe. Different countries can vary greatly in their economic, cultural, and political makeup. Even countries that are located in close proximity with one another may be very different. Thus, international firms need to group their world markets into segments with distinct buying needs and behaviors. Go to the homepage for EBay (www.ebay.com) and take a look at some of their international sites (they are located at the bottom of the main page). How have the international sites been adapted to meet local markets?

8.   Key Term: Measurable

One of the requirements for effective market segmentation is that the segment must be measurable. This means that the size of the segment, its purchasing power, and profile must all be able to be measured. You may have what you believe would be a good market segment, but if you cannot measure the segment, how would you know if it is viable to market to the segment? Visit Nielsen Media Research (www.nielsenmedia.com) and take a look at the variety of market reports that are available to subscribers. This will give you a feel of the type, quality, and quantity of segmentation data available from just one source.

9.   Key Term: Concentrated Marketing

Concentrated marketing (also called niche marketing) is a market coverage strategy that is particularly appropriate to use when company resources are limited. A company choosing to employ a niche marketing strategy is devoting its resources to go after a large share of a small segment (or niche), instead of going after a small share of a larger market. Find two companies that employ concentrated marketing strategies.

10.   Key Term: Individual Marketing

The ultimate example of micromarketing is individual marketing. Individual marketing is the tailoring of products and marketing programs to the needs and preferences of individual consumers. The advent of advanced web technology has made it easier for some companies to employ this version of micromarketing. Look at Audi's website (www.audiusa.com). How is Audi using technology to make use of individual marketing?

Marketing ADventure Exercises

1.   Ad Interpretation Challenge: Market Segmentation
        Ad: Apparel—Levi's Diamond Jeans

The first thing a company must do, in the design of a customer-driven marketing strategy, is to decide which customers it will serve. Market segmentation is dividing a market into smaller groups with distinct needs, characteristics, or behaviors that might require separate products or marketing mixes. Take a look at this Levi's ad. Based on this ad, Levi's has done a nice job of segmenting the women's jean market. They are not attempting to service everyone. What market do you believe Levi's is targeting?

2.   Ad Interpretation Challenge: Geographic Segmentation
        Ad: Student Choice

Geographic segmentation is one of many methods of market segmentation available to the marketer. Geographic segmentation is dividing a market into different geographical units such as nations, regions of a country, states, or even neighborhoods. Find an ad that is based on geographic segmentation.

3.   Ad Interpretation Challenge: Demographic Segmentation
        Ad: Services and B2B—University of Toronto

The most popular and widely used form of market segmentation is demographic segmentation. Demographic segmentation is so popular, in part, due to the fact that demographics are easier to measure than other segmentation variables. Demographic segmentation is the dividing of a market into groups based on variables such as age, gender, income, education, or other easily observable characteristic. Look at the ads for the University of Toronto. What would you say is the demographic segmentation variable is use here?

4.   Ad Interpretation Challenge: Gender Segmentation
        Ad: Student Choice

Gender segmentation is dividing the market into groups on the basis of gender. Gender segmentation has long been used in clothing, cosmetics, and magazines. Find an ad for a product that you believe is targeted to men. How could this product (or ad) be altered to be more appealing to women?

5.   Ad Interpretation Challenge: Income Segmentation
        Ad: Autos—Hyundai

Income segmentation is dividing the market into different groups on the basis of overall income. This form of segmentation has long been used by marketers of products and services such as automobiles, jewelry, travel, and financial services. Income segmentation is a valuable form of market segmentation at both the upper ends of the income categories and at the lower ends. Too frequently we think of using income segmentation at only the high end. Take a look at Hyundai. How might they position themselves to appeal more to lower income market segments?

6.   Ad Interpretation Challenge: Psychographic Segmentation
       Ad: Apparel—Umbro

People in the same demographic group may have very different likes and dislikes. They may possess very different psychographic profiles. Psychographic segmentation is dividing a market into different groups based on social class, lifestyle, or personality characteristics. How is Umbro using psychographic segmentation?

7.   Ad Interpretation Challenge: Occasions Based Segmentation
       Ad: Services and B2B: 24 Hour Fitness

Sometimes we can group buyers together on the basis of when they purchase or use a product (or service). Culture and habit many times dictate when we typically use some products. For example, the most popular nights for consumers to eat a meal out in a restaurant are Friday and Saturday. Most yogurts are consumed in the morning during the time we typically eat breakfast. How might occasions based segmentation have been behind the company 24 Hour Fitness?

8.   Ad Interpretation Challenge: Undifferentiated Marketing
       Ad: Student Choice

Undifferentiated (or mass) marketing is a market-coverage strategy in which a firm decides to ignore market segment differences and go after the whole market with one offer. This strategy focuses on what is common in the needs of consumers rather than what is unique or different about them. Look through the offered advertisements and try to locate one that is using an undifferentiated marketing approach.

9.   Ad Interpretation Challenge: Niche Marketing
       Ad: Newspapers and TV—Football Channel

Sometimes you do not want to be a player in the larger markets. Sometimes it makes more sense to use your limited resources to become a big player in a small market. Concentrated marketing (niche marketing) is just that. Instead of going after a small share of a large market, niche marketers go after a large share of a smaller market. Look at the Football Channel. Why would this company be considered playing in a niche market?

10.   Ad Interpretation Challenge: Individual Marketing
        Ad: Student Choice

Individual marketing is the tailoring of products and marketing programs to the needs and wants of individual customers. Individual marketing has also been called *one-to-one marketing* and *mass customization*. Find an ad that promotes this concept of individual marketing.

Chapter 8
Products, Services, and Brands: Building Customer Value

Learning Objectives

1. Define *product* and the major classifications of products and services
2. Describe the decisions companies make regarding their individual products and services, product lines, and product mixes
3. Discuss branding strategy—the decisions companies make in building and managing their brands
4. Identify the four characteristics that affect the marketing of a service and the additional marketing considerations that services require

Chapter Overview

In this and the next chapter, we look at how companies develop and manage products and brands. The product is usually the first and most basic marketing consideration. This chapter begins with a deceptively simple question: *What is a product?* After addressing this question, we look at ways to classify products in consumer and business markets. Then we discuss the important decisions that marketers make regarding individual products, product lines, and product mixes. Next, we look into the critically important issue of how marketers build and manage brands. Finally, we examine the characteristics and marketing requirements of a special form of product—services.

Chapter Outline

1. INTRODUCTION

Many old-timers still think of Las Vegas as "Sin City." The new Vegas has reinvented itself as a luxury destination. To visitors, Vegas is an emotional connection, a total brand experience. The research showed that the when people come to Las Vegas, they're a little naughtier. "We found that [the Las Vegas experience] centered on adult freedom," says Ralenkotter. "People could stay up all night and do things they wouldn't normally do in their own towns." Based on these consumer insights, the LVCVA coined a now-familiar catchphrase—"Only Vegas: What happens here, stays here." "It's all about branding," says CEO Ralenkotter. "The slogan captures the city's experiences rather than amenities, the image that Las Vegas represents freedom."

Opening Vignette Questions

1. What 'product' is Las Vegas selling?
2. Who would you consider to be their target market?
3. What is the 'Las Vegas' brand?

2. WHAT IS A PRODUCT?

A product is anything that can be offered to a market for attention, acquisition, use, or consumption that might satisfy a want or need. Broadly defined, "products" also include services, events, persons, places, organizations, ideas, or mixes of these. Services are a form of product that consists of activities, benefits, or satisfactions offered for sale that are essentially intangible and do not result in the ownership of anything.

2.1 Products, Services, and Experiences

A company's market offering often includes both tangible goods and services. At one extreme, the offer may consist of a *pure tangible good,* such as soap or toothpaste. At the other extreme are *pure services,* for which the offer consists primarily of a service. To differentiate their offers, marketers are creating and managing customer *experiences* with their brands or company.

2.2 Levels of Product and Services

Product planners need to think about products and services on three levels.

1. Core customer value
2. Actual product.
3. Augmented product

2.3 Product and Service Classifications

There are two main classification of products: *consumer products* and *industrial products.*

2.3.1 Consumer Products

Consumer products are products and services bought by final consumers for personal consumption. Consumer products include (see Table 8.1):

- Convenience products are consumer products and services that customers usually buy frequently, immediately, and with a minimum of comparison and buying effort.
- Shopping products are less frequently purchased consumer products and services that customers compare carefully on suitability, quality, price, and style.
- Specialty products are consumer products and services with unique characteristics or brand identification for which a significant group of buyers is willing to make a special purchase effort.
- Unsought products are consumer products that the consumer either does not know about or knows about but does not normally think of buying.

2.3.2 Industrial Products

Industrial products are those purchased for further processing or for use in conducting a business. The three groups of industrial products and services are:

- *Materials and parts* include raw materials and manufactured materials and parts.
- *Capital items* are industrial products that aid in the buyer's production or operations, including installations and accessory equipment.
- *Supplies and services* include operating supplies and maintenance and repair services.

2.4 Organizations, Persons, Places, and Ideas

Organization marketing consists of activities undertaken to create, maintain, or change the attitudes and behavior of target consumers toward an organization. *Person marketing* consists of activities undertaken to create, maintain, or change attitudes or behavior toward particular people. *Place marketing* involves activities undertaken to create, maintain, or change attitudes or behavior toward particular places. Social marketing is the use of commercial marketing concepts and tools in programs designed to influence individuals' behavior to improve their well-being and that of society.

3. PRODUCT AND SERVICE DECISIONS

3.1 Individual Product and Service Decisions

3.1.1 Product and Service Attributes

- Developing a product or service involves defining the benefits that it will offer. These benefits are communicated and delivered by product attributes such as *quality*, *features*, and *style and design*.
- Product Quality is creating customer value and satisfaction.
- *Total quality management (TQM)* is an approach in which all the company's people are involved in constantly improving the quality of products, services, and business processes.
- *Product quality* has two dimensions: level and consistency. The quality level means performance quality or the ability of a product to perform its functions. Quality conformance means quality consistency, freedom from defects, and consistency in delivering a targeted level of performance.
- Product Features are a competitive tool for differentiating the company's product from competitors' products. The company should periodically survey buyers who have used the product and ask these questions: How do you like the product? Which specific features of the product do you like most? Which features could we add to improve the product?
- Product Style and Design is another way to add customer value. *Style* describes the appearance of a product. *Design* contributes to a product's

usefulness as well as to its looks.

3.1.2   Branding

A **brand** is a name, term, sign, symbol, or design, or a combination of these, that identifies the maker or seller of a product or service.

3.1.3   Packaging

Packaging involves designing and producing the container or wrapper for a product.

3.1.3   Labeling

Labels perform several functions.
- The label *identifies* the product or brand.
- The label *describes* several things about the product.
- The label *promotes* the brand.

Labeling also raises concerns. As a result, several federal and state laws regulate labeling. The most prominent is the Fair Packaging and Labeling Act of 1966.

3.1.4   Product Support Services

The first step is to survey customers periodically to assess the value of current services and to obtain ideas for new ones. Next, the company can take steps to fix problems and add new services that will both delight customers and yield profits to the company.

3.2 Product Line Decisions

A product line is a group of products that are closely related because they function in a similar manner, are sold to the same customer groups, are marketed through the same types of outlets, or fall within given price ranges.
- *Product line length* is the number of items in the product line.
- *Product line filling* involves adding more items within the present range of the line.
- *Product line stretching* occurs when a company lengthens its product line beyond its current range. Companies located at the upper end of the market can stretch their lines *downward*. Companies located at the lower end of the market can stretch their product lines *upward*. Companies located in the middle range of the market can stretch their lines in *both directions*.

3.3 Product Mix Decisions

Product mix (or product portfolio) consists of all the product lines and items that a particular seller offers for sale. A company's product mix has four dimensions: width, length, depth, and consistency.

- Product mix *width* refers to the number of different product lines the company carries.
- Product mix *length* refers to the total number of items the company carries within its product lines.
- Product mix *depth* refers to the number of versions offered of each product in the line.
- Product mix *consistency* refers to how closely related the various product lines are in end use, production requirements, distribution channels, or some other way.

The company can increase its business in four ways.
1. It can add new product lines, widening its product mix.
2. It can lengthen its existing product lines.
3. It can add more versions of each product, deepening its product mix.
4. It can pursue more product line consistency.

4. BRANDING STRATEGY: BUILDING STRONG BRANDS

Some analysts see brands as *the* major enduring asset of a company. Brand Equity is the positive differential effect that knowing the brand name has on customer response to the product or service. Young & Rubicam's Brand Asset Evaluator measures brand strength along four consumer perception dimensions:

1. *differentiation* (what makes the brand stand out),
2. *relevance* (how consumers feel it meets their needs),
3. *knowledge* (how much consumers know about the brand), and
4. *esteem* (how highly consumers regard and respect the brand).

Brand valuation is the process of estimating the total financial value of a brand.

High brand equity provides a company with many competitive advantages.
- High level of consumer brand awareness and loyalty.
- More leverage in bargaining with resellers.
- More easily launch line and brand extensions.
- Defense against fierce price competition.
- Forms the basis for building strong and profitable customer relationships.

The fundamental asset underlying brand equity is *customer equity*—the value of the customer relationships that the brand creates.

4.1 Building Strong Brands

4.1.1 Brand Positioning

Marketers can position brands at any of three levels.
1. They can position the brand on *product attributes.*
2. They can position the brand with a desirable *benefit*.
3. They can position the brand on *beliefs and values.*

4.1.2 Brand Name Selection

Desirable qualities for a brand name include the following:

- It should suggest something about the product's benefits and qualities.
- It should be easy to pronounce, recognize, and remember.
- The brand name should be distinctive.
- It should be extendable.
- The name should translate easily into foreign languages.
- It should be capable of registration and legal protection.

4.1.3 Brand Sponsorship

A manufacturer has four sponsorship options.
- The product may be launched as a *manufacturer's brand* (or national brand).
- The manufacturer may sell to resellers who give it a *private brand* (also called a *store brand* or *distributor brand*).
- The manufacturer can market *licensed brands*.
- Two companies can join forces and *cobrand* a product

4.2 National Brands Versus Store Brands

National brands (or manufacturers' brands) have long dominated the retail scene. In recent times, an increasing number of retailers and wholesalers have created their own store brands (or *private brands*).

4.3 Licensing

Name and character licensing has grown rapidly in recent years. Annual retail sales of licensed products in the United States and Canada have grown from only $4 billion in 1977 to $55 billion in 1987 and more than $187 billion today.

4.4 Cobranding

Cobranding occurs when two established brand names of different companies are used on the same product.

4.5 Brand Development

A company has four choices when it comes to developing brands (see Figure 8.4).
- Line Extensions occur when a company extends existing brand names to new forms, colors, sizes, ingredients, or flavors of an existing product category.
- Brand Extensions extend a current brand name to new or modified products in a new category.
- Multibranding introduces additional brands in the same category.
- New Brands.
- Megabrand strategy—weeding out weaker brands and focusing their marketing dollars only on brands that can achieve the number-one or number-two market share positions in their categories.

4.6 Managing Brands

The *brand experience* is customers coming to know a brand through a wide range of contacts and touchpoints. Companies need to periodically audit their brands' strengths and weaknesses.

5. SERVICES MARKETING

5.1 Nature and Characteristics of a Service

A company must consider four service characteristics when designing marketing programs: *intangibility*, *inseparability*, *variability*, and *perishability* (see Figure 8.5).

- Service intangibility means that services cannot be seen, tasted, felt, heard, or smelled before they are bought.
- Service inseparability means that services cannot be separated from their providers, whether the providers are people or machines. Because the customer is also present as the service is produced, *provider-customer interaction* is a special feature of services marketing.
- Service variability means that the quality of services depends on who provides them as well as when, where, and how they are provided.
- Service perishability means that services cannot be stored for later sale or use.

5.2 Marketing Strategies for Service Firms

5.2.1 The Service-Profit Chain

In a service business, the customer and front-line service employee *interact* to create the service. The service-profit chain consists of five links:

- Internal service quality: *superior employee selection and training, a quality work environment, and strong support for those dealing with customers, which results in...*

85

- Satisfied and productive service employees: *more satisfied, loyal, and hardworking employees, which results in...*
- Greater service value: *more effective and efficient customer value creation and service delivery, which results in...*
- Satisfied and loyal customers: *satisfied customers who remain loyal, repeat purchase, and refer other customers, which results in...*
- Healthy service profits and growth: *superior service firm performance.*

5.2.2 Service marketing requires *internal marketing* and *interactive marketing*. (Figure 8.6).

Service companies face three major marketing tasks: They want to increase their *service differentiation, service quality*, and *service productivity*.

5.2.3 Managing Service Differentiation

Service companies can differentiate their service *delivery* by having more able and reliable customer-contact people, by developing a superior physical environment in which the service product is delivered, or by designing a superior delivery process. Service companies can work on differentiating their *images* through symbols and branding.

5.2.4 Managing Service Quality

Service quality is harder to define and judge than product quality. Service quality will always vary, depending on the interactions between employees and customers. Good *service recovery* can turn angry customers into loyal ones.

5.2.5 Managing Service Productivity

Service firms are under great pressure to increase service productivity.
- They can train current employees better or hire new ones who will work harder or more skillfully.
- They can increase the quantity of their service by giving up some quality.
- They can harness the power of technology.

Student Exercises

1.   Key Term: Product

What is a product? A product is defined as ANYTHING that can be offered to a market for attention, acquisition, use, or consumption that might satisfy a need or a want. So, as you can see, "product" has a very broad definition. Keep in mind that products are more than just tangible goods. Consider your college or university. What products does your school have?

2.   Key Term: Core Benefit

What is the buyer really buying? This is the most basic level of customer value a product provides. This is the core benefit. When product planners are thinking about products to offer in the marketplace, it is necessary to think of the product at this most basic of levels. Take a look at Canon digital cameras (www.canonusa.com). At its most basic level, what are the core benefits Canon is offering to consumers of its cameras?

3.   Key Term: Convenience Products

Consumer products are products and services bought by final consumers for their personal use. Marketers typically classify these products into three levels, based on how the consumer goes about buying them. Convenience goods are those products (and services) that consumers typically buy frequently, immediately, and without much product comparison or buying effort. Look at the homepage of Procter and Gamble (www.pg.com). Examine all of the different products and brands that they offer to consumers. Which of these product categories would you classify as convenience products?

4.   Key Term: Unsought Products

Unsought products present unique challenges to marketers. These are products that the consumer either does not know about or knows about but does not normally think of buying. The use of the modern windmill to generate electricity for the home is one such typically unsought product. Take a look at http://www.nrel.gov/wind/ and www.windmill.com for basic information on this technology and available products. How would you try to "get the word out" regarding this product?

5.   Key Term: Place Marketing

Place marketing involves activities undertaken to create, maintain, or change attitudes or behaviors toward particular places. Towns, cities, states, regions, or even entire countries compete to attract visitors, conventions, industries, and new residents. The New Orleans and Mississippi Gulf Coast areas are still reeling from the devastating effects of Hurricane Katrina. Take a look at the web marketing efforts of New Orleans (www.neworleansonline.com) and the Mississippi Gulf Coast region (www.gulfcoast.org). What are these regions doing to try and entice travelers back to visit?

6.   Key Term: Product Quality

One of the primary positioning tools available to the marketer is product quality. Product quality can be defined in many ways, but it really centers on creating customer satisfaction and customer value. The American Society for Quality defines quality as the characteristics of a product or service that bear on its ability to satisfy stated or implied customer needs. How would you rate the quality of your school's products?

7.   Key Term: Branding

The name, term, sign, symbol, or design that identifies the maker or the seller of a product of services is knows as its brand. Branding can definitely add value to a product. Brands help consumers identify products that might benefit them. Additionally, brands say something about product quality and consistency. Buyers who always buy the same brands always know what they are getting. What do the automotive brands Toyota (www.toyotausa.com), Kia (www.kia.com), and Volvo (www.volvocars.us) say to you about the products?

8.   Key Term: Packaging

Traditionally, the primary function of the package was to protect and hold the product. Companies are realizing the power of good packaging to create instant consumer recognition of the company and/or the brand. Not too long ago, the package was just considered something to hold the actual product; however, today, the package is an integral part of the product. Find a product for which you believe the packaging is a very meaningful and integral part of that product.

9.   Key Term: Product Line

A product line is a group of products that are closely related because they function in a similar manner, are sold to the same customer groups, are marketed through the same types of outlets, or fall within given price ranges. Look at the J. Peterman Company (www.jpeterman.com). What product lines does this merchant carry?

10.   Key Term: Brand Extension

A brand extension extends a current brand name to new or modified products in a new category. A brand extension gives a new product instant recognition and faster acceptance. However, if not carefully considered, a brand extension may confuse the image of the main brand, damaging its credibility. Read about Sea Ray boats (www.searay.com). If you were Sea Ray and considering a brand extension, what type of product might you consider?

Marketing ADventure Exercises

1. **Ad Interpretation Challenge: Product**
   Ad: Services and B2B—Leo's

A product is defined as anything that can be offered to a market for attention, acquisition, use, or consumption that might satisfy a need or a want. Is Leo's Sports Club a product?

2. **Ad Interpretation Challenge: Core Benefit**
   Ad: Electronics—Fujifilm

When product planners are thinking about products to offer in the marketplace, it is necessary to think of the product at this most basic of levels. A product's core benefit is the basic problem-solving benefits or services consumers seek in the purchase of a product. Think about this ad for Fujifilm. What would you say is the core benefit being offered by this product?

3. **Ad Interpretation Challenge: Convenience Products**
   Ad: Student Choice

Convenience goods are those products that consumers typically buy frequently, immediately, and without much product comparison or buying effort. Convenience products are usually low priced and marketers place them in many locations to make them readily available where customers shop. Find an ad that is promoting a convenience product.

4. **Ad Interpretation Challenge: Organization Marketing**
   Ad: Nonprofit Corporate Images—The Archdiocese

Many times, organizations carry out activities to sell the organization itself. Organization marketing consists of activities undertaken to create, maintain, or change the attitudes and behavior of target consumers toward an organization. Consider this ad for the Archdiocese. How does this type of marketing differ from traditional product marketing?

5. **Ad Interpretation Challenge: Social Marketing**
   Ad: Student Choice

Social marketing is, in essence, the marketing of social ideas. The Social Marketing Institute defines social marketing as the use of commercial marketing concepts and tools in programs designed to influence individuals' behavior to improve their well-being and that of society. Find an ad that exemplifies social marketing. What are the ideals the ad is forwarding?

6.	Ad Interpretation Challenge: Product Features
	Ad: Food and Beverage—Tabasco

Features are a competitive tool for differentiating a company's product from those offered by the competition. One unique feature can effectively distance a company's product from its competition, giving it that competitive advantage. Look at the ad for Tabasco. What is the unique feature of this product that the company hopes sets it apart from all others?

7.	Ad Interpretation Challenge: Packaging
	Ad: Student Choice

At one time, the primary function of the package was to protect and hold the product. Companies are realizing the power of good packaging to create instant consumer recognition of the company and/or the brand. Today, the package is an integral part of the product. Find an ad for a product for which you believe the packaging is a very meaningful and integral part of that product.

8.	Ad Interpretation Challenge: Product Line
	Ad: Autos—Jaguar

A product line is a group of products that are closely related because they function in a similar manner, are sold to the same customer groups, are marketed through the same types of outlets, or fall within given price ranges. A company can lengthen its product line by stretching. Product line stretching occurs when a company lengthens its product line beyond what it is currently offering. A company can stretch its line upward, downward, or both directions. A company must me mindful not to stretch its line to the extent that its core customers rebel. Sometimes a company can go too far, by lengthening its product line to include versions of the product its consumers do not recognize as belonging. Consider Jaguar. What dangers, if any, do you believe Jaguar is facing by lengthening its product line?

9.	Ad Interpretation Challenge: Product Mix
	Ad: Apparel—Levi's

The product mix (or product portfolio) is the set of all product lines and items that a particular seller offers for sale. Take a look at the Levis' ads offered. Also, log on to their website (www.us.levi.com). Examine the consistency of their product mix.

10.	Ad Interpretation Challenge: Brand Extensions
	Ad: Autos—Honda

A brand extension extends a current brand name to new or modified products in a new category. A brand extension gives a new product instant recognition and faster acceptance. However, if not carefully considered, a brand extension may confuse the image of the main brand, damaging its credibility. Take a look at the ads for Honda (both car and motorcycle). How do you believe Honda was able to successfully extend their brand from one form of transportation to another form (or forms) of transportation, in the U.S. market?

Chapter 9
New-Product Development and Product
Life-Cycle Strategies

Learning Objectives

1. Explain how companies find and develop new-product ideas.
2. List and define the steps in the new-product development process and the major considerations in managing this process.
3. Describe the stages of the product life cycle.
4. Describe how marketing strategies change during the product's life cycle.
5. Discuss two additional product and services issues: socially responsible product decisions and international product and services marketing.

Chapter Overview

In this chapter, we'll look into two product topics:
1. Developing new products

2. Managing products through their life cycles.

New-product development is risky, and many new products fail. The first part of this chapter lays out a process for finding and growing successful new products. In the second part of the chapter, we see that every product passes through several life-cycle stages and that each stage poses new challenges requiring different marketing strategies and tactics. Finally, we look at two additional considerations, social responsibility in product decisions and international product and services marketing.

Chapter Outline

1. INTRODUCTION

Then things took an ugly turn for Apple. In 1985, after tumultuous struggles with the new president he'd hired only a year earlier, Steve Jobs left Apple. With Jobs gone, Apple's creative fires cooled. By the mid- to late-1990s, Apple's sales had plunged to $5 billion, 50 percent off previous highs. Yet Apple has engineered a remarkable turnaround. Last year's sales soared to a record $24 billion, more than triple sales just three years earlier. After returning, Jobs next unleashed Mac OS X. The iMac and Mac OS X put Apple back on the map in personal computing. The iPod ranks as one of the greatest consumer electronics hits of all time. By March of 2008, Apple had sold more than 119 million iPods and more than four billion songs. The iPod captures more than 70 percent of the music player market. Thus, almost overnight, it seems, Steve Jobs has transformed Apple from a failing niche computer maker to a major force in consumer electronics, digital music and video, and who knows what else in the future. And he's done it through innovation.

Opening Vignette Questions

1. What was the cause of Apple's fall from grace?
2. How did Steve Jobs engineer Apple's stunning turnaround?
3. What did *Fortune* mean when it stated, "There [Apple], innovation is a way of life."

2. NEW-PRODUCT DEVELOPMENT STRATEGY

A firm can obtain new products in two ways.
1. *Acquisition*—by buying a whole company, a patent, or a license to produce someone else's product.
2. New-product development efforts.

There are a number of reasons new products may fail.

3. THE NEW-PRODUCT DEVELOPMENT PROCESS
Figure 9.1 shows the eight major steps in the *new-product development process.*

3.1 Idea Generation

Idea generation is the systematic search for new-product ideas.

3.1.1 Internal Idea Sources

Using **internal sources**, the company can find new ideas through formal research and development. Or it can pick the brains of employees—from executives to scientists, engineers, and manufacturing staff to salespeople.

3.1.2 External Idea Sources

Companies can also obtain good new-product ideas from any of a number of external sources, such as *distributors and suppliers* or even competitors. Perhaps the most important source of new-product ideas is *customers* themselves.

3.2 Idea Screening

The first idea-reducing stage is idea screening, which helps spot good ideas and drop poor ones as soon as possible.

3.3 Concept Development and Testing

A product idea is an idea for a possible product that the company can see itself offering to the market. A product concept is a detailed version of the idea stated in meaningful consumer terms. A product image is the way consumers perceive an actual or potential product.

3.3.1 Concept Development

In concept development, several descriptions of the product are generated to find out how attractive each concept is to customers. From these concepts, the best one is chosen.

3.3.2 Concept Testing

Concept testing calls for testing new-product concepts with groups of target consumers.

3.4 Marketing Strategy Development

Marketing strategy development is designing an initial marketing strategy for introducing this car to the market. The *marketing strategy statement* consists of three parts.
1. A description of the target market; the planned value proposition; and the sales, market share, and profit goals for the first few years.
2. Outline of the product's planned price, distribution, and marketing budget for the first year.
3. Description of the planned long-run sales, profit goals, and marketing mix strategy.

3.5 Business Analysis

Business analysis involves a review of the sales, costs, and profit projections for a new product to find out whether they satisfy the company's objectives.

3.6 Product Development

In product development, R&D or engineering develops the product concept into a physical product. The product development step calls for a large jump in investment.

3.7 Test Marketing

Test marketing is the stage at which the product and marketing program are introduced into realistic market settings. Standardized test markets occur when the company finds a small number of representative test cities, conducts a full marketing campaign in these cities, and uses store audits, consumer and distributor surveys, and other measures to gauge product performance.

Drawbacks include:
1. Costly
2. Time consuming
3. Competitors can monitor results
4. Competitors get early look at your new product.

Controlled Test Markets track individual consumer behavior for new products from television set to the checkout counter. These markets are composed of stores that have agreed to carry new products for a fee. Such test markets provide in-depth purchasing data not possible with retail point-of-sale data alone. Also, the system allows companies to evaluate their specific marketing efforts.

Drawbacks include:
1. Competitors can monitor results
2. Competitors get early look at your new product
3. Limited number of markets may not be representative of overall market.

Simulated Test Markets are basically simulated shopping environments. The company shows ads and promotions for a variety of products, including the one being tested, to a sample of consumers. It gives consumers a small amount of money and invites them to a store where they may keep the money or use it to buy items.

3.8 Commercialization

Commercialization is introducing the new product into the market.
Decisions must be made concerning:
- Timing,
- Where to launch the new product
- Market rollout.

4. MANAGING NEW-PRODUCT DEVELOPMENT

4.1 Customer-Centered New-Product Development

New-product development must be customer centered. Customer-centered new-product development focuses on finding new ways to solve customer problems and create more customer-satisfying experiences.

4.2 Team-Based New-Product Development

Under the sequential product development approach, one company department works individually to complete its stage of the process before passing the new product along to the next department and stage. This orderly, step-by-step process can help bring control to complex and risky projects. But it also can be dangerously slow. In order to get their new products to market more quickly, many companies use a team-based new-product development approach.

Under this approach, company departments work closely together in cross-functional teams, overlapping the steps in the product development process to save time and increase effectiveness. Instead of passing the new product from department to department, the company assembles a team of people from various departments that stay with the new product from start to finish.

4.3 Systematic New-Product Development

An innovation management system can be used to collect, review, evaluate, and manage new-product ideas. The innovation management system approach yields two favorable outcomes.

1. It helps create an innovation-oriented company culture.
2. It will yield a larger number of new-product ideas, among which will be found some especially good ones.

5. PRODUCT LIFE-CYCLE STRATEGIES

Figure 9.2 shows a typical product life cycle (PLC), the course that a product's sales and profits take over its lifetime.

5.1 The product life cycle has five distinct stages:

5.1.1   Product development begins when the company finds and develops a new-product idea. During product development, sales are zero and the company's investment costs mount.

5.1.2   Introduction is a period of slow sales growth as the product is introduced in the market. Profits are nonexistent in this stage because of the heavy expenses of product introduction.

5.1.3   Growth is a period of rapid market acceptance and increasing profits.

5.1.4   Maturity is a period of slowdown in sales growth because the product has achieved acceptance by most potential buyers. Profits level off or decline because of increased marketing outlays to defend the product against competition.

5.1.5   Decline is the period when sales fall off and profits drop.

The PLC concept can describe a product class (gasoline-powered automobiles), a product form (SUVs), or a brand (the Ford Escape). Product classes have the longest life cycles. Product forms have the standard PLC shape. Product brand PLC can change quickly because of changing competitive attacks and responses.

The PLC can be applied to styles, fashions, and fads (Figure 9.3).
• A style is a basic and distinctive mode of expression.

- A fashion is a currently accepted or popular style in a given field.
- Fads are temporary periods of unusually high sales driven by consumer enthusiasm and immediate product or brand popularity.

5.2 Strategies for each of the other life-cycle stages:

5.2.1 Introduction Stage: The introduction stage starts when the new product is first launched. In this stage, profits are negative or low, promotion spending is relatively high, only basic versions of the product are produced.

5.2.2 Growth Stage: The growth stage is where sales begin to climb quickly. New competitors will enter the market. They will introduce new product features, and the market will expand. The increase in competitors leads to an increase in the number of distribution outlets. Prices remain stable. Profits increase during the growth stage.

5.2.3 Maturity Stage: The maturity stage is characterized by slowing product growth. The slowdown in sales growth results in many producers with many products to sell. Competitors begin marking down prices, increasing their advertising and sales promotions, and upping their product-development budgets to find better versions of the product. These steps lead to a drop in profit. Product managers should consider modifying the market, product, and marketing mix. In modifying the market, the company tries to increase the consumption of the current product. In modifying the product, the company tries changing characteristics such as quality, features, style, or packaging to attract new users and to inspire more usage. In modifying the marketing mix, the company tries changing one or more marketing mix elements.

5.2.4 Decline Stage: The sales of most product forms and brands eventually dip. This is the decline stage. Management may decide to *maintain* its brand without change in the hope that competitors will leave the industry. Management may decide to *harvest* the product, which means reducing various costs (plant and equipment, maintenance, R&D, advertising, sales force) and hoping that sales hold up. Management may decide to *drop* the product from the line.

6. ADDITIONAL PRODUCT AND SERVICE CONSIDERATIONS

6.1 Product Decisions and Social Responsibility

Marketers should consider public policy issues and regulations regarding acquiring or dropping products, patent protection, product quality and safety, and product warranties. Regarding new products, the government may prevent companies from adding products through acquisitions if the effect threatens to lessen competition. Manufacturers must comply with specific laws regarding product quality and safety. Congress passed the

Magnuson-Moss Warranty Act in 1975. The act requires that full warranties meet certain minimum standards, including repair "within a reasonable time and without charge" or a replacement or full refund if the product does not work "after a reasonable number of attempts" at repair.

6.2 International Product and Services Marketing

International product and service marketers face special challenges.
- They must figure out what products and services to introduce and in which countries.
- They must decide how much to standardize or adapt their products and services for world markets.
- Packaging presents new challenges for international marketers.

The trend toward growth of global service companies will continue, especially in banking, airlines, telecommunications, and professional services.

Student Exercises

1.   Key Term: New Product Development

New product development is the development of original products, product improvement, product innovations, and new brands through the firm's own R&D efforts. Innovation can be very risky and very expensive. About 90 percent of all new products fail. Review the information regarding Apple's iPhone (www.apple.com/iphone). What do you think of this product? Do you believe it will "revolutionize" the cell phone market, as Apple states, or will it not live up to expectations?

2.   Key Term: Idea Generation

Companies must develop new products, but the odds are stacked against them. To have a chance at success, a company must carry out strong new-product planning and set up a systematic new-product development process for finding and growing new products. The first stage in this process is known as idea generation. Idea generation is the systematic search for new product ideas. Take a look at the work Frog Design has done for Victoria's Secret (www.frogdesign.com) in the revitalization of its retail design system for its new New York store. How do you believe the stage of idea generation played a part in this revitalization?

3.   Key Term: Concept Development

An attractive product idea must be developed into a product concept. A product concept is a detailed version of the new product idea stated in meaningful terms the consumer understands. Typically, a company will develop alternative product concepts and then find out how attractive each concept is to the customer, choosing the best one for further development. Look again at the Apple iPhone (www.apple.com/iphone). Develop three alternative product concepts for the iPhone Apple may have wanted to consider.

4.   Key Term: Test Marketing

Test marketing is the stage at which the product and marketing program are introduced into more realistic market settings. Test marketing gives the marketer experience with marketing the product before going to the great expense of full introduction. It allows the company to test the product and it entire marketing program. Imagine you were the marketer of a fashion-forward jean, different from anything currently on the market. You are preparing to test market your jeans before going nationwide. Where and how might you consider conducting your test market?

5.   Key Term: Product Life Cycle

The course of a product's sales and profits over its lifetime is known as the Product Life Cycle. It involves five distinct stages – product development, introduction, growth, maturity, and decline. Find a product that represents each of these stages.

6.   Key Term: Fashion

A fashion is a currently accepted or popular style in a given field. Fashions tend to grow slowly, remain popular for an extended period of time, and slowly decline to be replaced by the next fashion. Everyone knows of Morton Salt and the Morton Salt Girl. Go to www.mortonsalt.com. Take a look at how the dress of the little girl has changed through the years in response to changing American fashion.

7.   Key Term: Decline Stage

The last stage of the product life cycle is the decline stage. Products experiencing sales decline and profit decay occupy this unenviable stage. Take a look at the home audio component offering of Pioneer Electronics (www.pioneerelectronics.com). What product or products would you consider to occupy the decline stage?

8.   Key Term: Fads

Fads are temporary periods of unusually high sales driven by consumer enthusiasm and immediate product or brand popularity. Fads don't last long. Two recent fads of the fashion industry were the sailor look and the poncho. Both of these were introduced to great fanfare. Both experienced rapid run-ups in sales. Both saw their sales quickly come crashing down. What is a product do you consider to be a fad today?

9.   Key Term: Introduction Stage

The introduction stage begins when the product is first launched into the marketplace. Introducing a product takes time, and sales are likely to be slow. At this stage, profits are low (or negative) due to the low sales and the need to spend high sums of money to attract customers and build inventories. It takes time to develop adequate sales to lift a product to the next stage. Companies introducing the Blu-ray DVD disk and players are experiencing these uncomfortable growing pains. Take a look at www.blu-ray.com to learn more about this new technology. What is necessary for Blu-ray to move out of the introduction stage and on to the growth stage?

10.   Key Term: Social Responsibility

Marketers must carefully consider public policy issues and regulations involving introducing, acquiring, marketing, or dropping products or product quality and safety. Businesses are corporate citizens and, as such, must act with the well-being of the consumer in mind. How is the MillerCoors Brewing Company (www.millercoors.com) responding to the public policy issues surrounding underage drinking?

Marketing ADventure Exercises

1.   Ad Interpretation Challenge: Idea Generation
        Ad: Food & Beverage – Altoids

New-product development begins with idea generation – the systematic search for new-product ideas. Typically, companies have to generate many ideas in order to find a few good ones. Altoids, an unusual breath mint, is one of those "good" ideas. Your job is to take Altoids to the "next level." Using the currently available versions of Altoids, what new product ideas can you generate?

2.   Ad Interpretation Challenge: Idea Screening
        Ad: Food & Beverage – Heinz

The basic purpose of idea generation is to generate a large number of potential product ideas. The basic purpose of idea screening is to reduce that large number to a more manageable number. Idea screening helps spot potentially good products and drops the unworkable ones early on. Take a look at Heinz (www.heinz.com). Go to their new product introductions and take a look at the newest products in the Heinz line. Are there any products here that you would have had screened out during the idea screening stage?

3.   Ad Interpretation Challenge: Concept Testing
        Ad: Food & Beverage – Gatorade

Concept testing calls for testing new-product concepts with groups of target customers. The concepts can be presented to customers either physically or symbolically. Think about Gatorade. (You can go to www.gatorade.com to learn more about their products.) Imagine that Gatorade were considering introducing a version of their best-selling thirst quencher that was in capsule format. The product concept reads: "Gatorade in an easy to swallow capsule." Think about how you might present this concept symbolically (in words) to consumers for the purpose of conducting a concept test.

4.   Ad Interpretation Challenge: Test Marketing
        Ad: Electronics – Motorola

The stage of the new-product development process in which the product and marketing program are introduced into more realistic market settings is known as the test market. Test marketing gives the marketer a little experience with marketing the product before going to the great expense of full introduction. Consider this ad for Motorola V8088 cell phone. How might Motorola have test marketed this product prior to its national introduction?

5.   Ad Interpretation Challenge: Commercialization
        Ad: Student Choice

If the company chooses to go ahead after the test marketing stage and launch the new product into the market, they are entering the commercialization phase. Commercialization, a very expensive stage, is the final stage of the new-product development process. Commercialization is the introduction of a new product into the market. Find an ad that is designed to assist in this commercialization process. Find an ad that is "introducing" a new product to the marketplace.

6.   Ad Interpretation Challenge: Fashion
        Ad: Apparel - Student Choice

A fad is a currently accepted or popular style in a given field. Fashions tend to grow slowly, remain popular for a while, and then decline slowly. However, the underlying product remains. Look through the apparel ads offered. Find one that you believe is promoting a fashion.

7.   Ad Interpretation Challenge: Introduction Stage
        Ad: Student Choice

The introduction stage begins when the product is first launched and introduced to the market. No doubt, introduction takes time, and sales growth is bound to be slow initially. During this phase, competitors are few. The basic promotion strategy is to induce consumer trial of the product. Find an ad that is promoting consumer trial.

8.   Ad Interpretation Challenge: Growth Stage
      Ad: Electronics - LG

The growth stage of the product life cycle is characterized by products which are experiencing rapidly rising sales, an expanding distribution system, and an increasing number of competitors. Products in this stage typically appeal to the early adopter. Flat screen televisions (i.e., LCD or plasma) are a growth stage product. Take a look at this ad for flat FRONT televisions (they still have a picture tube, but the front of the screen is flat) manufactured by LG – a product in the mature stage. How would you alter this ad to indicate a product occupying the growth stage?

9.   Ad Interpretation Challenge: Decline Stage
      Ad: Electronics – Fuji Film

It is inevitable that, at some point, a product's sales will slow down and then begin to go down. At this point, the product enters into the decline phase of the product life cycle. Here, you find many producers with many products to sell; however, the numbers are less than when the product was in the mature stage. If you were the marketer of Fuji Film, a product one would consider definitely in the decline stage of the product life cycle, how would you attempt to make you product viable?

10.   Ad Interpretation Challenge: Social Responsibility
      Ad: Student Choice

Corporations are social institutions. As such, they must exhibit stewardship of our fragile planet and its limited resources. Marketers must be socially aware and socially responsible. Find an ad that is exhibiting the marketers believe in their social responsibility.

Chapter 10
Pricing: Understanding and
Capturing Customer Value

Learning Objectives

1. Answer the question "What is price?" and discuss the importance of pricing in today's fast changing environment.
2. Discuss the importance of understanding customer value perceptions when setting prices.
3. Discuss the importance of company and product costs in setting prices.
4. Identify and define the other important external and internal factors affecting a firm's pricing decisions.

Chapter Overview

Firms successful at creating customer value with the other marketing mix activities must capture this value in the prices they earn. Despite its importance, many firms do not handle pricing well. In this chapter, we begin with the question, What is a price? Next, we look at customer-value perceptions, costs, and other factors that marketers must consider when setting prices. Price can be defined as the sum of all the values that customers give up in order to gain the benefits of having or using a product or service. Pricing decisions are subject to an incredibly complex array of company, environmental, and competitive forces. Finally, we examine pricing strategies for new-product pricing, product mix pricing, price adjustments, and dealing with price changes.

Chapter Outline

1. INTRODUCTION

Trader Joe's is not really a gourmet food store. Then again, it's not a discount food store either. It's actually a bit of both. One of America's hottest retailers, Trader Joe's has put its own special twist on the food price-value equation – call it "cheap gourmet." Trader Joe's describes itself as an "island paradise" where "value, adventure, and tasty treasures are discovered, every day." Customers don't just shop at Trader Joe's, they experience it. Shelves bristle with an eclectic assortment of gourmet-quality grocery items. Trader' Joe's stocks only a limited assortment of about 2,000 specialty products (compared with 45,000 items found at a Safeway). However, the assortment is uniquely Trader Joe's. A special store atmosphere, exclusive gourmet products, helpful and attentive associates – this all sounds like a recipe for high prices. Not so at Trader Joe's. How does Trade Joe's keep it gourmet prices so low? It all starts with lean operations and a near-fanatical focus on saving money. Trader Joe's also saves money by spending almost nothing on advertising. It's all about value and price – what you get for what you pay.

Opening Vignette Questions
  1. What do you believe to be the 'secret' to Trader Joe's success?
  2. How does Trader Joe's keep prices so low (compared to Whole Foods, for example)?
  3. Is Trader Joe's a gourmet store?

2. WHAT IS A PRICE?

In the narrowest sense, price is the amount of money charged for a product or service. More broadly, price is the sum of all the values that customers give up in order to gain the benefits of having or using a product or service. Price is the only element in the marketing mix that produces revenue. Price is one of the most flexible marketing mix elements.

3. FACTORS TO CONSIDER WHEN SETTING PRICES

Figure 10.1 summarizes the major considerations in setting price.

3.1 Customer Perceptions of Value

In the end, the customer will decide whether a product's price is right.

3.1.1 Value-Based Pricing

Value-based pricing uses buyers' perceptions of value, not the seller's cost, as the key to pricing. Price is considered along with the other marketing mix variables *before* the marketing program is set. Cost-based pricing is product driven. "Good value" is not the same as "low price." Two types of value-based pricing are *good-value pricing* and *value-added pricing*.

- Good-Value Pricing. Good-value pricing is offering just the right combination of quality and good service at a fair price. *Everyday low pricing (EDLP)*. EDLP involves charging a constant, everyday low price with few or no temporary price discounts. *High-low pricing* involves charging higher prices on an everyday basis but running frequent promotions to lower prices temporarily on selected items.

- Value-Added Pricing. Value-added pricing is the strategy of attaching value-added features and services to differentiate their offers and thus support higher prices.

3.2 Company and Product Costs

Cost-based pricing involved setting prices based on the costs for producing, distributing, and selling the product plus a fair rate of return for its effort and risk.

3.2.1 Types of Costs

Fixed costs (also known as overhead) are costs that do not vary with production or sales level. Variable costs vary directly with the level of production. They are called variable because their total varies with the number of units produced. Total costs are the sum of the fixed and variable costs for any given level of production.

3.2.2 Costs at Different Levels of Production

To price wisely, management needs to know how its costs vary with different levels of production. Figure 10.3A shows the typical short-run average cost curve (SRAC). Figure 10.3B shows the long-run average cost curve (LRAC).Average cost tends to fall with accumulated production experience. This is shown in Figure 10.4. This drop in the average cost with accumulated production experience is called the experience curve (or the learning curve).A single-minded focus on reducing costs and exploiting the experience curve will not always work. The aggressive pricing might give the product a cheap image. The strategy also assumes that competitors are weak and not willing to fight it out by meeting the company's price cuts. Finally, while the company is building volume under one technology, a competitor may find a lower-cost technology that lets it start at prices lower than those of the market leader, who still operates on the old experience curve.

3.2.3 Cost-Based Pricing

The simplest pricing method is cost-plus pricing—adding a standard markup to the cost of the product. Markup pricing remains popular for many reasons.
- Sellers are more certain about costs than about demand.
- When all firms in the industry use this pricing method, prices tend to be similar and price competition is thus minimized.
- Many people feel that cost-plus pricing is fairer to both buyers and sellers.

3.2.4 Break-Even Analysis and Target Profit Pricing

Another cost-oriented pricing approach is break-even pricing, or a variation called target profit pricing. The firm tries to determine the price at which it will break even or make the target profit it is seeking. Target pricing uses the concept of a break-even chart that shows the total cost and total revenue expected at different sales volume levels. Figure 10.5 shows a break-even chart. The manufacturer should consider different prices and estimate break-even volumes, probable demand, and profits for each. This is done in Table 10.1.

3.3 Other Internal and External Considerations Affecting Price Decisions

3.3.1 Overall Marketing Strategy, Objectives, and Mix

General pricing objectives might include survival, current profit maximization, market share leadership, or customer retention and relationship building. Price is only one of the marketing mix tools that a company uses to achieve its marketing objectives. Price decisions must be coordinated with product design, distribution, and promotion decisions to form a consistent and effective integrated marketing program. Companies often position their products on price and then tailor other marketing mix decisions to the prices they want to charge. Target costing starts with an ideal selling price based on customer-value considerations, and then targets costs that will ensure that the price is met. Companies may deemphasize price and use other marketing mix tools to create nonprice positions.

3.3.2 Organizational Considerations

In small companies, prices are often set by top management rather than by the marketing or sales departments. In large companies, pricing is typically handled by divisional or product line managers. In industrial markets, salespeople may be allowed to negotiate with customers within certain price ranges. In industries in which pricing is a key factor, companies often have pricing departments to set the best prices or to help others in setting them.

3.3.3 The Market and Demand

3.4 Pricing in Different Types of Markets

3.4.1 Pure competition

The market consists of many buyers and sellers trading in a uniform commodity. No single buyer or seller has much effect on the going market price. In a purely competitive market, marketing research, product development, pricing, advertising, and sales promotion play little or no role. Thus, sellers in these markets do not spend much time on marketing strategy.

3.4.2 Monopolistic competition

The market consists of many buyers and sellers who trade over a range of prices rather than a single market price. A range of prices occurs because sellers can differentiate their offers to buyers.

3.4.3 Oligopolistic competition

The market consists of a few sellers who are highly sensitive to each other's pricing and marketing strategies. There are few sellers because it is difficult for new sellers to enter the market.

3.4.4. Pure monopoly

The market consists of one seller. The seller may be a government monopoly, a private regulated monopoly, or a private nonregulated monopoly.

3.5 Analyzing the Price-Demand Relationship

The relationship between the price charged and the resulting demand level is shown in the demand curve (Figure 10.6). In the case of prestige goods, the demand curve sometimes slopes upward. Consumers think that higher prices mean more quality. In a monopoly, the demand curve shows the total market demand resulting from different prices. If the company faces competition, its demand at different prices will depend on whether competitors' prices stay constant or change with the company's own prices.

3.6 Price Elasticity of Demand

Price elasticity is how responsive demand will be to a change in price. If demand hardly changes with a small change in price, we say demand is inelastic. If demand changes greatly with a small change in price, we say the demand is elastic.

3.6.1 Competitors' Strategies and Prices

In assessing competitors' pricing strategies, the company should ask several questions.
- How does the company's market offering compare with competitors' offerings in terms of customer value?
- How strong are current competitors and what are their current pricing strategies?
- How does the competitive landscape influence customer price sensitivity?

3.6.2 Other External Factors

Economic conditions can have a strong impact on the firm's pricing strategies. The company must also consider what impact its prices will have on other parties in its environment, such as resellers and the government. *Social concerns* may have to be taken into account.

Student Exercises

1.   Key Term: Price

Price is defined as the amount of money charged for a product or service, or the sum of the values that consumer exchange for the benefits having or using the product or service. It is the only element of the marketing mix that produces revenue. Go to Hewlett-Packard home page (www.hp.com) and build for yourself the ultimate laptop computer. Determine the actual monetary price you would be charged, after all of the deals and discounts.

2.   Key Term: Price

Yes, it is the same term as given in Exercise 1; however, here it takes on a totally different dimension. Consider your decision to come to school. You paid (and are paying) a price (both tangible and intangible) for that decision. What price did you pay for this service (education) you are receiving?

3.   Key Term: Value-Based Pricing

Good pricing begins with a complete understanding of the value that a product or service creates for the customer. Value-based pricing uses the buyer's perception of value, not the seller's cost, as the key to pricing. Your text uses the example of the Bentley Continental automobile as an example of value-based pricing. Find another relatively expensive product that you believe is practicing value-based pricing.

4.   Key Term: Good-Value Pricing

More and more, marketers have been adopting good-value pricing strategies. In such a pricing strategy, marketers offer just the right combination of quality and good service at a lower, fair price. Go to a Wal-Mart store or look at Wal-Mart online (www.walmart.com). Find products that you believe the marketers have employed good-value pricing.

5.   Key Term: Value-Added Pricing

Value-added pricing is the practice of attaching value-added features and services to differentiate a company's offerings and to support charging higher prices. Lexus automobiles (www.lexus.com) (the luxury division of Toyota) utilize value-added pricing. The company charges premium prices for their cars. In addition to building and providing a high quality automobile, what value-added features and/or services do they provide to the customer?

6.   Key Term: Fixed Costs

Fixed costs are costs that do not vary with production or sales volume. Take a look at Tomasini Fine Linens (www.tomasini.cc), a high-end linen manufacturer based in Los Angeles. What are some of the fixed costs with which this company is faced?

7.   Key Term: Variable Costs

Variable costs vary directly with production volume. Typically, these are costs associated with the materials used in the manufacturer of the product. You only use the items if you make the product. Again, examine Tomasini Fine Linens (www.tomasinifinelinens.com) and the products they manufacture and market. What are some of the variable costs involved?

8.   Key Term: Cost-Based Pricing

Adding a standard markup to the cost of a product is known as cost-based pricing. It is the simplest form of pricing around. You just determine how much it costs you to produce the item and then you add a standard markup for profit. Consider Hot Springs Portable Spas (www.hotspring.com). Would a company such as this utilize cost-based pricing?

9.   Key Term: Oligopolistic Competition

Under oligopolistic competition, the market consists of a few large sellers who are very aware of each other's pricing and marketing strategies. They are few sellers in the market because it is difficult for new sellers to successfully enter the market. Outside of cars and computers (examples used in your text), what is a market dominated by oligopolistic competition?

10.   Key Term: Pure Monopoly

In a pure monopoly, the market consists of just one seller. Nonregulated monopolies are free to price their products at what the market will bear. What is an example of a nonregulated monopoly today?

Marketing ADventure Exercises

1.   Ad Interpretation Challenge: Price
        Ad: Services and B2B—University of Toronto

Price is the amount of money charged for a product or service, or the sum of the values that consumers exchange for the benefits of having or using the product or service. Look at this ad for the University of Toronto. What is the "price" the student must pay to attend?

2.   Ad Interpretation Challenge: Value-based Pricing
      Ad: Autos—Jaguar

Remember, "good value" and "low cost" are not necessarily the same thing. Value-based pricing is setting prices based on the buyer's perception of value rather than on the seller's cost. Consider the ad for Jaguar. How could a consumer consider this product a good value?

3.   Ad Interpretation Challenge: Good-Value Pricing
      Ad: General Retail—Target

More and more, marketers have adopted a policy of good-value pricing. Good-value pricing is offering to the consumer just the right combination of quality and good service at a reasonable price. Wal-Mart is the king of good-value pricing with its use of EDLP (everyday low pricing). How is Target able to compete in the battle of good-value pricing?

4.   Ad Interpretation Challenge: Cost-based Pricing
      Ad: Autos—Mercedes

Adding a standard markup to the cost of a product is known as cost-based pricing. It is the simplest form of pricing around. You just determine how much it costs you to produce the item and then you add a standard markup for profit. Consider Mercedes. Would a company such as this utilize cost-based pricing?

5.   Ad Interpretation Challenge: Fixed Costs
      Ad: Travel and Tourism—American Airlines

Fixed costs are costs that do not vary much with production or sales volume. These are costs the manufacturer must pay regardless of these factors. Think about American Airlines. What are some of the fixed costs with which this company is faced?

6.   Ad Interpretation Challenge: Variable Costs
      Ad: Travel and Tourism—American Airlines

Variable costs vary directly with production volume. Typically, these are costs associated with the materials used in the manufacturer of the product or service. Again, think about American Airlines. What are some of the variable costs with which this company is faced?

7.   Ad Interpretation Challenge: Cost-Plus Pricing
      Ad: Student Choice

Adding a standard markup to the cost of a product or service is known as cost-plus pricing. It is the simplest form of pricing around. You just determine how much is costs

you to produce the item and then you add a standard markup for profit. Find an ad for a product or company that would use cost-plus pricing.

8.   Ad Interpretation Challenge: Monopolistic Competition
        Ad: Food and Beverage—Heinz

When a market consists of many buyers and sellers who trade over a range of prices rather than a single market price, monopolistic competition exists. Buyers see differences in sellers' products and make purchase decisions accordingly. How does Heinz ketchup compete in this monopolistic competitive environment?

9.   Ad Interpretation Challenge: Inelastic Demand
        Ad: Student Choice

The less elastic the demand for a product, the more it makes sense for the seller to raise the price of the product. Buyers are less price sensitive when the product they are buying is unique or when it is high in quality. Find an ad for a product which would most likely have an inelastic demand.

10.   Ad Interpretation Challenge: Elastic Demand
        Ad: Student Choice

The more elastic the demand for a product or service, the more it makes sense to possibly lower the price of your product. Because of elastic demand, the lower the price, the greater the demand created for the product or service. Find an ad for a product or service which you believe experiences elastic demand.

Chapter 11
Pricing Strategies

Learning Objectives

1. Describe the major strategies for pricing imitative and new products.
2. Explain how companies find a set of prices that maximize the profits from the total product mix.
3. Discuss how companies adjust their prices to take into account different types of customers and situations.
4. Discuss the key issues related to initiating and responding to price changes.

Chapter Overview

In this chapter, we look at pricing strategies available to marketers – new-product pricing strategies, product mix pricing strategies, price adjustment strategies, and price reaction strategies. A company does not set a single price, but rather a pricing structure that covers different items in its line. This pricing structure changes over time as products move through their life cycles. The company adjusts its prices to reflect changes in costs and demand and to account for variations in buyers and situations. As the competitive environment changes, the company considers when to initiate price changes and when to respond to them. This chapter examines the major pricing strategies available to marketers. The chapter covers new-product pricing strategies for products in the introductory stage of the product life cycle, product mix strategies for related products in the product mix, price adjustment strategies that account for customer differences and changing situations, and strategies for initiating and responding to price changes.

Chapter Outline

1. INTRODUCTION

HP, Epson, Canon, and Lexmark have long dominated the $50 billion printer industry with a maddening "razor-and-blades" pricing strategy (as in give away the razor, then make your profits on the blades). They sell printers at little or not profit. But once you own the printer, you're stuck buying their grossly overpriced, high-margin replacement ink cartridges. Enter Kodak – with a unique solution. Kodak recently introduced its first line of printers – EasyShare All-in-One printers – with a revolutionary pricing strategy that threatens to turn the entire inkjet printer industry upside-down. Kodak sells its printers at premium prices with no discounts, and then sells the ink cartridges for less. EasyShare printers sell for about $50 more than comparable printers sold by competitors. EasyShare ink cartridges go for about half that of prevailing competitors. Using new technology, EasyShare ink cartridges use much less ink to make a print and the cartridges contain no electronics (competitor's cartridges use much more ink and contain some electronics in the cartridge). This allows Kodak to charge less for its cartridges. Kodak introduced the ThINK campaign to re-educate consumers about printer and ink pricing. It's too soon to tell whether Kodak's new pricing strategy is working, but early results are promising.

Opening Vignette Questions

1. What unique pricing strategy has Kodak introduced with its line of EasyShare printers?
2. How has the competition responded to this new competitor in the marketplace?
3. What is the "razor-and-blades" pricing strategy used so widely in the industry?

2. NEW-PRODUCT PRICING STRATEGIES

Companies bringing out a new product face the challenge of setting prices for the first time. They can choose between two broad strategies.

2.1 Market-Skimming Pricing

Many companies that invent new products set high initial prices to "skim" revenues layer-by-layer from the market. This is called market-skimming pricing.
Market skimming makes sense only under certain conditions.

- The product's quality and image must support its higher price, and enough buyers must want the product at that price.
- The costs of producing a smaller volume cannot be so high that they cancel the advantage of charging more.
- Competitors should not be able to enter the market easily and undercut the high price.

2.2 Market-Penetration Pricing

Rather than setting a high price to skim off small but profitable market segments, some companies use market-penetration pricing. They set a low initial price in order to penetrate the market quickly and deeply—to attract a large number of buyers quickly and win a large market share.

Several conditions must be met for this low-price strategy to work.
- The market must be highly price sensitive so that a low price produces more market growth.
- Production and distribution costs must fall as sales volume increases.

- The low price must help keep out the competition, and the penetration pricer must maintain its low-price position—otherwise, the price advantage may be only temporary.

3. PRODUCT MIX PRICING STRATEGIES

3.1 Product Line Pricing

Companies usually develop product lines rather than single products. In product line pricing, management must decide on the price steps to set between the various products in a line. The price steps should take into account cost differences between the products in the line, customer evaluations of their different features, and competitors' prices. In many industries, sellers use well-established price points for the products in their line. The seller's task is to establish perceived quality differences that support the price differences.

3.2 Optional Product Pricing

Many companies use optional-product pricing—offering to sell optional or accessory products along with their main product. Pricing these options is a sticky problem. The company has to decide which items to include in the base price and which to offer as options.

3.3 Captive Product Pricing

Companies that make products that must be used along with a main product are using captive-product pricing. Producers of the main products often price them low and set high markups on the supplies. In the case of services, this strategy is called two-part pricing. The price of the service is broken into a fixed fee plus a variable usage rate. The service firm must decide how much to charge for the basic service and how much for the variable usage. The fixed amount should be low enough to induce usage of the service; profit can be made on the variable fees.

3.4 By-Product Pricing

Using by-product pricing, a manufacturer will seek a market for by-products and should accept any price that covers more than the cost of storing and delivering them. By-products can even turn out to be profitable.

3.5 Product Bundle Pricing

Using product bundle pricing, sellers often combine several of their products and offer the bundle at a reduced price. Price bundling can promote the sales of products consumers might not otherwise buy, but the combined price must be low enough to get them to buy the bundle.

4. PRICE-ADJUSTMENT STRATEGIES

Companies usually adjust their basic prices to account for various customer differences and changing situations. The six price adjustment strategies are summarized in Table 11.2.

4.1 Discount and Allowance Pricing

Most companies adjust their basic price to reward customers for certain responses, such as early payment of bills, volume purchases, and off-season buying. The many forms of discounts include a cash discount—a price reduction to buyers who pay their bills promptly. A typical example is "2/10, net 30," which means that although payment is due within 30 days, the buyer can deduct 2 percent if the bill is paid within 10 days. A quantity discount is a price reduction to buyers who buy large volumes. Such discounts provide an incentive to the customer to buy more from one given seller, rather than from many different sources. A functional discount (trade discount) is offered by the seller to trade-channel members who perform certain functions, such as selling, storing, and record keeping. A seasonal discount is a price reduction to buyers who buy merchandise or services out of season. Allowances are another type of reduction from list price. Trade-in allowances are price reductions given for turning in an old item when buying a new one. Promotional allowances are payments or price reductions to reward dealers for participating in advertising and sales support programs.

4.2 Segmented Pricing

Companies will often adjust their basic prices to allow for differences in customers, products, and locations. In segmented pricing, the company sells a product or service at two or more prices, even though the difference in prices is not based on differences in costs. Under customer-segment pricing, different customers pay different prices for the same product or service. Under product form pricing, different versions of the product are priced differently but not according to differences in their costs. Under location pricing, a company charges different prices for different locations, even though the cost of offering each location is the same. Using time pricing, a firm varies its prices by the season, the month, the day, and even the hour. Segmented pricing goes by many names. Some in the airline industry call it revenue management. Airlines, hotels, and restaurants call it yield management.

For segmented pricing to be an effective strategy, certain conditions must exist.
- The market must be segmentable, and the segments must show different degrees of demand.
- The costs of segmenting and watching the market cannot exceed the extra revenue obtained from the price difference.
- The segmented pricing must also be legal.

4.3 Psychological Pricing

Price says something about the product. For example, many consumers use price to judge quality. In using psychological pricing, sellers consider the psychology of prices and not simply the economics. Another aspect of psychological pricing is reference prices—prices that buyers carry in their minds and refer to when looking at a given product.

- The reference price might be formed by noting current prices, remembering past prices, or assessing the buying situation.
- Sellers can influence or use these consumers' reference prices when setting price.

For most purchases, consumers don't have all the skill or information they need to figure out whether they are paying a good price. They may rely on certain cues that signal whether a price is high or low. Even small differences in price can signal product differences.

4.4 Promotional Pricing

With promotional pricing, companies will temporarily price their products below list price and sometimes even below cost to create buying excitement and urgency.

Promotional pricing takes several forms.

- The seller may simply offer *discounts* from normal prices to increase sales and reduce inventories.
- Supermarkets and department stores will price a few products as *loss leaders* to attract customers to the store in the hope that they will buy other items at normal markups.
- Sellers will also use special-event pricing in certain seasons to draw more customers.
- Manufacturers sometimes offer *cash rebates* to consumers who buy the product from dealers within a specified time; the manufacturer sends the rebate directly to the customer.
- Some manufacturers offer *low-interest financing*, longer warranties, or *free maintenance* to reduce the consumer's "price."

Promotional pricing can have adverse effects.
- Used too frequently and copied by competitors, price promotions can create "deal-prone" customers who wait until brands go on sale before buying them.
- Constantly reduced prices can erode a brand's value in the eyes of customers.
- Marketers sometimes use price promotions as a quick fix instead of sweating through the difficult process of developing effective longer-term strategies for building their brands.
- The frequent use of promotional pricing can also lead to industry price wars. Such price wars usually play into the hands of only one or a few competitors—those with the most efficient operations.

4.5 Geographical Pricing

A company also must decide how to price its products for customers located in different parts of the country or world.

- FOB-origin pricing is a practice that means the goods are placed free on board (hence, FOB) a carrier. At that point the title and responsibility pass to the customer, who pays the freight from the factory to the destination.
- Uniform-delivered pricing is the opposite of FOB pricing. Here, the company charges the same price plus freight to all customers, regardless of their location. The freight charge is set at the average freight cost.
- Zone pricing falls between FOB-origin pricing and uniform-delivered pricing. The company sets up two or more zones. All customers within a given zone pay a single total price; the more distance the zone, the higher the price.
- Using basing-point pricing, the seller selects a given city as a "basing point" and charges all customers the freight cost from that city to the customer location, regardless of the city from which the goods are actually shipped. Some companies set up multiple basing points to create more flexibility: they quote freight charges from the basing-point city nearest to the customer.

The seller who is anxious to do business with a certain customer or geographical area might use freight-absorption pricing. Using this strategy, the seller absorbs all or part of the actual freight charges in order to get the desired business.

4.6 Dynamic Pricing

Dynamic pricing offers many advantages for marketers. Internet sellers can mine their databases to gauge a specific shopper's desires, measure his or her means, and instantaneously tailor products to fit that shopper's behavior, and price products accordingly. Many B2B marketers monitor inventories, costs, and demand at any given moment and adjust prices instantly. Buyers also benefit from the Web and dynamic pricing.

4.7 International Pricing

Companies that market their products internationally must decide what prices to charge in the different countries in which they operate. In some cases, a company can set a uniform worldwide price. However, most companies adjust their prices to reflect local market conditions and cost considerations. The price that a company should charge in a specific country depends on many factors, including economic conditions, competitive situations, laws and regulations, and development of the wholesaling and retailing system. Consumer perceptions and preferences also may vary from country to country, calling for different prices. Or the company may have different marketing objectives in various world markets that require changes in pricing strategy. Costs play an important role in setting international prices. Travelers abroad are often surprised to find that goods that are relatively inexpensive at home may carry outrageously higher price tags in other countries. In some cases, such price escalation may result from differences in selling strategies or market conditions. In most instances, however, it is simply a result of the higher costs of selling in another country—the additional costs of product modifications, shipping and insurance, import tariffs and taxes, exchange rate fluctuations, and physical distribution.

5. PRICE CHANGES

Companies often face situations in which they must initiate price changes or respond to price changes by competitors.

5.1 Initiating Price Changes

5.1.1 Initiating Price Cuts

Several situations may lead a firm to consider cutting its price.
- One such circumstance is excess capacity. In this case, the firm needs more business and cannot get it through increased sales effort, product improvement, or other measures.
- Another situation leading to price changes is falling market share in the face of strong price competition.
- A company may also cut prices in a drive to dominate the market through lower costs. Either the company starts with lower costs than its competitors, or it cuts prices in the hope of gaining market share that will further cut costs through larger volume.

5.1.2 Initiating Price Increases

A successful price increase can greatly increase profits.
- A major factor in price increases is cost inflation. Rising costs squeeze profit margins and lead companies to pass cost increases along to customers.
- Another factor leading to price increases is over demand. When a company cannot supply all that its customers need, it can raise prices, ration products to customers, or both.

Companies can increase their prices in a number of ways to keep up with rising costs. Prices can be raised almost invisibly by dropping discounts and adding higher-priced units to the line. Or prices can be pushed up openly. In passing price increases on to customers, the company must avoid being perceived as a price gouger. Companies also need to think of who will bear the brunt of increased prices. Price increases should be supported by company communications telling customers why prices are being increased. Whenever possible, the company should consider ways to meet higher costs or demand without raising prices.

5.1.3 Buyer Reactions to Price Changes

Customers do not always interpret price changes in a straightforward way. A brand's price and image are often closely linked. A price change, especially a drop in price, can adversely affect how consumers view the brand.

5.1.4 Competitor Reactions to Price Changes

Competitors are most likely to react when the number of firms involved is small, when the product is uniform, and when the buyers are well informed about products and prices. The company must guess each competitor's likely reaction. If all competitors behave alike, this amounts to analyzing only a typical competitor. In contrast, if the competitors do not behave alike, then separate analyses are necessary.

5.2 Responding to Price Changes

If a company decides that effective action can and should be taken, it might make any of four responses.

- It could reduce its price to match the competitor's price. The company should try to maintain its quality as it cuts prices.
- The company might maintain its price but raise the perceived value of its offer. It could improve its communications, stressing the relative quality of its product over that of the lower-price competitor.
- The company might improve quality and increase price, moving its brand into a higher-price position. The higher quality justifies the higher price that in turn preserves the company's higher margins.
- The company might launch a low-price "fighting brand"—adding a lower-price item to the line or creating a separate lower-price brand. This is necessary if the particular market segment being lost is price sensitive and will not respond to arguments of higher quality.

6. PUBLIC POLICY AND PRICING

Price competition is a core element of our free-market economy. In setting prices, companies are not usually free to charge whatever prices they wish. Many federal, state, and even local laws govern the rules of fair play in pricing. The most important pieces of legislation affecting pricing are the Sherman, Clayton, and Robinson-Patman acts, initially adopted to curb the formation of monopolies and to regulate business practices that might unfairly restrain trade.

6.1 Pricing within Channel Levels

Federal legislation on price-fixing states that sellers must set prices without talking to competitors. Otherwise, price collusion is suspected. Sellers are also prohibited from using predatory pricing—selling below cost with the intention of punishing a competitor or gaining higher long-run profits by putting competitors out of business. This protects small sellers from larger ones who might sell items below cost temporarily or in a specific locale to drive them out of business.

6.2 Pricing across Channel Levels

The Robinson-Patman Act seeks to prevent unfair price discrimination by ensuring that sellers offer the same price terms to customers at a given level of trade. Price discrimination is allowed if the seller can prove that its costs are different when selling to different retailers.

Or the seller can discriminate in its pricing if the seller manufactures different qualities of the same product for different retailers. The seller has to prove that these differences are proportional. Retail (or resale) price maintenance is prohibited—a manufacturer cannot require dealers to charge a specified retail price for its product. Although the seller can propose a manufacturer's suggested retail price to dealers, it cannot refuse to sell to a dealer who takes independent pricing action, nor can it punish the dealer by shipping late or denying advertising allowances.

Deceptive pricing occurs when a seller states prices or price savings that mislead consumers or are not actually available to consumers. This might involve bogus reference or comparison prices, as when a retailer sets artificially high "regular" prices then announces "sale" prices close to its previous everyday prices. Deceptive pricing issues include scanner fraud and price confusion. The widespread use of scanner-based computer checkouts has led to increasing complaints of retailers overcharging their customers. Price confusion results when firms employ pricing methods that make it difficult for consumers to understand just what price they are really paying. Treating customers fairly and making certain that they fully understand prices and pricing terms is an important part of building strong and lasting customer relationships.

Student Exercises

1.   Key Term: Market-Skimming Pricing

When you set a price high for a new product to skim maximum revenues layer by layer from the segments willing to pay the high price, you are employing a market-skimming pricing strategy. Your text provides a good example of market-skimming pricing in the discussion regarding HDTV. Find another such example of a new product.

2.   Key Term: Market-Penetration Pricing

Market-penetration pricing is when a marketer sets a low price for a new product in order to attract a large number of buyers and a large market share. They set a low initial price in order to penetrate the market quickly and deeply. Look at the website for JR Cigars (www.jrcigars.com). JR Cigars is the largest seller of high quality cigars in the United States. How would you say they have used market-penetration pricing to their advantage?

3.   Key Term: Product-Line Pricing

Companies typically develop product lines rather than just one single product. It makes sense for them to offer multiple versions of a product, each with its own combination of consumer benefits and features to match the varying needs of customers. In product-line pricing, management must decide on the price steps to set between the various versions of the product. Apple's iPod is a great example. Examine the various iPod offerings (www.apple.com) and specify the differences between products their pricing.

4.   Key Term: Optional-Product Pricing

Many companies use optional-product pricing—offering to sell optional or accessory products along with their main product. Cars are a great example of optional-product pricing. Typically, you begin with the base car and then add on all of the bell-and-whistles that make it uniquely yours. Build yourself a SAAB (www.saabusa.com) and see how much the price changes from the base, once you add on items you believe you can not live without.

5.   Key Term: Captive-Product Pricing

There exist some secondary products that are only used in conjunction with the main product. These are known as captive products and the pricing of them is known as captive-product pricing. If you own the main product you have to buy the secondary product. Your text gives the example of razor blade cartridges and ink cartridges. Find other products that are priced using this strategy.

6.   Key Term: By-Product Pricing

By-product pricing is setting a price for by-products in order to make the main product's price more attractive. In the production of many products, there are often by-products left over. If you cannot get rid of these leftovers it will impact the price of the main product. In some instances, by-products have turned out to be profitable. Your text uses the example of MeadWestvaco. Find another example of a by-product that has become a profitable product in its own right.

7.   Key Term: Product Bundle Pricing

Using product bundle pricing, sellers often combine several of their products and offer the bundle at a reduced prices. Price bundling can promote the sales of products the consumer might not otherwise buy. Look at the website for Expedia, the online travel services company (www.expedia.com). Explore their site and examine the ways in which they use product bundle pricing to boost sales.

8. Key Term: Psychological Pricing

Psychological pricing is a pricing approach that considers the psychology of prices and not simply the economics—the price is used to say something about the product. For example, consumers usually perceive higher-priced products as having higher quality. Even though the products may be virtually identical, in the absence of additional information, most consumers will choose the higher-priced version. Take a look at the web pages for Nordstrom's Department Stores (www.nordstroms.com). Go to men's dress shirts and look at the different versions of the classic white dress shirt. Which ones do you believe are of the highest quality?

9. Key Term: Reference Price

Prices that the consumer may carry with them (either in their minds or written down) and refer to when looking at a given product are known as reference prices. Sellers have realized the importance of such prices and now will many times provide the customer with a reference price. Buyers should be careful about over-relying on such seller-provided references. Log on to Overstock (www.overstock.com) and spend some time reviewing their use of reference pricing. How effective do you believe its use to be?

10. Key Term: Promotional Pricing

Promotional pricing is temporarily pricing products below the list price to increase short-term sales by creating a sense of excitement or urgency. Look around and find a retail merchant that makes good use of promotional pricing.

Marketing ADventure Exercises

1. Ad Interpretation Challenge: Market-Skimming Pricing
   Ad: Electronics—Sony HS Series

When you set a price high for a new product to skim maximum revenues layer-by-layer from the segments willing to pay the high price, you are employing a market-skimming pricing strategy. Take a look at this ad for the Sony HS Series projection television. Do you believe this product would employ market-skimming pricing?

2. Ad Interpretation Challenge: Market-Penetration Pricing
   Ad: Student Choice

Market-penetration pricing is when a marketer sets a low price for a new product in order to attract a large number of buyers and quickly capture a large market share. They set a low initial price in order to penetrate the market quickly and deeply. Find an ad for a product that you believe would do well with market-penetration pricing.

3.   Ad Interpretation Challenge: Product Line Pricing
        Ad: Apparel—Levi's

Setting the price steps between various products in a product line based on cost differences between the products, customer evaluations of different features, and competitors' prices is known as product line pricing. How has Levi's employed product line pricing in jeans?

4.   Ad Interpretation Challenge: Optional-Product Pricing
        Ad: Autos—Ford

Many companies use optional-product pricing—offering to sell optional or accessory products for use with and along with their main product. Cars are a great example of optional-product pricing. Typically, you begin with the base car and then add on all of the bell-and-whistles that make it uniquely yours. Consider the ads for Ford (or for any car). How do the ads typically inform you that the vehicle is priced utilizing the optional-product pricing strategy?

5.   Ad Interpretation Challenge: Captive-Product Pricing
        Ad: Student Choice

Captive-product pricing is the pricing of optional or accessory products along with the main product. These are products that are made to be used along with the main product and cannot, in fact, be used independently. Find an ad for a product that would typically employ captive-product pricing.

6.   Ad Interpretation Challenge: Product Bundle Pricing
        Ad: Cosmetics and Pharmaceuticals—Edge

Using product bundle pricing, sellers will often combine several of their products and offer the bundle to the consumer at a reduced price. In this manner, sellers may be able to sell items to consumers they would normally purchase singularly. Think about the ad for Edge shaving gel. How might this product be bundled with other products to create an appealing package for the customer?

7.   Ad Interpretation Challenge: Psychological Pricing
        Ad: Cosmetics and Pharmaceuticals—Edge

Price says something about the product. In using psychological pricing, sellers consider the psychology of prices and not simply the economics. How might the marketers of Edge shaving gel use psychological pricing to convey a message of quality to consumers?

8.   Ad Interpretation Challenge: Reference Prices
      Ad: General Retail—World's Biggest

Reference prices are the prices that consumers carry with them in their minds and refer to when looking at a given product. Merchants can help the consumer in this by having reference prices readily available to shoppers for comparison purposes. Consider the ads for World's Biggest Bookstore. How are they using the concept of reference prices?

9.   Ad Interpretation Challenge: Promotional Pricing
      Ad: Student Choice

Promotional pricing is the temporary pricing of products below the list price for the purpose of creating a buying excitement and urgency. Such pricing serves to get customers into the store. Find an ad for a product that could make good use of promotional pricing.

10.   Ad Interpretation Challenge: Dynamic Pricing
      Ad: Travel and Tourism—AeroMexico

Dynamic pricing is adjusting prices continually to meet the characteristics and needs of individual customers and situations. How might AeroMexico use dynamic pricing?

Chapter 12
Marketing Channels: Delivering Customer Value

Learning Objectives

1. Explain why companies use marketing channels and discuss the functions these channels perform
2. Discuss how channel members interact and how they organize to perform the work of the channel
3. Identify the major channel alternatives open to a company
4. Explain how companies select, motivate, and evaluate channel members
5. Discuss the nature and importance of marketing logistics and integrated supply chain management

Chapter Overview

An individual firm's success depends not only on how well *it* performs but also on how well its *entire marketing channel* competes with competitors' channels. To be good at customer relationship management, a company must also be good at partner relationship management. The first part of this chapter explores the nature of marketing channels and the marketer's channel design and management decisions. We then examine physical distribution—or logistics—an area that is growing dramatically in importance and sophistication.

Chapter Outline

1. INTRODUCTION

Surprisingly, the number one U.S. rental car company is Enterprise Rent-A-Car. Enterprise left number two Hertz behind in the late 1990s. How did Enterprise become such a dominating industry leader? What contributed most to Enterprise taking the lead was an industry-changing, customer-driven distribution strategy. While competitors such as Hertz and Avis focused on serving travelers at airports, Enterprise developed a new distribution doorway to a large and untapped segment. It opened off-airport, neighborhood locations that provided short-term car-replacement rentals for people whose cars were wrecked, stolen, or being serviced. Enterprise founder, Jack Taylor, discovered the unmet customer need and located his rental offices in center-city and neighborhood areas. These locations also have Taylor a cost advantage. Taylor's groundbreaking strategy worked and the business grew quickly. Enterprise continued to focus steadfastly on what it called the "home-city" market. Branch managers developed strong relationships with local auto insurance adjusters, dealership sales and service personnel, and body shops and service garages. Many of Enterprise's customers had no way to get to the rental agency location to pick up their car, so Enterprise developed the strategy of picking the customer up and bringing them in; hence the famous tag-line "Pick Enterprise. We'll Pick You Up." In late 2007, Enterprise purchased the Vanguard Car Rental Group, which owned the National and Alamo brands. This gave Enterprise a combined 27.4% of the airport market. That combined with the more than 55% share of the off-airport market, makes Enterprise the runaway leader. Enterprise continues to move forward. It has developed WeCar, a car-sharing program. WeCar members pay a $35 annual membership fee. They can then rent conveniently located, fuel-efficient cars for $10 per hour or $30 overnight. Thus, Enterprise continues to move ahead aggressively with its winning distribution strategy.

Opening Vignette Questions

1. How did Enterprise become the industry leader?
2. What has been the secret of its distribution strategy? How has it provided value to its clients?
3. Describe the value provided by the WeCar concept.
4. How can Hertz or Avis compete?

2. SUPPLY CHAINS AND THE VALUE DELIVERY NETWORK

The *supply chain* consists of "upstream" and "downstream" partners. Upstream from the company is the set of firms that supply the raw materials, components, parts, information, finances, and expertise needed to create a product or service. Marketers have traditionally focused on the "downstream" side of the supply chain—on the *marketing channels* (or *distribution channels*) that look forward toward the customer. A better term would be *demand chain* because it suggests a *sense-and-respond* view of the market. Under this view, planning starts with the needs of target customers, to which the company responds by organizing a chain of resources and activities with the goal of creating customer value. As defined in Chapter 2, a value delivery network is made up of the company, suppliers, distributors, and ultimately customers who "partner" with each other to improve the performance of the entire system.

3. THE NATURE AND IMPORTANCE OF MARKETING CHANNELS

Producers try to forge a marketing channel (or distribution channel)—a set of interdependent organizations that help make a product or service available for use or consumption by the consumer or business user.

3.1 How Channel Members Add Value

Figure 12.1 shows how using intermediaries can provide economies. The role of marketing intermediaries is to transform the assortments of products made by producers into the assortments wanted by consumers. Members of the marketing channel perform many key functions. Some help to complete transactions:

- *Information:* Gathering and distributing marketing research and intelligence information about actors and forces in the marketing environment needed for planning and aiding exchange.

- *Promotion*: Developing and spreading persuasive communications about an offer.
- *Contact*: Finding and communicating with prospective buyers.
- *Matching*: Shaping and fitting the offer to the buyer's needs, including activities such as manufacturing, grading, assembling, and packaging.
- *Negotiation*: Reaching an agreement on price and other terms of the offer so that ownership or possession can be transferred.

Others help to fulfill the completed transactions:

- *Physical distribution*: Transporting and storing goods.
- *Financing*: Acquiring and using funds to cover the costs of the channel work.
- *Risk taking*: Assuming the risks of carrying out the channel work.

3.2 Number of Channel Levels

A channel level is each layer of marketing intermediaries that performs some work in bringing the product and its ownership closer to the final buyer. The *number of intermediary levels* indicates the *length* of a channel. (Figure 12.2) A direct marketing channel has no intermediary levels; the company sells directly to consumers. An indirect marketing channel contains one or more intermediaries. From the producer's point of view, a greater number of levels mean less control and greater channel complexity.

4. CHANNEL BEHAVIOR AND ORGANIZATION

4.1 Channel Behavior

A marketing channel consists of firms that have partnered for their common good. Each channel member depends on the others. Each channel member plays a specialized role in the channel. The channel will be most effective when each member assumes the tasks it can do best. Disagreements over goals, roles, and rewards generate channel conflict. *Horizontal conflict* occurs among firms at the same level of the channel. *Vertical conflict* occurs between different levels of the same channel.

4.2 Vertical Marketing Systems

A conventional distribution channel consists of one or more independent producers, wholesalers, and retailers. Each is a separate business seeking to maximize its own profits, perhaps even at the expense of the system as a whole. A vertical marketing system (VMS) consists of producers, wholesalers, and retailers acting as a unified system. One channel member owns the others, has contracts with them, or wields so much power that they must all cooperate. (Figure 12.3) There are three main types of Vertical Marketing Systems:

- A Corporate VMS integrates successive stages of production and distribution under single ownership.

- A Contractual VMS consists of independent firms at different levels of production and distribution who join together through contracts to obtain more economies or sales impact than each could achieve alone.
- The franchise organization is the most common type of contractual relationship— a channel member called a *franchisor* links several stages in the production-distribution process.

There are three types of franchises:
- The *manufacturer-sponsored retailer franchise system*—for example, Ford and its network of independent franchised dealers.
- The *manufacturer-sponsored wholesaler franchise system*—Coca-Cola licenses bottlers (wholesalers) in various markets who buy Coca-Cola syrup concentrate and then bottle and sell the finished product to retailers in local markets.
- The *service-firm-sponsored retailer franchise system*—examples are found in the auto-rental business (Avis), the fast-food service business (McDonald's), and the motel business (Ramada Inn).

In an Administered VMS, leadership is assumed not through common ownership or contractual ties but through the size and power of one or a few dominant channel members.

Horizontal Marketing Systems: Two or more companies at one level join together to follow a new marketing opportunity.

Multichannel Distribution Systems (often called *hybrid marketing channels*): Occurs when a single firm sets up two or more marketing channels to reach one or more customer segments. (Figure 12.4)

4.3 Changing Channel Organization

Disintermediation occurs when product or service producers cut out intermediaries and go directly to final buyers, or when radically new types of channel intermediaries displace traditional ones.

5. CHANNEL DESIGN DECISIONS

Marketing channel design calls for analyzing consumer needs, setting channel objectives, identifying major channel alternatives, and evaluating them.

5.1 Analyzing Consumer Needs

The company must balance consumer needs not only against the feasibility and costs of meeting these needs but also against customer price preferences.

5.2 Setting Channel Objectives

Companies should state their marketing channel objectives in terms of targeted levels of customer service. The company should decide which segments to serve and the best channels to use in each case. The company's channel objectives are influenced by the nature of the company, its products, its marketing intermediaries, its competitors, and the environment. Environmental factors such as economic conditions and legal constraints may affect channel objectives and design.

5.3 Identifying Major Alternatives

5.3.1 Types of Intermediaries

A firm should identify the types of channel members available to carry out its channel work.

5.3.2 Number of Marketing Intermediaries

Companies must also determine the number of channel members to use at each level. Three strategies are available:

- Intensive distribution: Ideal for producers of convenience products and common raw materials. It is a strategy in which they stock their products in as many outlets as possible.
- Exclusive distribution: Purposely limit the number of intermediaries handling their products. The producer gives only a limited number of dealers the exclusive right to distribute its products in their territories.
- Selective distribution: This is the use of more than one, but fewer than all, of the intermediaries who are willing to carry a company's products.

5.3.3 Responsibilities of Channel Members

The producer and intermediaries need to agree on the terms and responsibilities of each channel member. They should agree on price policies, conditions of sale, territorial rights, and specific services to be performed by each party.

5.4 Evaluating the Major Alternatives

Using economic criteria, a company compares the likely sales, costs, and profitability of different channel alternatives. Using control issues means giving them some control over the marketing of the product, and some intermediaries take more control than others. Using adaptive criteria means the company wants to keep the channel flexible so that it can adapt to environmental changes.

5.5 Designing International Distribution Channels

In some markets, the distribution system is complex and hard to penetrate, consisting of many layers and large numbers of intermediaries. At the other extreme, distribution systems in developing countries may be scattered, inefficient, or altogether lacking. Sometimes customs or government regulation can greatly restrict how a company distributes products in global markets.

6. CHANNEL MANAGEMENT DECISIONS

Marketing channel management calls for selecting, managing, and motivating individual channel members and evaluating their performance over time.

6.1 Selecting Channel Members

When selecting intermediaries, the company should determine what characteristics distinguish the better ones.

6.2 Managing and Motivating Channel Members

The company must sell not only through the intermediaries but to and with them. Most companies practice strong partner relationship management (PRM) to forge long-term partnerships with channel members.

6.3 Evaluating Channel Members

The company should recognize and reward intermediaries who are performing well and adding good value for consumers. Those who are performing poorly should be assisted or, as a last resort, replaced. Finally, manufacturers must be sensitive to their dealers.

7. PUBLIC POLICY AND DISTRIBUTION DECISIONS

Exclusive distribution occurs when the seller allows only certain outlets to carry its products. Exclusive dealing occurs when the seller requires that these dealers not handle competitors' products. Exclusive arrangements exclude other producers from selling to these dealers. This brings exclusive dealing contracts under the scope of the Clayton Act of 1914. Exclusive territorial agreements occur when the producer agrees not to sell to other dealers in a given area, or the buyer may agree to sell only in its own territory. Full-line pricing occurs when producers of a strong brand sell it to dealers only if the dealers will take some or all of the rest of the line. This is also known as a tying agreement. In general, sellers can drop dealers "for cause."

8. MARKETING LOGISTICS AND SUPPLY CHAIN MANAGEMENT

8.1 Nature and Importance of Marketing Logistics

Marketing logistics—also called physical distribution—involves planning, implementing, and controlling the physical flow of goods, services, and related information from points of origin to points of consumption to meet customer requirements at a profit. Marketing logistics involves *outbound distribution* (moving products from the factory to resellers and ultimately to customers), *inbound distribution* (moving products and materials from suppliers to the factory) and *reverse distribution* (moving broken, unwanted, or excess products returned by consumers or resellers). It involves the entire supply chain management—managing upstream and downstream value-added flows of materials, final goods, and related information among suppliers, the company, resellers, and final consumers (Figure 12.5).Companies today are placing greater emphasis on logistics for several reasons.

- Companies can gain a powerful competitive advantage by using improved logistics to give customers better service or lower prices.
- Improved logistics can yield tremendous cost savings to both the company and its customers.
- The explosion in product variety has created a need for improved logistics management.
- Improvements in information technology have created opportunities for major gains in distribution efficiency.

8.2 Goals of the Logistics System

The goal of marketing logistics should be to provide a *targeted* level of customer service at the least cost.

8.3 Major Logistics Functions

8.3.1 Warehousing

A company must decide on how many and what types of warehouses it needs and where they will be located. Storage warehouses store goods for moderate to long periods. Distribution centers are designed to move goods rather than just store them.

8.3.2 Inventory Management

Just-in-time logistics systems: Producers and retailers carry only small inventories of parts or merchandise, often only enough for a few days of operations.

8.3.3 Transportation

Trucks have increased their share of transportation steadily and now account for nearly 35 percent of total cargo ton-miles (more than 60 percent of actual tonnage). Trucks are highly flexible in their routing and time schedules, and they can usually offer faster service than railroads. They are efficient for short hauls of high-value merchandise. Railroads account for 31 percent of total cargo ton-miles moved. They are one of the most cost-effective modes for shipping large amounts of bulk products—coal, sand, minerals, and farm and forest products—over long distances. Water carriers account for 11 percent of cargo ton-miles, transport large amounts of goods by ships and barges on U.S. coastal and inland waterways. Although the cost of water transportation is very low for shipping bulky, low-value, nonperishable products, it is the slowest mode and may be affected by the weather. Pipelines account for 16 percent of cargo ton-miles, are a specialized means of shipping petroleum, natural gas, and chemicals from sources to markets. Air carriers transport less than 5 percent of the nation's goods. Airfreight rates are much higher than rail or truck rates. The Internet carries digital products from producer to customer via satellite, cable, or phone wire.

Intermodal transportation: Combining two or more modes of transportation.

- Piggyback: Rail and trucks;
- Fishyback: Water and trucks;
- Trainship: Water and rail;
- Airtruck: Air and trucks.

8.3.4 Logistics Information Management

Electronic data interchange (EDI) is the computerized exchange of data between organizations. Vendor-managed inventory (VMI) systems or continuous inventory replenishment systems, is the customer sharing real-time data on sales and current inventory levels with the supplier. The supplier then takes full responsibility for managing inventories and deliveries.

8.4 Integrated Logistics Management

Integrated logistics management is a concept that recognizes that providing better customer service and trimming distribution costs require teamwork, both inside the company and among all the marketing channel organizations.

8.4.1 Cross-Functional Teamwork Inside the Company

The goal of integrated supply chain management is to harmonize all of the company's logistics decisions. Close working relationships among departments can be achieved in several ways.

- Permanent logistics committees, made up of managers responsible for different physical distribution activities.
- Supply chain manager positions that link the logistics activities of

functional areas.

- System-wide supply chain management software.

8.4.2 Building Logistics Partnerships

Cross-functional, cross-company teams: For example, P&Gers work jointly with their counterparts at Wal-Mart to find ways to squeeze costs out of their distribution system.

Shared projects: For example, Home Depot allows key suppliers to use its stores as a testing ground for new merchandising programs.

8.4.3 Third-Party Logistics

Third-party logistics (3PL) providers help clients tighten up overstuffed supply chains, slash inventories, and get products to customers more quickly and reliably. (Also called outsourced logistics or contract logistics.) Companies use third-party logistics providers for several reasons.

- These providers can often do it more efficiently and at lower cost.
- Outsourcing logistics frees a company to focus more intensely on its core business.
- Integrated logistics companies understand increasingly complex logistics environments.

Student Exercises

1. Key Term: Value Delivery Network

A value delivery network is the network made up of the company, suppliers, distributors, and ultimately customers who partner with each other to improve the performance of the entire system. Take a look at Mountain Valley Spring Company (www.mountainvalleyspring.com). Mountain Valley Spring is a well-known producer of premium spring water. Review their site. Make a list of the members of their "partner community."

2. Key Term: Marketing Channel

Very few producers really sell their goods directly to the final user. Most use some kind of intermediary to bring their products to market. The set of independent organizations that help make a product or service available for use or consumption by the consumer (or business user) is known as the marketing channel. What marketing channel does computer manufacturer Gateway (www.gateway.com) uses to get their product to the ultimate (final) consumer?

3.   Key Term: Direct Marketing Channel

A direct marketing channel is a marketing channel that has no intermediary levels. The company sells directly to the consumer. Your texts points out Mary Kay cosmetics and Amway as examples of the direct marketing channel. Find two more.

4.   Key Term: Indirect Marketing Channel

An indirect marketing channel is any form of marketing channel that is not direct from the company to the customer. Indirect marketing channels involve one or more layers of intermediaries. Go to Starbuck's homepage (www.starbucks.com). What are the different indirect marketing channels Starbucks uses to get its products to the coffee drinker?

5.   Key Term: Horizontal Channel Conflict

Channel conflict occurs when there is disagreement among marketing channel members on goals and roles. Horizontal channel conflict occurs between firms at the same level of the channel. Think about the gas station where you typically buy gas. How could they come in conflict with other local stations owned by the same company?

6.   Key Term: Vertical Channel Conflict

Vertical channel conflict occurs between different levels of the same channel. It occurs even more frequently than does horizontal channel conflict. Your text gives you the example Goodyear using different channels to sell its tires. Take a look at Subway (www.subway.com). Currently, you can find a Subway store almost anywhere, it seems. Think of another form of distribution that Subway might enter in to that would potentially create vertical channel conflict with its existing stores.

7.   Key Term: Conventional Distribution Channel

A conventional distribution channel is a channel consisting of one or more independent producers, wholesalers, and retailers, each a separate business seeking to maximize its own profits even at the expense of profits for the system as a whole. No one channel member has much control over any of the other channel members. Every member is out for what is good for them, without regard to other channel members. Consider Green Giant vegetables (www.greengiant.com). Describe the conventional distribution channel you believe this company would use to get their frozen and canned vegetables to you, the consumer.

8.   Key Term: Vertical Marketing System (VMS)

A vertical marketing system consists of producers, wholesalers, and retailers acting as a unified system—in contrast to the adversarial nature of a conventional distribution channel. The VMS may be dominated by the producer, the wholesaler, or the retailer.

Take a look at Goodyear (www.goodyear.com). Your text talks a lot about the relationship of Goodyear and its dealers. Describe the VMS used by Goodyear.

9.   Key Term: Administered VMS

An administered VMS is a vertical marketing system that coordinates successive stages of production and distribution, not through common ownership or contractual ties, but through the size or power of one of the members. Other than the examples of administered VMS given in your text think of another.

10.   Key Term: Exclusive Distribution

When a manufacturer gives a limited number of dealers the exclusive right to distribute the company's products in their territories it is known as exclusive distribution. Exclusive distribution is often found in the distribution of luxury automobiles and prestige women's clothing. The dealers of these products are few and far between. Exclusive distribution aids in enhancing the product image and contributes to larger markups. Find another product that makes use of an exclusive distribution channel.

Marketing ADventure Exercises

1.   Ad Interpretation Challenge: Value Delivery Network
      Ad: Apparel—Puma

A value delivery network is the network made up of the company, suppliers, distributors, and ultimately customers who partner with each other to improve the performance of the entire system. The idea of such a network is to improve the performance of the network with the result being higher profits for the channel members and a fair price to the consumer. Think about this Puma ad. Make a list of all members of value delivery network that would have an impact on this product.

2.   Ad Interpretation Challenge: Direct Marketing Channel
      Ad: Student Choice

A direct marketing channel has no intermediaries. The product goes from the company to the final consumer. Find an ad for a product that is sold through the direct marketing channel.

3.   Ad Interpretation Challenge: Channel Conflict
      Ad: Food and Beverage—Cool Drinking Water

Disagreements often occur among channel members on goals and roles—who should do what and who should get what. Describe the possible channel conflicts that you believe could arise regarding the marketing of this product.

4.   Ad Interpretation Challenge: Vertical Channel Conflict
      Ad: Electronics—LG

Vertical conflict is conflict between two members at different levels in the channel. Vertical conflict is a very common occurrence. Companies must manage this conflict to keep it from getting out of hand. Think about LG Electronics. How might they unwittingly create vertical conflict?

5.   Ad Interpretation Challenge: Horizontal Channel Conflict
      Ad: Autos—Ford

Horizontal channel conflict occurs among firms at the same level of the channel. Give a situation in which a Ford dealer might express horizontal channel disagreement with Ford Inc.

6.   Ad Interpretation Challenge: Vertical Marketing System
      Ad: Student Choice

A vertical marketing system is a distribution channel structure in which all channel member's work as a unified system. One channel member owns the others, has contracts with them, or has so much power that they all cooperate. Find an example of an ad for a company that would likely utilize a VMS.

7.   Ad Interpretation Challenge: Vertical Marketing System—Student Decision
      Ad: General Retail—Hallmark

Review the information on vertical marketing systems (VMS). Remember, in a VMS, one channel member owns the others, has contracts with them, or has so much power that they all cooperate. Three basic types of VMS exist—corporate, franchise, or administered. Study Hallmark, Inc. (www.hallmark.com). Pay particular attention to the relationship between Hallmark (the company) and Hallmark stores. What type of VMS does Hallmark employ?

8.   Ad Interpretation Challenge: Administered VMS
      Ad: General Retail—Target

An administered VMS is a vertical marketing system that coordinates successive stages of production and distribution, not through common ownership or contractual ties, but through the size and power of one of the parties. Consider Target. Why would you say Target operates an administered VMS?

9.   Ad Interpretation Challenge: Multichannel Distribution Systems
      Ad: General Retail—Hallmark

A multichannel distribution system is a distribution system in which a single firm sets ups two or more marketing channels to reach one or more customer segments. More and more companies are turning to such distribution systems as customer segments and channel possibilities have proliferated. What multiple channels of distribution does Hallmark employ?

10. Ad Interpretation Challenge: Intensive Distribution
     Ad: Student Choice

Intensive distribution occurs when the company stocks their product in as many outlets as possible. The goal is to have the product everywhere that consumers may be. You want the product to be readily available so the consumer does not have to search for it. Find an ad for a product that you would consider a candidate for intensive distribution.

Chapter 13
Retailing and Wholesaling

Learning Objectives

1. Explain the role of retailers in the distribution channel and describe the major types of retailers.
2. Describe the major retailer marketing decisions.
3. Discuss the future of retailing.
4. Explain the major types of wholesalers and their marketing objectives.

Chapter Overview

This chapter is a continuation of the prior chapter on marketing channels; it provides more detail on retailing and wholesaling, two very important concepts in the value delivery network. Retailers can be classified according to several characteristics, including the amount of service they offer, the breadth and depth of their product lines, the relative prices they charge, and how they are organized. The major decisions retailers make are centered on their target market and positioning, their product assortment and services, their price, their promotion strategies, and where they are located. The wheel of retailing concept says that many new retailing forms begin as low-margin, low-price, low-status operations. They challenge established retailers, and then the new retailers' success leads them to upgrade their facilities and offer more services. In turn, their costs increase, and eventually they become like the conventional retailers they replaced. The cycle begins again. There are many types of wholesalers, including merchant wholesalers, agents and brokers, and manufacturers' sales branches and offices.

Chapter Outline

1. INTRODUCTION

Costco is trouncing Wal-Mart at its own low-price game. With about the same number of members but 60 fewer stores, Costco outsells Sam's Club by 50 percent. Its $64 billion in sales makes Costco the nation's fourth-largest retailer, behind only Wal-Mart, Home Depot, and Kroger, and one step ahead of Target. How is Costco beating Sam's Club at its own low-price game? The two retailers are very similar in many ways. But inside the store, Costco adds a certain merchandising magic that Sam's Club just can't match. Both Costco and Sam's Club excel at low-cost operations and low prices. As one industry analyst puts it, "While Wal-Mart stands for low prices, Costco is a retail treasure hunt, where one's shopping cart could contain a $50,000 diamond ring resting on top of a vat of mayonnaise." Costco brings flair to an otherwise dreary setting. Mixed in with its regular stock of staples, Costco features a glittering, constantly-shifting array of one-time specials such as discounted Prada bags, Calloway gold clubs, or Kenneth Cole Bags—deals you just won't find at Sam's Club.

Opening Vignette Questions

1. How would you compare Costco and its product offerings to what you would find in a typical Wal-Mart store?
2. How has Costco been able to beat Sam's at its own low-price game?
3. What are the basic differences in the merchandise mix at a Costco and a Sam's?
4. What is Costco's value proposition?

2. RETAILING

Retailing includes all the activities involved in selling products or services directly to final consumers for their personal, nonbusiness use. Retailers: Businesses whose sales come primarily from retailing. Many marketers are now embracing the concept of shopper marketing, the idea that the retail store itself is an important marketing medium. In recent years nonstore retailing has been growing much faster than has store retailing.

2.1 Types of Retailers

Self-service retailers serve customers who are willing to perform their own "locate-compare-select" process to save time or money. Limited-service retailers provide more sales assistance because they carry more shopping goods about which customers need information. Full-service retailers include high-end specialty stores and first-class department stores. Salespeople assist customers in every phase of the shopping process.

2.2 Product Line

Specialty stores carry narrow product lines with deep assortments within those lines. Department stores carry a wide variety of product lines. In recent years, department stores have been squeezed between more focused and flexible specialty stores on the one hand, and more efficient, lower-priced discounters on the other. Supermarkets are the most frequently shopped type of retail store. Supermarkets also have been hit hard by the rapid growth of out-of-home eating. Supermarkets' share of the groceries and consumables market plunged from 89 percent in 1988 to 50 percent in 2008. Convenience stores are small stores that carry a limited line of high-turnover convenience goods. Superstores are much larger than regular supermarkets and offer a large assortment of routinely purchased food products, nonfood items, and services. Supercenters (called hypermarkets in some countries) are very large combination food and discount stores. Category killers are superstores that are actually giant specialty stores. (Best Buy and Circuit City are examples.) Service retailers include hotels and motels, banks, airlines, colleges, hospitals, movie theaters, tennis clubs, bowling alleys, restaurants, repair services, hair salons, and dry cleaners. Service retailers in the United States are growing faster than product retailers.

2.3 Relative Prices

Discount stores sells standard merchandise at lower prices by accepting lower margins and selling higher volume. Off-price retailers offer products to fill the ultralow-price, high-volume gap by pricing lower than discount stores. The three main types of off-price retailers are:

- Independent off-price retailers either are independently owned and run or are divisions of larger retail corporations.
- Factory outlets—manufacturer-owned and operated stores—sometimes group together in factory outlet malls and value-retail centers.
- Warehouse clubs (or wholesale clubs or membership warehouses), operate in huge, drafty, warehouse-like facilities and offer few frills.

2.4 Organizational Approach

Chain stores are two or more outlets that are commonly owned and controlled. They have many advantages over independents.

- Their size allows them to buy in large quantities at lower prices and gain promotional economies.
- They can hire specialists to deal with areas such as pricing, promotion, merchandising, inventory control, and sales forecasting.

There are three forms of contractual associations:

- Voluntary chain—a wholesaler-sponsored group of independent retailers that engages in group buying and common merchandising.
- Retailer cooperative—a group of independent retailers that bands together to set up a jointly owned, central wholesale operation and conducts joint merchandising and promotion efforts.
- Franchise— The main difference between franchise organizations and other contractual systems is that franchise systems are normally based on some unique product or service; on a method of doing business. Franchises command approximately 40 percent of all retail sales in the United States.

Merchandising conglomerates are corporations that combine several different retailing forms under one central ownership. An example is Limited Brands, which operates The Limited, Express, Victoria's Secret, and others.

2.5 Retailer Marketing Decisions

Retailers are always searching for new marketing strategies to attract and hold customers. As shown in Figure 13.1, retailers face major marketing decisions.

Segmentation, Targeting, Differentiation, and Positioning Decisions

Too many retailers fail to define their target markets and positions clearly. They try to have "something for everyone" and end up satisfying no market well. In contrast, successful retailers define their target markets well and position themselves strongly.

Product Assortment and Services Decision

Retailers must decide on three major product variables:
Product assortment should differentiate the retailer while matching target shoppers' expectations.
Services mix can help set one retailer apart from another.
Store atmosphere is another important element in the reseller's product arsenal.

Price Decision

Most retailers seek either high markups on lower volume (most specialty stores) or low markups on higher volume (mass merchandisers and discount stores).
"High-low" pricing—charging higher prices on an everyday basis, coupled with frequent sales and other price promotions to increase store traffic, clear out unsold merchandise, create a low-price image, or attract customers who will buy other goods at full prices.
Everyday low pricing (EDLP), charging constant, everyday low prices with few sales or discounts.

Promotion Decision

Retailers use any or all of the promotion tools—advertising, personal selling, sales promotion, public relations, and direct marketing—to reach consumers.

2.5.5. Place Decision

It's very important that retailers select locations that are accessible to the target market in areas that are consistent with the retailer's positioning. Shopping centers are a group of retail businesses planned, developed, owned, and managed as a unit.

- Regional shopping centers, or regional shopping malls, are the largest and most dramatic shopping center, contains from 40 to over 200 stores, including two or more full-line department stores.
- Community shopping centers contain between 15 and 40 retail stores. It normally contains a branch of a department store or variety store, a supermarket, specialty stores, professional offices, and sometimes a bank.
- Neighborhood shopping centers or strip malls that generally contain between 5 and 15 stores. They are close and convenient for consumers.
- Power centers are huge unenclosed shopping centers consisting of a long strip of retail stores, including large, freestanding anchors. This is the current trend.
- Lifestyle centers are smaller malls with upscale stores, convenient locations, and non-retail activities such as dining and a movie theater.

2.6 The Future of Retailing

2.6.1 New Retail Forms and Shortening Retail Life Cycles

New retail forms continue to emerge to meet new situations and consumer needs, but the life cycle of new retail forms is getting shorter. The wheel-of-retailing concept states that many new types of retailing forms begin as low-margin, low-price, and low-status operations. The new retailers' success leads them to upgrade their facilities and offer more services, forcing them to increase their prices. Eventually, the new retailers become like the conventional retailers they replaced. The cycle begins again.

2.6.2 Growth of Nonstore Retailing

Americans are increasingly avoiding the hassles and crowds at malls by doing more of their shopping by phone or computer. Much of the anticipated growth in online sales will go to multichannel retailers—the click-and-brick marketers who can successfully merge the virtual and physical worlds.

2.6.3 Retail Convergence

The merging of consumers, products, prices, and retailers is called retail convergence. Such convergence means greater competition for retailers and greater difficulty in differentiating offerings.

2.6.4 The Rise of Megaretailers

The megaretailers are shifting the balance of power between retailers and producers. A relative handful of retailers now control access to enormous numbers of consumers, giving them the upper hand in their dealings with manufacturers.

2.6.5 Growing Importance of Retail Technology

Many retailers now routinely use technologies such as touch-screen kiosks, customer-loyalty cards, electronic shelf labels and signs, handheld shopping assistants, smart cards, and self-scanning checkout systems.

2.6.6 Global Expansion of Major Retailers

Retailers with unique formats and strong brand positioning are increasingly moving into other countries. Many are expanding internationally to escape mature and saturated home markets. Most U.S retailers are still significantly behind Europe and Asia when it comes to global expansion.

2.6.7 Retail Stores as "Communities" or "Hangouts"

With the rise in the number of people living alone, working at home, or living in isolated and sprawling suburbs, there has been a resurgence of establishments that, regardless of the product or service they offer, also provide a place for people to get together.

3. WHOLESALING

3.1 Wholesaling Activities

Wholesaling includes all activities involved in selling goods and services to those buying for resale or business use. Wholesalers are those firms engaged primarily in wholesaling activities. Wholesalers buy mostly from producers and sell mostly to retailers, industrial consumers, and other wholesalers. Wholesalers add value by performing one or more of the following channel functions:

- Selling and promoting: Wholesalers' sales forces help manufacturers reach many small customers at a low cost.
- Buying and assortment building: Wholesalers can select items and build assortments needed by their customers, thereby saving the consumers much work.
- Bulk-breaking: Wholesalers save their customers money by buying in carload lots and breaking bulk (breaking large lots into small quantities).
- Warehousing: Wholesalers hold inventories, thereby reducing the inventory costs and risks of suppliers and customers.
- Transportation: Wholesalers can provide quicker delivery to buyers because they are closer than the producers.
- Financing: Wholesalers finance their customers by giving credit, and they finance their suppliers by ordering early and paying bills on time.
- Risk bearing: Wholesalers absorb risk by taking title and bearing the cost of theft, damage, spoilage, and obsolescence.
- Market information: Wholesalers give information to suppliers and customers about competitors, new products, and price developments.
- Management services and advice: Wholesalers often help retailers train their salesclerks, improve store layouts and displays, and set up accounting and inventory control systems.

3.2 Types of Wholesalers

Wholesalers fall into three major groups. Merchant wholesalers are the largest single group of wholesalers, accounting for roughly 50 percent of all wholesaling. Merchant wholesalers include two broad types:

- Full-service wholesalers provide a full set of services.
- Limited-service wholesalers offer fewer services to their suppliers and customers.

Brokers and agents differ from merchant wholesalers in two ways: They do not take title to goods. They perform only a few functions.

A broker brings buyers and sellers together and assists in negotiation. Agents represent buyers or sellers on a more permanent basis. Manufacturers' agents (also called manufacturers' representatives) are the most common type of agent wholesaler. Manufacturers' sales branches and offices are wholesaling by sellers or buyers themselves rather than through independent wholesalers.

3.3 Wholesaler Marketing Decisions

3.3.1 Segmentation, Targeting, Differentiation, and Positioning Decisions

Like retailers, wholesalers must segment and define their target markets and differentiate and position themselves effectively—they cannot serve everyone.

3.3.2 Marketing Mix Decisions

Wholesalers add customer value though the products and services they offer. They are often under great pressure to carry a full line and to stock enough for immediate delivery. But this practice can damage profits. Price is an important wholesaler decision. Most wholesalers are not promotion minded.

3.4 Trends in Wholesaling

The industry remains vulnerable to one of the most enduring trends of the last decade—fierce resistance to price increases and the winnowing out of suppliers who are not adding value based on cost and quality. The distinction between large retailers and large wholesalers continues to blur. Wholesalers will continue to increase the services they provide to retailers—retail pricing, cooperative advertising, marketing and management information reports, accounting services, online transactions, and others. Finally, many large wholesalers are now going global.

Student Exercises

1.   Key Term: Retailing

Retailing is defined as all activities involved in selling goods or services directly to the final consumer for their personal, nonbusiness use. Look at Amazon (www.amazon.com) and National Cap and Set Screw Company (www.natlcap.com). Do both of these companies engage in retailing?

2.   Key Term: Self-Service Retailers

Self-service retailers serve customers who are willing to perform their own "locate-compare-select" process to save money. Self-service is the basis of all discount operations and is typically used by sellers of convenience goods and nationally branded, fast-moving shopping goods. This chapter opens with a discussion of Whole Foods. Would you consider Whole Foods a self-service retailer?

3.   Key Term: Specialty Store

Specialty stores carry narrow product lines with deep assortments within those lines. What are two specialty store chains?

4.   Key Term: Category Killer

A category killer is a giant specialty store that carries a very deep assortment of a particular line and is staffed by knowledgeable employees. In recent years category killers have experienced explosive growth. Category killers have come to dominate the retail landscape in recent years. Take a look at some category killers. Do you see any vulnerability which could cause them concern?

5.   Key Term: Superstores

A store much larger than a regular supermarket that offers a large assortment of routinely purchased food products, nonfood items, and services is commonly known as a superstore. Wal-Mart, Target, and Meijer (among others) all offer this supersized combination discount and grocery store. They are growing at the rate of 25% annually. Where is their weakness?

6.   Key Term: Discount Store

A discount store sells standard merchandise at lower prices by accepting lower margins and selling higher volume. In recent years, discount stores have been moving gradually upscale, selling higher quality merchandise and charging slightly higher prices. Your text spotlights Wal-Mart Stores (www.walmart.com). Take a look at Wal-Mart and briefly review their history, How has the focus of their stores changed over the years?

7.   Key Term: Factory Outlet

An off-price retail operation that is owned and operated by a manufacturer and that normally carries the manufacturer's surplus, discontinued, or irregular goods is known as a factory outlet. Factory outlet stores (and malls) have become one of the hottest growth areas in retailing. Take a look at Prime Outlets (www.primeoutlets.com), one of the largest operators of outlet mall in the country. How does the factory outlet mall differ from a traditional mall?

8.   Key Term: Power Center

A shopping center is a group of retail businesses planned, developed, owned, and managed as a unit. A power center is a huge unenclosed shopping center consisting of a long strip of retail stores, including large free-standing anchor stores. Each store has its own outside entrance. Why do you believe such centers have become increasingly popular in recent years?

9.   Key Term: The Wheel-of-Retailing Concept

The wheel-of-retailing concept is a concept of retailing that states new types of retailers typically begin as low-margin, low-price, low-status operations but later evolve into higher-priced, higher-service operations, eventually becoming like the conventional retailers they replaced. Think of an example of a retail format that has progressed through at least a portion of the wheel-of-retailing.

10.   Key Term: International Retailing

Retailers with unique formats and strong brand positioning are increasingly moving into other countries. Many are expanding internationally to escape mature and saturated markets at home. They feel they must expand internationally to continue to grow. Think of some of the issues these retailers may face.

Marketing ADventure Exercises

1.   Ad Interpretation Challenge: Self-Service Retailer
        Ad: Cosmetics and Pharmaceuticals—Edge

Self-service retailers serve customers who are willing to perform their own "locate-compare-select" process to save money. Self-service is the basis of all discount operations and is typically used by sellers of convenience goods and nationally branded, fast-moving shopping goods. Edge shaving gel is a typical product found in a self-service retailer. What type of information should the packaging of this product provide to assist the consumer in the "locate-compare-select" process?

2.   Ad Interpretation Challenge: Specialty Store
        Ad: Student Choice

A specialty store is a retail store that carries a narrow product line with a deep assortment within that line. The increasing use of market segmentation, market targeting, and product specialization has resulted in a greater need for stores that focus on specific products and segments. Find an ad for a retailer that you would consider a specialty store.

3.   Ad Interpretation Challenge: Department Store
        Ad: Electronics—LG

A department store is a retail organization that carries a wide variety of product lines—each line is operated as a separate department managed by specialist buyers or merchandisers. In recent years, department stores have been squeezed by both the discounters and the specialty stores. Why might you find a product such as this LG television in a department store?

4.   Ad Interpretation Challenge: Supermarket
        Ad: Food and Beverage—Heinz

Large, low-cost, low-margin, high-volume, self-service stores that carry a wide variety of grocery and household products are known as supermarkets. Why is it necessary to sell products such as Heinz ketchup through such stores?

5.   Ad Interpretation Challenge: Category Killer
        Ad: General Retail –World's Biggest

The category killer is a relatively new type of retail format. Category killers are in essence giant specialty stores that carry a very deep assortment of a particular line of product and are staffed by knowledgeable employees. What advantages does the consumer gain from shopping a store such as World's Biggest Bookstore?

6.   Ad Interpretation Challenge: Discount Stores
        Ad: Student Choice

Discount stores are retailers that sell standard merchandise at lower prices by accepting lower margins and making up for it by higher volume. Of the offered ads, find one for a discount store.

7.   Ad Interpretation Challenge: Off-Price Retailers
        Ad: Apparel—Levis

Off-price retailers are a type of retailer that buys at less-than-regular wholesale prices and sell at less than retail. Off-price retailers are a relatively new retail format that has come into existence as the traditional discount store has traded up. Under what situation would a product such as Levi's New Collection Diamond Jeans wind up at an off-price retailer?

8.   Ad Interpretation Challenge: Franchise
        Ad: Student Choice

A franchise is a contractual association between a manufacturer, wholesaler, or service organization (a franchiser) and independent businesspeople (franchisees) who buy the right to own and operate one or more units in the franchise system. Franchises now control over 40 percent of all U.S. sales. Locate an ad for a U.S.–based franchise.

9.   Ad Interpretation Challenge: Retail Positioning
      Ad: General Retail—Target

Retailers must define their target markets and positioning clearly. Otherwise, they do not project a clear image to the consumer. Wal-Mart has successfully positioned itself as the low-cost provider. How can Target successfully compete?

10.   Ad Interpretation Challenge: The Wheel-of-Retailing Concept
       Ad: General Retail—Worlds Biggest

The wheel-of-retailing concept states that new types of retailers typically begin as low-margin, low-price, low-status operations but later evolve into higher-priced, higher-service operations, eventually becoming like the conventional retailers they replaced. World's Biggest Bookstore seems to be in the beginning stages of the wheel. If they are not careful, how might they evolve and eventually become obsolete?

Chapter 14
Communicating Customer Value:
Integrated Marketing Communications Strategy

Learning Objectives

1. Define the five promotion mix tools for communicating customer value.
2. Discuss the changing communications landscape and the need for integrated marketing communications
3. Outline the communications process and the steps in developing effective marketing communications.
4. Explain the methods for setting the promotion budget and factors that affect the design of the promotion mix.

Chapter Overview

Companies must do more than just create customer value. They must also use promotion to clearly and persuasively communicate that value. Promotion is not a single tool but, rather, a mix of several tools. Under the concept of integrated marketing communications, the company must carefully coordinate these promotion elements to deliver a clear, consistent, and compelling message about the organization and its brands. The chapter begins with an introduction to the various promotion mix tools. Next, we examine the rapidly changing communications environment and the need for intergraded marketing communications. Finally, the chapter discusses the steps in developing marketing communications and the promotion budgeting process.

Chapter Outline

1. INTRODUCTION

Today, most advertisers are scrambling to make sense of the Web. The digital revolution has created a kind of "media divide," pitting traditional media such as television against the new-age digital media. Consumer giant Unilever was recently anointed Digital Marketer of the Year. Interestingly, the company doesn't really do digital campaigns as such. Unilever has made Web and digital tactics just another important part of its mainstream marketing. None of Unilever's digital efforts was purely a digital campaign. Instead, each digital effort was carefully integrated with other media and marketing tactics. For example, Suave's "In the Motherhood" webisodes are only a small part of a much larger integrated communications campaign for the brand. It starts with television spots featuring real mothers. The TV ads pull customers onto two related Web sites. Public relations ahs also played a role in the Suave campaign. Thus, the entire Suave campaign – television, digital, and public relations – is all integrated to create a "sisterhood" of moms and to deliver the brand's "Say yes to beauty" positioning. One powerful result of integrating digital with traditional media is what has been called "superdistribution," the idea of getting Web programs picked up by other media. One of the best examples is Dove's "Evolution" video. "Evolution" has racked up over 20 million views on YouTube and other video sites. But throw in viewership via everything from TV news and talk shows to classrooms and general word-of-mouth, and global viewership has exceeded 400 million. To put that in perspective, that level of distribution equates to some $150 million worth of free media coverage. Unilever understands that the growing shift to digital doesn't really change the fundamentals much. If anything it means brand managers have to be more firmly grounded in what their brands are about in order to clearly and consistently define the brands across an exploding array of old and new media.

Opening Vignette Questions

1. How has Unilever successfully crossed the "media divide?"
2. What role has public relations played in the Suave campaign?
3. What is "superdistribution?"

2. THE PROMOTION MIX

A company's total promotion mix—also called its marketing communications mix—consists of the specific blend of advertising, sales promotion, public relations, personal selling, and direct-marketing tools that the company uses to pursue its advertising and marketing objectives.

Definitions of the five major promotion tools are:
- Advertising: Any paid form of nonpersonal presentation and promotion of ideas, goods, or services by an identified sponsor
- Sales promotion: Short-term incentives to encourage the purchase or sale of a product or service
- Public relations: Building good relations with the company's various publics by obtaining favorable publicity, building up a good corporate image, and handling or heading off unfavorable rumors, stories, and events
- Personal selling: Personal presentation by the firm's sales force for the purpose of making sales and building customer relationships
- Direct marketing: Direct connections with carefully targeted individual consumers to both obtain an immediate response and cultivate lasting customer relationships—using telephone, mail, fax, e-mail, the Internet, and other tools to communicate directly with specific customers.

3. INTEGRATED MARKETING COMMUNICATIONS

3.1 The New Marketing Communications Landscape

Several major factors are changing the face of today's marketing communications.

- Consumers are changing. They are better informed and more communications empowered.
- Marketing strategies are changing. As mass markets have fragmented, marketers are shifting away from mass marketing. More and more, they are developing focused marketing programs designed to build closer relationships with customers in more narrowly defined micromarkets.
- Sweeping changes in communications technology are causing remarkable changes in the ways in which companies and customers communicate with each other.

3.2 The Shifting Marketing Communications Model

Although television, magazines, and other mass media remain very important, their dominance is declining. Advertisers are now adding a broad selection of more-specialized and highly targeted media to reach smaller customer segments. The new media range from specialty magazines, cable television channels, and video on demand (VOD) to Internet catalogs, e-mail, podcasts, cell phones, and online social networks. Companies are doing less broadcasting and more narrowcasting. Many large advertisers are shifting their advertising budgets away from network television in favor of more targeted, cost-effective, interactive, and engaging media. It seems likely that the new marketing communications model will consist of a shifting mix of both traditional mass media and a wide array of exciting new, more-target, more-personalized media.

3.3 The Need for Integrated Marketing Communications

Customers don't distinguish between message sources the way marketers do. In the consumer's mind, advertising messages from different media and different promotional approaches all become part of a single message about the company. Conflicting messages from these different sources can result in confused company images and brand positions.

Today, more companies are adopting the concept of integrated marketing communications (IMC). Under this concept, as illustrated in Figure 14.1, the company carefully integrates and coordinates its many communications channels to deliver a clear, consistent, and compelling message about the organization and its brands. IMC calls for recognizing all contact points where the customer may encounter the company, its products, and its brands. Each brand contact will deliver a message, whether good, bad, or indifferent. The company must strive to deliver a consistent and positive message with each contact. IMC builds brand identity and strong customer relationships by tying together all of the company's messages and images. Brand messages and positioning are coordinated across all communication activities and media.

4. A VIEW OF THE COMMUNICATION PROCESS

Integrated marketing communications involves identifying the target audience and shaping a well-coordinated promotional program to obtain the desired audience response. Today, marketers are moving toward viewing communications as managing the customer relationship over time. Because customers differ, communications programs need to be developed for specific segments, niches, and even individuals. The communications process should start with an audit of all the potential contacts target customers may have with the company and its brands. To communicate effectively, marketers need to understand how communication works. Communication involves the nine elements shown in Figure 14.2.

- Sender: The party sending the message to another party
- Encoding: The process of putting thought into symbolic form
- Message: The set of symbols that the sender transmits
- Media: The communication channels through which the message moves from sender to receiver
- Decoding: The process by which the receiver assigns meaning to the symbols encoded by the sender
- Receiver: The party receiving the message sent by another party
- Response: The reactions of the receiver after being exposed to the message
- Feedback: The part of the receiver's response communicated back to the sender
- Noise: The unplanned static or distortion during the communication process that results in the receiver's getting a different message than the one the sender sent.

5. STEPS IN DEVELOPING EFFECTVE MARKETING COMMUNICATION

There are several steps in developing an effective integrated communications and promotion program.

5.1 Identifying the Target Audience

A marketing communicator starts with a clear target audience in mind. The audience may be potential buyers or current users, those who make the buying decision or those who influence it. The audience may be individuals, groups, special publics, or the general public. The target audience will heavily affect the communicator's decisions on what will be said, how it will be said, when it will be said, where it will be said, and who will say it.

5.2 Determining the Communication Objectives

Once the target audience has been defined, the marketing communicator must decide what response is sought. The marketing communicator needs to know where the target audience now stands and to what stage it needs to be moved. The target audience may be in any of six buyer-readiness stages, the stages consumers normally pass through on their way to making a purchase. (See Figure 14.3) The communicator must first build awareness and knowledge. Assuming target consumers know about the product, how do they feel about it? These stages include liking (feeling favorable about the product), preference, (preferring it to other brands), and conviction (believing that the product is best for them).

Some members of the target market might be convinced about the product, but not quite get around to making the purchase. The communicator must lead these consumers to take the final step. Actions might include offering special promotional prices, rebates, or premiums.

5.3 Designing a Message

Having defined the desired audience response, the communicator turns to developing an effective message. The message should get Attention, hold Interest, arouse Desire, and obtain Action (a framework known as the AIDA model). In putting the message together, the marketing communicator must decide what to say (message content) and how to say it (message structure and format).

5.3.1 Message Content

The communicator has to figure out an appeal or theme that will produce the desired response. There are three types of appeals.
- Rational appeals relate to the audience's self-interest. They show that the product will produce the desired benefits.
- Emotional appeals attempt to stir up either negative or positive emotions that can motivate purchase. Communicators may use positive emotional appeals such as love, pride, joy, and humor. Communicators can also use negative emotional appeals, such as fear, guilt, and shame that get people to do things they should or to stop doing things they shouldn't.
- Moral appeals are directed to the audience's sense of what is "right" and "proper." They are often used to urge people to support social causes such as a cleaner environment, better race relations, equal rights for women, and aid to the disadvantaged.

5.3.2 Message Structure

The communicator must also decide how to handle three message structure issues.
- The first is whether to draw a conclusion or leave it to the audience. Recent research suggests that in many cases, rather than drawing a conclusion, the advertiser is better off asking questions and letting buyers come to their own conclusions.
- The second message structure issue is whether to present the strongest arguments first or last. Presenting them first gets strong attention but may lead to an anticlimactic ending.
- The third message structure issue is whether to present a one-sided argument (mentioning only the product's strengths) or a two-sided argument (touting the product's strengths while also admitting its shortcomings).

5.3.3 Message Format

The marketing communicator also needs a strong format for the message. In a print ad, the communicator has to decide on the headline, copy, illustration, and color. To attract attention, advertisers use novelty and contrast; eye-catching pictures and headlines; distinctive formats; message size and position; and color, shape, and movement. If the message is to be carried on television or in person, then all these elements plus body language have to be planned. Presenters plan their facial expressions, gestures, dress, posture, and hairstyles. If the message is carried on the product or its package, the communicator has to watch texture, scent, color, size, and shape.

5.4 Choosing Media

The communicator now must select channels of communication. There are two broad types of communication channels – personal and nonpersonal.

5.4.1 Personal Communication Channels

In personal communication channels, two or more people communicate directly with each other. Some personal communication channels are controlled directly by the company. Other personal communications about the product may reach buyers through channels not directly controlled by the company. Word-of-mouth influence has considerable effect in many areas. Companies can take steps to put personal communication channels to work for them. They can create marketing programs that will generate favorable word-of-mouth communications about their brands. Companies can create opinion leaders—people whose opinions are sought by others—by supplying influencers with the product on attractive terms or by educating them so that they can inform others. Buzz marketing involves cultivating opinion leaders and getting them to spread information about a product or service to others in their communities.

5.4.2 Nonpersonal communication channels

Nonpersonal communication channels are media that carry messages without personal contact or feedback. Major media include print media, broadcast media, display media, and online media. Atmospheres are designed environments that create or reinforce the buyer's leanings toward buying a product. Events are staged occurrences that communicate messages to target audiences. Nonpersonal communication affects buyers directly. Communications first flow from television, magazines, and other mass media to opinion leaders and then from these opinion leaders to others. Thus, opinion leaders step between the mass media and their audiences and carry messages to people who are less exposed to media. This suggests that mass communicators should aim their messages directly at opinion leaders, letting them carry the message to others.

5.5 Selecting a Message Source

The message's impact on the target audience is also affected by how the audience views the communicator. Messages delivered by highly credible sources are more persuasive. Marketers often hire celebrity endorsers to deliver their message. But companies must be careful when selecting celebrities to represent their brands.

5.6 Collecting Feedback

After sending the message, the communicator must research its effect on the target audience. This involves asking the target audience members whether they remember the message, how many times they saw it, what points they recall, how they felt about the message, and their past and present attitudes toward the product and company. The communicator would also like to measure behavior resulting from the message—how many people bought a product, talked to others about it, or visited the store. Feedback on marketing communications may suggest changes in the promotion program or in the product offer itself.

6. SETTING THE TOTAL PROMOTION BUDGET AND MIX

How does the company decide on the total promotion budget and its division among the major promotional tools to create the promotion mix?

6.1 Setting the Total Promotion Budget

One of the hardest marketing decisions facing a company is how much to spend on promotion. We look at four common methods used to set the total budget for advertising.

6.1.1 Affordable Method

Some companies use the affordable method: They set the promotion budget at the level they think the company can afford. Unfortunately, this method of setting budgets completely ignores the effects of promotion on sales.

6.1.2 Percentage-of-Sales Method

Other companies use the percentage-of-sales method, setting their promotion budget at a certain percentage of current or forecasted sales. Or they budget a percentage of the unit sales price. The percentage-of-sales method has advantages.
- It is simple to use
- It helps management think about the relationship between promotion spending, selling price, and profit per unit.

However, it wrongly views sales as the cause of promotion rather than as the result. The percentage-of-sales budget is based on availability of funds rather than on opportunities. It may prevent the increased spending sometimes needed to turn around falling sales. Because the budget varies with year-to-year sales, long-range planning is difficult. Finally, the method does not provide any basis for choosing a specific percentage, except what has been done in the past or what competitors are doing.

6.1.3 Competitive-Parity Method

Other companies use the competitive-parity method, setting their promotion budgets to match competitors' outlays. They monitor competitors' advertising or get industry promotion spending estimates from publications or trade associations, and then set their budgets based on the industry average.

6.1.4 Objective-and-Task Method

The most logical budget-setting method is the objective-and-task method, whereby the company sets its promotion budget based on what it wants to accomplish with promotion.

This budgeting method entails:
- Defining specific promotion objectives,
- Determining the tasks needed to achieve these objectives,
- Estimating the costs of performing these tasks.

The sum of these costs is the proposed promotion budget. The advantage of the objective-and-task method is that it forces management to spell out its assumptions about the relationship between dollars spent and promotion results. But it also is the most difficult method to use. Often, it is hard to figure out which specific tasks will achieve stated objectives.

6.2 Shaping the Overall Promotion Mix

The concept of integrated marketing communications suggests that the company must blend the promotion tools carefully into a coordinated promotion mix. Companies within the same industry differ greatly in the design of their promotion mixes.

6.2.1 The Nature of Each Promotion Tool

Each promotion tool has unique characteristics and costs. Marketers must understand these characteristics in selecting their mix of tools.

Advertising can reach masses of geographically dispersed buyers at a low cost per exposure, and it enables the seller to repeat the message many times. Beyond its reach, large-scale advertising says something positive about the seller's size, popularity, and success. Because of advertising's public nature, consumers tend to view advertised products as more legitimate. Advertising also has some shortcomings. Although it reaches many people quickly, advertising is impersonal

156

and cannot be as directly persuasive as can company salespeople. For the most part, advertising can carry on only a one-way communication with the audience, and the audience does not feel that it has to pay attention or respond. In addition, advertising can be very costly.

Personal selling is the most effective tool at certain stages of the buying process, particularly in building up buyers' preferences, convictions, and actions. A sales force requires a longer-term commitment than does advertising—advertising can be turned on and off, but sales force size is harder to change. Personal selling is also the company's most expensive promotion tool.

Sales promotion includes a wide assortment of tools—coupons, contests, cents-off deals, premiums, and others—all of which have many unique qualities. They attract consumer attention, offer strong incentives to purchase, and can be used to dramatize product offers and to boost sagging sales. Sales promotions invite and reward quick response. Sales promotion effects are often short-lived.

Public relations is very believable—news stories, features, sponsorships, and events seem more real and believable to readers than ads do. Public relations can reach many prospects that avoid salespeople and advertisements—the message gets to the buyers as "news" rather than as a sales-directed communication.

Direct marketing has four distinctive characteristics:
- Direct marketing is less public: The message is normally directed to a specific person.
- Direct marketing is immediate and
- Direct marketing is customized: Messages can be prepared very quickly and can be tailored to appeal to specific consumers.
- Direct marketing is interactive: It allows a dialogue between the marketing team and the consumer, and messages can be altered depending on the consumer's response.

Thus, direct marketing is well suited to highly targeted marketing efforts and to building one-to-one customer relationships.

6.2.2 Promotion Mix Strategies

Marketers can choose from two basic promotion mix strategies. Figure 14.4 contrasts the two strategies.

A push strategy involves "pushing" the product through distribution channels to final consumers. The producer directs its marketing activities (primarily personal selling and trade promotions) toward channel members to induce them to carry the product and to promote it to final consumers.

Using a pull strategy, the producer directs its marketing activities (primarily advertising and consumer promotion) toward final consumers to induce them to buy the product. If the pull strategy is effective, consumers will then demand the product from channel members, who will in turn demand it from producers.

The effects of different promotion tools also vary with stages of the product life cycle.
- In the introduction stage, advertising and public relations are good for producing high awareness, and sales promotion is useful in promoting early trial. Personal selling must be used to get the trade to carry the product.
- In the growth stage, advertising and public relations continue to be powerful influences, whereas sales promotion can be reduced because fewer incentives are needed.
- In the mature stage, sales promotion again becomes important relative to advertising. Buyers know the brands, and advertising is needed only to remind them of the product.
- In the decline stage, advertising is kept at a reminder level, public relations is dropped, and salespeople give the product only a little attention. Sales promotion, however, might continue strong.

6.3 Integrating the Promotion Mix

Having set the promotion budget and mix, the company must now take steps to see that all of the promotion mix elements are smoothly integrated.

Here is a checklist for integrating the firm's marketing communications.
- Start with customer touch points.
- Analyze trends—internal and external—that can affect the company's ability to do business.
- Audit the pockets of communications spending throughout the organization.
- Identify all contact points for the company and its brands.
- Team up in communications planning.
- Create compatible themes, tones, and quality across all communications media.
- Create performance measures that are shared by all communications elements.
- Appoint a director responsible for the company's persuasive communications efforts.

7. SOCIALLY RESPONSIBLE MARKETING COMMUNICATION

In shaping its promotion mix, a company must be aware of the large body of legal and ethical issues surrounding marketing communications.

7.1 Advertising and Sales Promotion

By law, companies must avoid false or deceptive advertising. Advertisers must not make false claims, such as suggesting that a product cures something when it does not. They must avoid ads that have the capacity to deceive, even though no one actually may be deceived. Sellers must avoid bait-and-switch advertising that attracts buyers under false pretenses. A company's trade promotion activities are also closely regulated. For example, under the Robinson-Patman Act, sellers cannot favor certain customers through their use of trade promotions. They must make promotional allowances and services available to all resellers on proportionately equal terms. Companies can use advertising and other forms of promotion to encourage and promote socially responsible programs and actions.

7.2 Personal Selling

A company's salespeople must follow the rules of "fair competition." Most states have enacted deceptive sales acts that spell out what is not allowed.

Student Exercises

1.   Key Term: The Promotion Mix

The specific blend of advertising, sales promotion, public relations, personal selling, and direct-marketing tools that the company uses to persuasively communicate customer value and build customer relationships is known as the promotion mix. This blend is different for every company, with some companies heavily employing all facets of the mix, while other companies only make use of specific mix components. Take a look at your university. Describe the promotion mix it employees.

2.   Key Term: Integrated Marketing Communication

Under the concept of integrated marketing communication (IMC), the company carefully integrates its many communications channels to deliver a clear, consistent, and compelling message about the organization and its brands. IMC calls for recognizing all contact points where the customer may encounter the company and its brands. Take a look at the Apple iPhone (www.apple.com). How do you believe IMC can play a key role in the success of this new product?

3.   Key Term: Noise

Noise is defined as the unplanned static or distortion which occurs during the communication process. This static may result in the receiver's getting a different message than the one the sender sent or intended. Think about a local television commercial for your favorite Mexican restaurant. What noise might interfere with the viewer's reception of the ad??

4.   Key Term: Decoding

Decoding is the part of the communication process in which the receiver assigns meaning to the symbols encoded by the sender. For example, a reader views an ad and interprets the words and illustrations it contains. Sometimes this can go awry. Go to BCBG's website (www.bcbg.com). How might a viewer decode the message here in a manner contrary to that intended by BCBG?

5.   Key Term: Message Content—Rational Appeals

The marketer has to figure out an appeal or theme that will produce the desired response. The rational appeal is one possibility. In a rational appeal, the marketer tries to relate the audience's self-interest. They show that the product will produce the desired benefits. Take a look at Audi USA (www.audiusa.com). Think of a couple of rational appeals Audi might use to provide information to consumers.

6.   Key Term: Message Content—Emotional Appeals

The emotional appeal is another method a marketer may use to attempt to produce the desired response in the consumer. Emotional appeals attempt to stir up either positive or negative emotions that can motivate a consumer to action. Rogaine is a product designed to help rejuvenate hair growth. Log on to Rogaine's webpage (www.rogaine.com). How is the emotional appeal used by this company?

7.   Key Term: Personal Communication Channel

A personal communication channel is a channel through which two or more people communicate directly with each other—including face-to-face on the phone, through mail or email, or even through an internet "chat." Personal communication channels are effective because they allow for personal addressing and feedback. You walk into your local Best Buy store. What personal communication channels may come into play?

8.   Key Term: Word-of-Mouth Influence

Word-of-mouth influence is derived from personal communication about a product between target buyers and neighbors, friends, family members, and associates. Personal influence, such as word-of-mouth, carries great weight for products that are expensive, risky, or highly visible. Trip Advisor is an internet website devoted to providing customer reviews about destinations worldwide. This type of customer-driven site is of enormous value to many travelers considering a holiday at an unfamiliar site. Take a look at Trip Advisor (www.tripadvisor.com). Type in a search for a specific destination or hotel (such as the Sandals Resorts property in the Bahamas) and read some of the reviews. How might such information influence your travel decisions?

9.   Key Term: Buzz Marketing

Buzz marketing involves cultivating opinion leaders and getting them to spread information about a product or service to others in their communities. Consider the Palm Treo Smartphone (go to www.palm.com/us/ to learn about it). Why might buzz marketing be a viable method of supplying information to the market?

10.   Key Term: Nonpersonal Communication Channel

Nonpersonal communication channels are media that carry messages without personal contact or feedback. They include media, atmospheres, and events. Go back and look again at the Palm Treo Smartphone (www.palm.com/us/). What nonpersonal communication channels do you believe would be useful in getting information about this phone out?

Marketing ADventure Exercises

1.   Ad Interpretation Challenge: The Promotion Mix
       Ad: Advertising—Universal McCann

The promotion mix is the specific blend of advertising, sales promotion, public relations, personal selling, and direct marketing tools that the company uses to persuasively communicate customer value and build customer relationships. Look at this ad for Universal McCann. Are they limiting themselves?

2.   Ad Interpretation Challenge: Narrowcasting
       Ad: Auto—Audi

A proliferation of new media formats has generated a shift in the way many marketers are doing business. These new media include specialty magazines, cable television channels, video on demand, and product placement in television shows and movies. This allows marketers to more finely tune their promotional efforts to more carefully reach their target markets. All of this is contributing to companies doing less broadcasting and more narrowcasting. How might Audi utilize narrowcasting to more effectively get the word out regarding the new Audi A2?

3.   Ad Interpretation Challenge: Mass-Media Communication
       Ad: Student Choice

Mass-media communication allows marketers to reach large groups of people efficiently through the use of mass media, such as television or newspaper advertising. Find an ad for a product that could make good use of a mass-media communication strategy.

4.   Ad Interpretation Challenge: Integrated Marketing Communications (IMC)
      Ad: Auto—Chrysler

Under the concept of integrated marketing communication (IMC), the company carefully integrates its many communications channels to deliver a clear, consistent, and compelling message about the organization and its brands. IMC calls for recognizing all contact points where the customer may encounter the company and its brands. Each of these points of contact will deliver a message about the product. The goal of IMC is to have the same message delivered at each contact point. Consider this ad for Chrysler. How might IMC be utilized to standardize the message Chrysler is using?

5.   Ad Interpretation Challenge: Noise
      Ad: Newspaper and TV—Cartoon Network

Noise is unplanned static or distortion during the communication process, which results in the receiver getting a different message than the one the sender sent. Examine this magazine ad for the Cartoon Network. What possible noise could interfere with the proper interpretation of this ad?

6.   Ad Interpretation Challenge: Receiver
      Ad: Auto—Audi A2

The receiver is the party receiving the message sent by another party. The message creator must have in mind specifically who will be receiving the ad so that the most effective message can be created and the most useful delivery format utilized. Take a look at this ad for the Audi A2. Who is the intended receiver of this advertisement?

7.   Ad Interpretation Challenge: Buyer-Readiness Stages
      Ad: Auto—Mercedes C Class

Buyer-readiness stages are the stages that consumers normally pass through on their way to purchase, including awareness, knowledge, liking, preference, conviction, and purchase. Take a look at this ad for the new Mercedes C Class automobile. What buyer-readiness stage is this ad targeting?

8.   Ad Interpretation Challenge: Emotional Appeal
      Ad: Student Choice

Emotional appeals attempt to stir up either positive or negative emotions that can motivate purchase. Communicators may use positive emotional appeals such as love, pride, or joy. Find an ad for a product or service that is based on an emotional appeal.

9.   Ad Interpretation Challenge: Humorous Appeal
       Ad: Financial—Fame

Properly used, humor can capture attention, make people feel good, and give a brand personality. Take a look at this ad for F.A.M.E. How does it use humor to get its point across?

10.   Ad Interpretation Challenge: Word-of-Mouth Influence
       Ad: Auto—Ford

Word-of-mouth influence is derived from personal communication about a product between target buyers and neighbors, friends, family members, and associates. Personal influence, such as word-of-mouth, carries great weight for products that are expensive, risky, or highly visible. Consider Ford. If you were in the market for this product, how might word-of-mouth play a role in your decision?

Chapter 15
Advertising and Public Relations

Learning Objectives

1. Define the role of advertising in the promotion mix.
2. Describe the major decisions involved in developing an advertising program.
3. Define the role of public relations in the promotion mix.
4. Explain how companies use public relations to communicate with their publics.

Chapter Overview

In this chapter, we look at advertising and public relations. Advertising involves communicating the company's or brand's value proposition by using paid media to inform, persuade, and remind consumers. Public relations involve building good relations with various company publics – from consumers and the general public to the media, investor, donor, and government publics. As with all of the promotion mix tools, advertising and public relations must be blended into the overall integrated marketing communications program.

Chapter Outline

1. INTRODUCTION

Until about ten years ago, GEICO was a little-known player in the auto insurance industry. But now, thanks in large part to an industry-changing advertising campaign featuring a likable spokes-lizard, an indignant clan of cavemen, and an enduring tagline, GEICO has grown to become a major industry player. Like all good advertising, the GEICO campaign began with a simple but enduring theme. Every single one of the more than 150 commercials produced in the campaign drives home the now-familiar tagline: "15 minutes could save you 15 percent or more on car insurance." In 1999, GEICO ran a 15-second spot in which the now-famous, British-accented gecko calls a press conference and pleads: "I am a gecko, not to be confused with a GEICO, which could save you hundreds on car insurance. So stop calling me." Then came the cavemen. The company's new advertising slogan is "It's so easy to use GEICO.com, even a caveman could do it." The indignant cavemen have taken on a cult status all their own. Not only have the gecko and cavemen helped GEICO grow, they've changed the face of the auto insurance industry.

Opening Vignette Questions
1. Through their catchy advertising campaigns, GEICO is pursuing which advertising objective?
2. How has GEICO used public relations to promote their brand?

164

3. Can GEICO continue to use this same advertising campaign indefinitely? If not, what would you suggest for them next?

2. ADVERTISING

Figure 15.1 show the four decisions made when developing an advertising program.
- Setting advertising objectives
- Setting the advertising budget
- Developing advertising strategy
- Evaluating advertising campaigns

2.1 Setting Advertising Objectives

Advertising objectives should be based on past decisions about the target market, positioning, and the marketing mix, which define the job that advertising must do in the total marketing program. An advertising objective is a specific communication task to be accomplished with a specific target audience during a specific period of time. Advertising objectives can be classified by primary purpose (Table 12.1):
- Informative advertising is used heavily when introducing a new product category.
- Persuasive advertising becomes important as competition increases. Here, the company's objective is to build selective demand.
- Comparative advertising is directly or indirectly comparing one brand with another.
- Reminder advertising is important for mature products—it helps to maintain customer relationships and keep consumers thinking about the product.

2.2 Setting the Advertising Budget

Specific factors to consider when setting the budget include share of the product life cycle and market share.

2.3 Developing the Advertising Strategy

Advertising strategy consists of two major elements:
- Creating advertising *messages*
- Selecting advertising *media*

2.3.1 Creating the Advertising Message

Breaking Through the Clutter. Just to gain and hold attention, today's advertising messages must be better planned, more imaginative, more entertaining, and more rewarding to consumers.

Many marketers are now subscribing to a new merging of advertising and entertainment, dubbed "Madison & Vine."

Message Strategy. The first step in creating effective advertising messages is to plan a message strategy—to decide what general message will be communicated to consumers. Developing an effective message strategy begins with identifying customer benefits that can be used as advertising appeals. The advertiser must next develop a compelling creative concept—or "big idea"—that will bring the message strategy to life in a distinctive and memorable way.

Advertising appeals should have three characteristics:
- They should be meaningful.
- Appeals must be believable.
- Appeals should be distinctive.

Message Execution. The advertiser has to turn the big idea into an actual ad execution that will capture the target market's attention and interest. Execution styles include the following:
- Slice of life: This style shows one or more "typical" people using the product in a normal setting.
- Lifestyle: This style shows how a product fits in with a particular lifestyle.
- Fantasy: This style creates a fantasy around the product or its use. For instance, many ads are built around dream themes.
- Mood or image: This style builds a mood or image around the product or service, such as beauty, love, or serenity.
- Musical: This style shows people or cartoon characters singing about the product.
- Personality symbol: This style creates a character that represents the product.
- Technical expertise: This style shows the company's expertise in making the product.
- Scientific evidence: This style presents survey or scientific evidence that the brand is better or better liked than one or more other brands.
- Testimonial evidence or endorsement: This style features a highly believable or likable source endorsing the product.

The advertiser must choose a tone, words, and format for the ad.

Consumer-Generated Messages. Taking advantage of today's interactive technologies, many companies are now tapping consumers for message ideas or actual ads. If used carefully, consumer-generated advertising efforts can produce big benefits.

2.3.2 Selecting Advertising Media

The major steps in advertising media selection are (1) deciding on reach, frequency, and impact; (2) choosing among major media types; (3) selecting specific media vehicles; and (4) deciding on media timing.

Deciding on Reach, Frequency, and Impact.

Reach is a measure of the percentage of people in the target market who are exposed to the ad campaign during a given period of time. Frequency is a measure of how many times the average person in the target market is exposed to the message. The advertiser must decide on the desired media impact—the qualitative value of a message exposure through a given medium. Typically, the advertiser wants to choose media that will engage consumers rather than simply reach them.

Choosing Among Major Media Types.

The media planner has to know the reach, frequency, and impact of each of the major media types. As summarized in Table 15.2, the major media types are newspapers, television, direct mail, radio, magazines, outdoor, and the Internet. Each medium has advantages and limitations. Media planners must also decide between narrowcasting and shotgun approaches.

Selecting Specific Media Vehicles. The media planner now must choose the best media vehicles—specific media within each general media type. Media planners must compute the cost per thousand persons reached by a vehicle. The media planner must also consider the costs of producing ads for different media. The media planner must balance media costs against several media effectiveness factors.
- Audience quality.
- Audience engagement.
- Editorial quality.

Deciding on Media Timing. The advertiser must decide how to schedule the advertising over the course of a year. Some marketers do only seasonal advertising. The advertiser has to choose the pattern of the ads.
- Continuity means scheduling ads evenly within a given period.
- Pulsing means scheduling ads unevenly over a given time period.

2.4 Evaluating Advertising Effectiveness and Return on Advertising Investment

Advertising accountability and return on advertising investment have become hot issues for most companies.

2.5 Other Advertising Considerations

2.5.1 Organizing for Advertising

Different companies organize in different ways to handle advertising. In small companies, advertising might be handled by some-one in the sales department. Large companies set up advertising departments whose job it is to set the advertising budget, work with the advertising agency, and handle advertising not done by the agency. *Advertising agencies* employ specialists who can often perform advertising tasks better than the company's own staff. Most large advertising agencies have the staff and resources to handle all phases of an advertising campaign for its clients, from creating a marketing plan to developing ad campaigns and preparing, placing, and evaluating ads.

2.5.2 International Advertising Decisions

International advertisers face many complexities not encountered by domestic advertisers. The most basic issue concerns the degree to which global advertising should be adapted to the unique characteristics of markets in various countries. Standardization produces many benefits—lower advertising costs, greater global advertising coordination, and a more consistent worldwide image. There are also drawbacks. It ignores the fact that country markets differ greatly in their cultures, demographics, and economic conditions. Global advertisers face several special problems.

- Advertising media costs and availability differ vastly from country to country.
- Countries also differ in the extent to which they regulate advertising practices.
- Although advertisers may develop global strategies to guide their overall advertising efforts, specific advertising programs must usually be adapted to meet local cultures and customers, media characteristics, and advertising regulations.

3. PUBLIC RELATIONS

Public relations is building good relations with the company's various publics by obtaining favorable publicity, building up a good corporate image, and handling or heading off unfavorable rumors, stories, and events. Public relations departments may perform any or all of the following functions:

- Press relations or press agency: Creating and placing newsworthy information in the news media to attract attention to a person, product, or service.
- Product publicity: Publicizing specific products.
- Public affairs: Building and maintaining national or local community relations.
- Lobbying: Building and maintaining relations with legislators and government officials to influence legislation and regulation.
- Investor relations: Maintaining relationships with shareholders and others in the financial community.
- Development: Public relations with donors or members of nonprofit organizations to gain financial or volunteer support.

Public relations is used to promote products, people, places, ideas, activities, organizations, and even nations.

3.1 The Role and Impact of Public Relations

Public relations can have a strong impact on public awareness at a much lower cost than advertising can. The company does not pay for the space or time in the media. If the company develops an interesting story or event, it could be picked up by several different media, having the same effect as advertising that would cost millions of dollars.
It has more credibility than advertising. Public relations is sometimes described as a marketing stepchild because of its often limited and scattered use.

3.2 Major Public Relations Tools

Public relations professionals use several tools.

- PR professionals find or create favorable news about the company and its products or people.
- Speeches can also create product and company publicity.
- Another common PR tool is special events, ranging from news conferences, press tours, grand openings, and fireworks displays to laser shows, hot air balloon releases, multimedia presentations, start-studded spectaculars, or educational programs designed to reach and interest target publics.
- Public relations people also prepare written materials to reach and influence their target markets. These materials include annual reports, brochures, articles, and company newsletters and magazines.
- Audiovisual materials, such as films, slide-and-sound programs, and video and audio CDs, are being used increasingly as communication tools.
- Corporate identity materials can also help create a corporate identity that the public immediately recognizes.
- Companies can improve public goodwill by contributing money and time to public service activities.

Student Exercises

1.   Key Term: Advertising

Advertising is defined as any form of paid nonpersonal presentation and promotion of ideas, goods, or services by an identified sponsor. Advertising's goal is to move consumers through the buyer-readiness stages previously discussed. Advertising is a good way to inform and persuade. Take a look at Bucuti Beach Resort's website (www.bucuti.com/en/). The site is providing the viewer with information about the resort and about Aruba in general. Is this advertising?

2.   Key Term: Advertising Objectives

An advertising objective is a specific communication task to be accomplished with a specific target audience during a specific period of time. Advertising objectives are classified by their primary purpose—whether the aim is to inform, persuade, or remind.

Go to SuperClubs website (www.superclubs.com). What is the primary advertising objective of their site?

3.   Key Term: Reminder Advertising

One of the three basic advertising objectives is to remind. Reminder advertising is particularly important for mature products—it helps to maintain customer relationships and keep customers thinking about the product. What is a product that benefits from the use of reminder advertising?

4.   Key Term: Breaking Through the Clutter

There is so much advertising in the marketplace today that it can become little more than noise to the eyes and ears of the consumer. It becomes bothersome to the consumer. Likewise, it becomes an issue for the advertisers. The proliferation of ads means that marketers must work extra hard to make sure their ads break through the clutter of the market and stand out from the pack. If you were the marketing executive in charge of advertising Jamaica, what would you do to break through the clutter so that consumers would notice and pay attention to your product (Jamaica)?

5.   Key Term: Creative Concept

The creative concept is the compelling "big idea" that will bring the advertising message strategy to life in a distinctive and memorable manner. At this stage, simple message ideas become great ad campaigns. The newest advertising campaign designed to bring visitors to Australia is an example of one of these "big ideas." Go to www.australia.com. Discuss what you consider to be this "big idea."

6.   Key Term: Execution Style

Advertisers must turn the big idea into an actual ad execution that will capture the target market's attention and interest. Execution style is the approach, style, tone, works, and format used for executing an advertising message. Take a look at Couples Resorts in Jamaica (www.couples.com). What execution style is being employed here?

7.   Key Term: Advertising Media

Advertising media is the vehicle through which the advertising messages are delivered to their intended audiences. The major advertising media types are television, newspapers, direct mail, magazines, radio, outdoor, and the internet. Each medium has advantages and limitations. Read a little bit about Scion (www.scion.com). What forms of media do you believe would be most effective in reaching the intended Scion audience?

8.   Key Term: Alternative Media

Alternative media are those forms of media outside of the traditionally accepted formats. For example, Real Marketing 15.2, from your text discusses various forms of these alternative media—everything from miniature billboards on shopping cards to painted cows. Think again about Scion (www.scion.com). What are some alternative media formats you can think of that might be useful in getting the Scion name out to potential consumers?

9.   Key Term: Public Relations

Public relations is the building of good relationships with the company's various publics by obtaining favorable publicity, building a good corporate image, and handling or heading off unfavorable rumors, stories, and events. Britney Spears is an entertainer who seems to spend quite a bit of time in the news. Take a look at her website (www.britneyspears.com). How does the pop princess use public relations to try and enhance her public image?

10.   Key Term: Lobbying

One of the functions of public relations may be lobbying—the building and maintaining of relations with legislators and government officials to influence legislation and regulation. Consider the National Rifle Association (NRA) (www.nra.org). What role does lobbying play in the overall public relations campaign of the NRA?

Marketing ADventure Exercises

1.   Ad Interpretation Challenge: Advertising
      Ad: Apparel—Levi's New Collection Diamond Jean

Advertising is defined as any form of paid nonpersonal presentation and promotion of ideas, goods, or services by an identified sponsor. Advertising's goal is to move consumers through the buyer-readiness stages previously discussed. Advertising is a good way to inform and persuade. Take a look at this ad for Levi's. Do you view this ad as a good way to inform and persuade the consumer?

2.   Ad Interpretation Challenge: Reminder Advertising
      Ad: Student Choice

One of the three basic advertising objectives is to remind. Reminder advertising is particularly important for mature products—it helps to maintain customer relationships and keep customers thinking about the product. Take a look at the offered ads. Find one for a mature product that you believe is using reminder advertising.

3.   Ad Interpretation Challenge: Informative Advertising
      Ad: Auto—Hyundai Lean Burn

Another of the basic advertising objectives is to inform. Informative advertising is used heavily when introducing a new product category. In this case, the objective is to build primary demand. Consider this ad for Hyundai's lean burn engine (a high-efficiency engine). Why would this ad be considered an informative ad?

4.   Ad Interpretation Challenge: Persuasive Advertising
      Ad: Electronics—LG

Still another of the basic advertising objectives is to persuade. Persuasive advertising takes on greater importance as competition increases. Here, the company's objective is to build selective demand. Look at the ad for LG. Is this ad based on the objective of persuasion?

5.   Ad Interpretation Challenge: Advertising Budget
      Ad: Apparel—Levi's New Collection Diamond Jean

The advertising budget is the dollars and other resources allocated to a product or company advertising program. A brand's advertising budget is often related to its stage in the product life cycle. Take a look at this ad for Levi's New Collection Diamond Jean. Where would you place this product in the product life cycle and, as a result, how much of an advertising budget is required?

6.   Ad Interpretation Challenge: Breaking Through the Clutter
      Ad: Student Choice

There is so much advertising in the marketplace today that it can become little more than noise to the eyes and ears of the consumer. It becomes bothersome to the consumer. Likewise, it becomes an issue for the advertisers. The proliferation of ads means that marketers must work extra hard to make sure their ads break through the clutter of the market and stand out from the pack. Look at the offered ads. Locate one that seems to do a good job of breaking through the clutter.

7.   Ad Interpretation Challenge: Madison & Vine
      Ad: General Retail—Hallmark

"Madison & Vine' is a term that has come to represent the merging of advertising and entertainment in an effort to break through the clutter and create new avenues for reaching consumers with more engaging messages. It is becoming ever more important to entertain consumers. Go to Hallmark's home page (www.hallmark.com). Click on the link that takes you to hoops&yoyo—one of their collections of characters. Peruse the site. You will see that hoops&yoyo has been used in advertising and now has a line of products you can purchase. How are hoops&yoyo a meeting of Madison & Vine?

8.	Ad Interpretation Challenge: Execution Style
	Ad: Auto—Honda Motorcycles

Advertisers must turn the big idea into an actual ad execution that will capture the target market's attention and interest. Execution style is the approach, style, tone, works, and format used for executing an advertising message. Look at the ads for Honda motorcycles. What execution style would you say is being used in all of these ads?

9.	Ad Interpretation Challenge: Advertising Media
	Ad: Autos—Audi

Advertising media is the vehicle through which advertising messages are delivered to their intended audiences. The major advertising media types are television, newspapers, direct mail, magazines, radio, outdoor, and the Internet. Each medium has advantages and limitations. Take a look at this ad. What medium would you suggest carry this ad?

10.	Ad Interpretation Challenge: Advertising Media
	Ad: Newspapers and TV—MTV Masters

Yes, it is the same topical area as covered in the previous exercise, but here we are considering a different advertisement with different consequences. Take a look at this ad for MTV Masters. If you could rework and reformat this ad, what possible media do you believe would be useful in disseminating this information?

Chapter 16
Personal Selling and Sales Promotion

Learning Objectives

1. Discuss the role of a company's salespeople in creating value for customers and building customer relationships
2. Identify and explain the six major sales force management steps
3. Discuss the personal selling process, distinguishing between transaction-oriented marketing and relationship marketing
4. Explain how sales promotion campaigns are developed and implemented

Chapter Overview

This chapter concentrates on two more IMC elements—personal selling and sales promotion. Personal selling is the interpersonal arm of marketing communications, in which the sales force interacts with customers and prospects to build relationships and make sales. Sales promotion consists of short-term incentives to encourage purchase or sale of a product or service. Although this chapter examines personal selling and sales promotion as separate tools, they must be carefully integrated with other elements of the promotion mix.

Chapter Outline

1. INTRODUCTION

CDW Corporation, the nation's largest reseller of technology products and services, is thriving. The company owes its success to its highly effective "clicks and people" direct marketing strategy. CDW has traditionally targeted small and midsize businesses (SMBs). When someone says "salesperson", you may still think of the stereotypical "traveling salesman"—the fast-talking, ever-smiling peddler who travels his territory foisting his wares on reluctant customers. Such stereotypes, however, are out of date. Today, like CDW's account managers, most professional salespeople are well-educated, well-trained men and women who work to build valued customer relationships.

Opening Vignette Questions

1. What is the major role and responsibility of the account manager at CDW?
2. What benefit does the CDW@work extranet site provide to customers?
3. Is the salesperson obsolete at CDW? Why or why not?

2. PERSONAL SELLING

Robert Louis Stevenson once noted that "everyone lives by selling something."

2.1 The Nature of Personal Selling

Personal selling is one of the oldest professions in the world. The people who do the selling go by many names: salespeople, sales representatives, district managers, account executives, sales consultants, sales engineers, agents, and account development reps to name just a few. The term salesperson covers a wide range of positions. At one extreme, a salesperson might be an order taker, such as the department store salesperson standing behind the counter. At the other extreme are order getters, whose positions demand creative selling and relationship building for products and services ranging from appliances to industrial equipment.

2.2 The Role of the Sales Force

Personal selling is the interpersonal arm of the promotion mix. The role of personal selling varies from company to company. Some firms have no salespeople at all—for example, companies that sell only online or through catalogs, or companies that sell through manufacturer's reps, sales agents, or brokers. In most firms, however, the sales force plays a major role.

2.2.1 Linking the Company with Its Customers

The sales force serves as a critical link between a company and its customers.
- They represent the company to customers.
- They represent customers to the company.

2.2.2 Coordinating Marketing and Sales

A company can take several actions to help bring its marketing and sales functions closer together.
- It can increase communications between the two groups by arranging joint meetings and by spelling out when and with whom each group should communicate.
- The company can create joint assignments.
- The company can create joint objectives and reward systems for sales and marketing.
- They can appoint marketing-sales liaisons—people from marketing who "live with the sales force" and help to coordinate marketing and sales force programs and efforts.
- The firm can appoint a chief revenue officer (or chief customer officer)—a high-level marketing executive who oversees both marketing and sales.

3. MANAGING THE SALES FORCE

Sales force management is defined as the analysis, planning, implementation, and control of sales force activities. (Figure 16.1)

3.1 Designing Sales Force Strategy and Structure

3.1.1 Sales Force Structure

A company can divide sales responsibilities along any of several lines.

Territorial Sales Force Structure: Each salesperson is assigned to an exclusive geographic area and sells the company's full line of products or services to all customers in that territory.

Characteristics:
- The organization defines each salesperson's job and fixes accountability.
- The organization increases the salesperson's desire to build local customer relationships.
- Because each salesperson travels within a limited geographic area, travel expenses are relatively small.

Product Sales Force Structure: The sales force sells along product lines. This structure can lead to problems if a single large customer buys many different company products.

Customer Sales Force Structure: The sales force is organized along customer or industry lines. Separate sales forces may be set up for different industries, for serving current customers versus finding new ones, and for major accounts versus regular accounts.

Complex Sales Force Structures: A company often combines several types of sales force structures when it sells a wide variety of products to many types of customers over a broad geographic area.

3.1.2 Sales Force Size

Sales force size may range in size from only a few salespeople to tens of thousands. The workload approach means that a company first groups accounts into different classes according to size, account status, or other factors related to the amount of effort required to maintain them. It then determines the number of salespeople needed to call on each class of accounts the desired number of times.

3.1.3 Other Sales Force Strategy and Structure Issues

Outside (Field Sales force) and Inside Sales Forces. Outside salespeople travel to call on customers in the field. Inside salespeople conduct business from their offices via telephone, the Internet, or visits from buyers.

- Technical sales support people provide technical information and answers to customers' questions.
- Sales assistants provide administrative backup for outside salespeople.
- Telemarketers and Web sellers use the phone and Internet to find new leads and qualify prospects or to sell and service accounts directly.

Most companies now use team selling to service large, complex accounts. Sales teams can unearth problems, solutions, and sales opportunities that no individual salesperson could. Such teams might include experts from any area or level of the selling firm—sales, marketing, technical and support services, R&D, engineering, operations, finance, and others. In team selling situations, the salesperson shifts from "soloist" to "orchestrator."

Shortcomings of team selling:
- Salespeople who are used to having customers all to themselves may have trouble learning to work with and trust others on a team.
- Selling teams can confuse or overwhelm customers who are used to working with only one salesperson.
- Difficulties in evaluating individual contributions to the team selling effort can create some sticky compensation issues.

3.2 Recruiting and Selecting Salespeople

The best salespeople possess four key talents:
- Intrinsic motivation.
- Disciplined work style.
- The ability to close a sale.
- The ability to build relationships with customers.

When recruiting, companies should analyze the sales job itself and the characteristics of its most successful salespeople to identify the traits needed by a successful salesperson in their industry.

Sources of new potential hires:
- The human resources department gets names from current salespeople, using employment agencies, placing classified ads, searching the Web, and working through college placement services.
- Another source is to attract top salespeople from other companies.

3.3 Training Salespeople

Training programs have several goals.
- The training program must teach them about different types of customers and their needs, buying motives, and buying habits.
- It must teach them how to sell effectively and train them in the basics of the selling process.
- The training program teaches them about the company's objectives, organization, and chief products and markets, and about the strategies of major competitors.

Many companies are adding e-learning to their sales training programs.
Most e-learning is Web-based but many companies now offer on-demand training for PDAs, cell phones, and even video iPods.

3.4 Compensating Salespeople

Compensation is made up of several elements – a fixed amount, a variable amount, expenses, and fringe benefits. Management must decide what mix of compensation elements makes the most sense for each sales job. Different combinations of fixed and variable compensation give rise to four basic types of compensation plans:
- Straight salary,
- Straight commission,
- Salary plus bonus,
- Salary plus commission.

The average salesperson's pay consists of about 67 percent salary and 33 percent incentive pay. Compensation should direct salespeople force toward activities that are consistent with overall sales force and marketing objectives.

3.5 Supervising and Motivating Salespeople

The goal of supervision is to help salespeople "work smart" by doing the right things in the right ways. The goal of motivation is to encourage salespeople to "work hard" and energetically toward sales force goals.

Companies vary in how closely they supervise their salespeople.
- The annual call plan shows which customers and prospects to call on and which activities to carry out.
- The time-and-duty analysis shows the time the salesperson spends selling, traveling, waiting, taking breaks, and doing administrative chores. (Figure 16.2)

On average, active selling time accounts for only 10 percent of total working time!

Salespeople often need special encouragement to do their best. Organizational climate describes the feeling that salespeople have about their opportunities, value, and rewards for a good performance.

Sales quotas are standards stating the amount they should sell and how sales should be divided among the company's products. Compensation is often related to how well salespeople meet their quotas.

Companies use various positive incentives to increase sales force effort.

- Sales meetings provide social occasions, breaks from routine, chances to meet and talk with "company brass," and opportunities to air feelings and to identify with a larger group.
- Companies also sponsor sales contests to spur the sales force to make a selling effort above what would normally be expected.
- Other incentives include honors, merchandise and cash awards, trips, and profit-sharing plans.

3.6 Evaluating Salespeople and Sales-Force Performance

Management sources of salesperson information:
- Sales reports,
- Call reports,
- Expense reports.

Formal evaluation forces management to develop and communicate clear standards for judging performance and provides salespeople with constructive feedback and motivates them to perform well.

As with other marketing activities, the company wants to measure its return on sales investment.

4. THE PERSONAL SELLING PROCESS

4.1 Steps in the Selling Process (Figure 16.3)

The selling process consists of seven steps:
- Prospecting and qualifying,
- Preapproach,
- Approach,
- Presentation and demonstration,
- Handling objections,
- Closing,
- Follow-up.

4.1.1 Prospecting and Qualifying

Prospecting is identifying qualified potential customers. The best source of prospects is referrals.

Qualifying a lead is knowing how to identify the good ones and screen out the poor ones.

4.1.2. Preapproach

The preapproach is the stage in which the salesperson learns as much as possible about the organization (what it needs, who is involved in the buying) and its buyers (their characteristics and buying styles).

4.1.3. Approach

During the approach step, the salesperson should know how to meet and greet the buyer and get the relationship off to a good start.

4.1.4. Presentation and Demonstration

During the presentation step of the selling process, the salesperson tells the "value story" to the buyer, showing how the company's offer solves the customer's problems.

4.1.5 Handling Objections

In handling objections, the salesperson should:
- Use a positive approach,
- Seek out hidden objections,
- Ask the buyer to clarify any objections,
- Take objections as opportunities,
- Turn the objections into reasons for buying.

4.1.6. Closing

Salespeople can use one of several closing techniques:
- Ask for the order,
- Review points of agreement,
- Offer to help write up the order,
- Ask whether the buyer wants this model or that one,

4.1.7. Follow-up

Follow-up is necessary if the salesperson wants to ensure customer satisfaction and repeat business.

4.2 Personal Selling and Managing Customer Relationships

Transaction orientation: Purpose is to help salespeople close a specific sale with a customer.

Relationship orientation: Purpose is to serve the customer over the long haul in a mutually profitable relationship.

5. SALES PROMOTION

Sales promotion consists of short-term incentives to encourage purchase or sales of a product or service.

5.1 Rapid Growth of Sales Promotion

Sales promotion tools are targeted toward final buyers (consumer promotions), retailers and wholesalers (trade promotions), business customers (business promotions), and members of the sales force (sales force promotions). Several factors have contributed to the rapid growth of sales promotion:

- Product managers face greater pressures to increase their current sales.
- The company faces more competition and competing brands are less differentiated.
- Advertising efficiency has declined.
- Consumers have become more deal oriented.

The growing use of sales promotion has resulted in promotion clutter. Consumers are increasingly tuning out promotions, weakening their ability to trigger immediate purchase.

5.2 Sales Promotion Objectives

Sales promotion objectives vary widely.

- Consumer promotions: Urge short-term customer buying or to enhance customer brand involvement.
- Trade promotions: Get retailers to carry new items and more inventory, buy ahead, or promote the company's products and give them more shelf space.
- Sales force: Get more sales force support for current or new products or getting salespeople to sign up new accounts.

Sales promotions should help to reinforce the product's position and build long-term customer relationships.

5.3 Major Sales Promotion Tools

Many tools can be used to accomplish sales promotion objectives. Descriptions of the main consumer, trade, and business promotion tools follow.

5.3.1 Consumer Promotions

The consumer promotions include a wide range of tools.

- Samples are offers of a trial amount of a product.
- Coupons are certificates that give buyers a saving when they purchase specified products.
- Cash refunds (or rebates) are like coupons except that the price reduction occurs after the purchase rather than at the retail outlet.
- Price packs (also called cents-off deals) offer consumers savings off the regular price of a product.
- Premiums are goods offered either free or at low cost as an incentive to buy a product.
- Advertising specialties, also called promotional products, are useful articles imprinted with an advertiser's name, logo, or message that are given as gifts to consumers.
- Point-of-purchase (POP) promotions include displays and demonstrations that take place at the point of sale.
- Contests, sweepstakes, and games give consumers the chance to win something.
- Event marketing (or event sponsorships) allows companies to create their own brand marketing events or serve as sole or participating sponsors of events created by others.

5.3.2 Trade Promotions

Trade promotions persuade resellers to carry a brand, give it shelf space, promote it in advertising, and push it to consumers. Manufacturers use several trade promotion tools:

- Offer a straight discount (also called a price-off, off-invoice, or off-list).
- Offer an allowance (usually so much off per case).
- Offer free goods.
- Offer push money.
- Offer free specialty advertising items.

5.3.3 Business Promotions

Business promotions are used to generate business leads, stimulate purchases, reward customers, and motivate salespeople.

- Conventions and trade shows: Firms selling to the industry show their products at the trade show.

- Sales contests: Contests for salespeople or dealers to motivate them to increase their sales performance over a given period.

5.4 Developing the Sales Promotion Program

Marketers must decide:
1. Size of the incentive.
2. Conditions for participation.
3. Promotion and distribution.
4. Length of the promotion.
5. Evaluation

Student Exercises

1.   Key Term: Personal Selling

Personal selling is the personal presentation by the firm's sales force for the purpose of making sales and building customer relationships. Today, most salespeople are well-educated, well-trained professionals who work to build and maintain long-term customer relationships. To get an idea of the current state of professionalism in personal selling take a look at the Journal of Personal Selling and Sales Management. Specifically, clink on the link that gives a description of the journal. (http://jpssm.org/general/jrnldesc.htm)

2.   Key Term: Salesperson

A salesperson is an individual representing a company to customers by performing one or more of the following activities: prospecting, communicating, selling, servicing, information gathering, and relationship building. The term "salesperson" covers a wide range of positions. Think about the salespeople at your favorite department store in the local mall. What functions to they really fulfill?

3.   Key Term: Sales Force Management

Sales force management is the analysis, planning, implementation, and control of sales force activities. It includes designing sales force strategy and structure and recruiting, selecting, training, supervising, compensating, and evaluating the firm's salespeople. Look at Limited Brands (www.limited.com), parent company to seven retail brands including Limited Stores and Victoria's Secret. How does Limited Brands use their website to assist in sales force management?

4.   Key Term: Territorial Sales Force Structure

A sales force organization that assigns each salesperson to an exclusive geographic territory in which that salesperson sells the company's full line is known as a territorial sales force structure. Take a look at IMS Health (www.imshealth.com), a health care consulting service. Look closely at the information they provide for the use of a territorial sales force.

5. Key Term: Product Sales Force Structure

Product sales force structure is a sales force organization under which salespeople specialize in selling only a portion of the company's products or lines. Under such a structure, salespeople become specialists in only a portion of the company's products; however, the depth of knowledge they have is great. Find a company you believe would be well suited for use of a product sales force structure.

6. Key Term: Customer Sales Force Structure

Customer sales force structure is a sales force organization under which salespeople specialize in selling only to certain customers or industries. Separate sales forces may be set up for different industries. Organizing the sales force around customers can help a company build closer relationships with important customers. Take a look at Wal-Mart Stores (www.walmart.com). How have companies used customer sales force structure to build closer relations with the retailing giant?

7. Key Term: Outside Sales Force

Outside sales people who travel to call on customers in the field are known as an outside sales force (or field sales force). Compared to a sales call from an inside sales person, outside sales calls are very expensive and time consuming, but sometimes necessary to deliver adequate customer contact. Find a company that you believe would employ and outside sales force.

8. Key Term: Inside Sales Force

An inside sales force is comprised of inside salespeople who conduct business from their offices via telephone, the internet, or visits from prospective buyers. Some inside salespeople provide support services for the outside sales forces. Other inside salespeople do much more than just provide support. Look at Office Depot's educational institution's webpage (www.officedepot.com). Examine how they make good use of an inside sales force to service the educational market.

9. Key Term: Prospecting

Prospecting is the first step in the personal selling process. This is the stage of the process in which the salesperson identifies qualified potential customers. If you were a company salesperson for Montecristo cigars (www.montecristo.com), looking for a new outlet, what all would go into your prospecting?

10. Key Term: Sales Promotion

A sales promotion is a short-term incentive to encourage the purchase or sale of a product or service. Whereas advertising offers reasons to buy a product or service, sales promotion offers reason to buy NOW. Find an example of a sales promotion.

Marketing ADventure Exercises

1.   Ad Interpretation Challenge: Personal Selling
        Ad: Student Choice

Personal selling is the personal presentation by the firm's sales force for the purpose of making sales and building customer relationships. Today, most salespeople are well-educated, well-trained professionals who work to build and maintain long-term customer relationships. Choose an ad for a product or service that you believe would be best served through personal selling.

2.   Ad Interpretation Challenge: Salesperson
        Ad: General Retail – Target

A salesperson is an individual representing a company to customers by performing one of more of the following activities: prospecting, communicating, selling, servicing, information gathering, and relationship building. The term 'salesperson' covers a wide range of positions. At one extreme, a salesperson might be largely an order taker. At the other extreme are order getters. What type of salesperson do you believe Target Stores would typically employ?

3.   Ad Interpretation Challenge: Territorial Sales Force Structure
        Ad: Food & Beverage – Heinz

A sales force organization that assigns each salesperson to an exclusive geographic territory in which that salesperson sells the company's full line is known as a territorial sales force structure. Why would H.J. Heinz Company choose to use a territorial sales force structure?

4.   Ad Interpretation Challenge: Product Sales Force Structure
        Ad: Electronics - Sony

Product sales force structure is a sales force organization under which salespeople specialize in selling only a portion of the company's products or lines. Under such a structure, salespeople become specialists in only a portion of the company's products; however, the depth of knowledge they have is great. Consider Sony. Why would Sony choose to use a product sales force structure?

5.   Ad Interpretation Challenge: Customer Sales Force Structure
        Ad: Apparel – Levi's

A sales force organization under which salespeople specialize in selling only to certain customers or industries is known as a customer sales force structure. Separate sales forces may be set up for different industries or for servicing major accounts versus regular accounts. Think about Levi Strauss & Company. Under what conditions can you see this company using a customer sales force structure?

6.   Ad Interpretation Challenge: Inside Sales Force
        Ad: Financial – H&R Block

Inside salespeople who conduct business from their offices via telephone, the internet, or visits from prospective buyers are known as the inside sales force. Why would the sales force of H&R Block be characterized as an inside sales force?

7.   Ad Interpretation Challenge: Team Selling
        Ad: Student Choice

Team selling occurs when a company uses teams of people from sales, marketing, engineering, finance, technical support, and possibly even upper management to service large, complex accounts. Find an ad for a product (or company) that you believe could make good use of the team selling concept.

8.   Ad Interpretation Challenge: Prospecting
        Ad: Services & B2B - EMS

Prospecting is the first step in the personal selling process. This is the stage of the process in which the salesperson identifies qualified potential customers. Prospects can be qualified by looking at their financial ability, special needs, location, and possibilities for growth. Look at the EMS Urgent Mail ad. If you were EMS, what features would you be looking for in your prospects?

9.   Ad Interpretation Challenge: Presentation
        Ad: Autos – Mercedes Keys

The presentation is the step in the selling process in which the salesperson tells the "product story" to the buyer, highlighting customer benefits. Look at this ad for Mercedes. If you were using this ad to take the place of the salesperson presentation, what "product story" would this ad tell?

10.   Ad Interpretation Challenge: Sales Promotion
        Ad: Food & Beverage - Snickers

A sales promotion is a short-term incentive to encourage the purchase or sale of a product or service. What type of sales promotion could Snickers use to encourage the purchase of their product?

Chapter 17
Direct and Online Marketing:
Building Direct Customer Relationships

Learning Objectives

1. Define direct marketing and discuss its benefits to customers and companies
2. Identify and discuss the major forms of direct marketing
3. Explain how companies have responded to the Internet and other powerful new technologies with online marketing strategies
4. Discuss how companies go about conducting online marketing to profitably deliver more value to customers
5. Overview the public policy and ethical issues presented by direct marketing.

Chapter Overview

This chapter looks at the final IMC element, direct marketing, and at its fastest-growing form, online marketing. In many ways direct marketing constitutes an overall marketing approach—a blend of communication and distribution channels all rolled into one. Remember, although this chapter examines direct marketing as a separate tool, it must be carefully integrated with the other elements of the promotion mix.

Chapter Outline

1. INTRODUCTION

When you think of shopping on the Web, chances are good that you think first of Amazon.com. Amazon sells everything. "We have the Earth's Biggest Selection," declares the company's Web site. From the start, Amazon has grown explosively. Its annual sales have rocketed from $15 million in 1996 to more than $15 billion today. Last year the company ranked fifth in the nation in return to shareholders, two spots above Apple. One study estimates that 52 percent of all consumers who went to the Internet to shop last year started at Amazon. Fifty percent of Amazon's sales come from overseas. What has made Amazon one of the world's premier direct marketers? To its core, the company is relentlessly customer driven. Everything at Amazon begins with the customer. Anyone at Amazon will tell you the company wants to do much more than just sell books and DVDs. It wants to deliver a special experience to every customer. Visitors to Amazon's Web site receive a unique blend of benefits: huge selection, good value, convenience, and what the company calls "discovery" – on the Web site, you're compelled to stay for a while, looking, learning, and discovering. Amazon is constantly on the lookout for innovative new ways to use the power of the Web and direct marketing to create more shopping selection, value, convenience, and discovery for customers. Says

Jeff Bezos, Amazon's founder, "We are not great advertisers. So we start with customers, figure out what they want, and figure out how to get it to them."

Opening Vignette Questions

1. What one key factor has made Amazon one of the world's premier direct marketers?
2. What does Amazon founder, Jeff Bezos, mean when he says they want to deliver a special experience to the customer?
3. What has caused some traditional brick-and-mortar merchants to turn to Amazon for help?
4. So, do you believe Amazon.com will become the Wal-Mart of the Web?

2. THE NEW DIRECT-MARKETING MODEL

Most companies still use direct marketing as a supplementary channel or medium. For a growing number of companies direct marketing constitutes a complete model for doing business. Firms employing this new direct model use it as the only approach.

3. GROWTH AND BENEFITS OF DIRECT MARKETING

Direct marketing has become the fastest-growing form of marketing. The Internet now accounts for about 20 percent of direct marketing-driven sales.

3.1 Benefits to Buyers
- Gives buyers ready access to a wealth of products.
- Gives buyers access to a wealth of comparative information about companies, products, and competitors.
- Is interactive and immediate.
- Gives consumers a greater measure of control.

3.2 Benefits to Sellers
- Can target small groups or individual consumers.
- Low-cost, efficient, speedy alternative for reaching their markets.
- Can offer greater flexibility.
- Gives sellers access to buyers that they could not reach through other channels.

4. CUSTOMER DATABASES AND DIRECT MARKETING

A customer database is an organized collection of comprehensive data about individual customers or prospects, including geographic, demographic, psychographic, and behavioral data.

In consumer marketing, the customer database might contain a customer's demographics (age, income, family members, birthdays), psychographics (activities, interests, and opinions), and buying behavior (buying preferences and the recency, frequency, and monetary value—RFM—of past purchases).

In business-to-business marketing, the customer profile might contain the products and services the customer has bought; past volumes and prices; key contacts (and their ages, birthdays, hobbies, and favorite foods); competing suppliers; status of current contracts; estimated customer spending for the next few years; and assessments of competitive strengths and weaknesses in selling and servicing the account.

Companies use their databases in many ways.
- To locate good potential customers and to generate sales leads.
- To learn about customers in detail.

5. FORMS OF DIRECT MARKETING

Figure 17.1 shows the major forms of direct marketing.
- Personal selling,
- Direct-mail marketing,
- Catalog marketing,
- Telephone marketing,
- Direct-response television marketing,
- Kiosk marketing,
- New digital direct marketing technologies,
- Online marketing. (Figure 17.1)

5.1 Direct Mail Marketing

Direct-mail marketing involves sending an offer, announcement, reminder, or other item to a person at a particular address. Direct mail (including both catalog and non-catalog mail) accounts for more than a third of all U.S. direct marketing sales.

Characteristics:
- Well suited to direct, one-to-one communication.
- Permits high target-market selectivity,
- Can be personalized,
- Is flexible,
- Allows easy measurement of results.
- Costs more than mass media per thousand people reached, people reached are much better prospects.

New forms of delivery have become popular, such as voice mail, text messaging, and e-mail. Voice mail is subject to the same do-not-call restrictions as telemarketing. Permission-based mobile marketing (via cell phones) is growing rapidly and e-mail is booming as a direct marketing tool.

5.2 Catalog Marketing

Catalog used to be defined as printed, bound piece of at least eight pages, selling multiple products, and offering a direct ordering mechanism. With Internet, more and more catalogs are going digital. A variety of Web-only catalogers have emerged, and most print catalogers have added Web-based catalogs.

Advantages of Web-based catalogs:
- Eliminate production, printing, and mailing costs.
- Allow real-time merchandising.

Printed catalogs are still thriving.
Advantages of printed catalogs:
- One of the best ways to convince consumers to use the online versions.
- Create emotional connections with customers.

5.3 Telephone Marketing

Telephone marketing involves using the telephone to sell directly to consumers and business customers. Telephone marketing now accounts for 20 percent of all direct marketing-driven sales. Business-to-business marketers also use telephone marketing extensively, accounting for more than 55 percent of all telephone marketing sales.
Outbound telephone marketing is used to sell directly to consumers and businesses. Inbound toll-free 800 (888, 877, 866) numbers are used to receive orders from television and print ads, direct mail, or catalogs. Do-not-call legislation (National Do-Not-Call Registry) has hurt the telemarketing industry, but not all that much. Do-not-call appears to be helping most direct marketers more than it's hurting them.

5.4 Direct-Response Television Marketing

Direct-response television marketing takes one of two major forms. Direct-response television advertising (DRTV) is television spots which describe a product and give customers a toll-free number or Web site for ordering. 30-minute or longer advertising programs are called infomercials. Home shopping channels are television programs or entire channels dedicated to selling goods and services.

5.5 Kiosk Marketing

Kiosks are information and ordering machines.

5.6 New Digital Direct Marketing Technologies

5.6.1 Mobile Phone Marketing

About 80 percent of consumers in the United States use cell phones and about 60 percent of those people also text message. Within five years, an estimated 40 percent of cell phone subscribers will use their phones to access the Web.

5.6.2   Podcasts and Vodcasts
The name podcast derives from Apple's iPod. With podcasting, consumers can download audio files (podcasts) or video files (vodcasts) via the Internet to an iPod or other handheld device, and then listen to or view them whenever they wish.

Interactive TV (ITV)

Interactive TV (ITV) lets viewers interact with television programming and advertising using their remote controls.

6. ONLINE MARKETING

Online marketing is the fastest-growing form of direct marketing.

6.1 Marketing and the Internet

The Internet, a vast public web of computer networks, connects users of all types all around the world to each other and to an amazingly large information repository. Internet household penetration in the United States is approximately 72 percent, with more than 221 million people now using the Internet at home or at work. The average U.S. Internet user spends some 70 hours a month surfing the Web at home and work. Worldwide, more than 540 million people now have Internet access.

Click-only companies operate only on the Internet. They include a wide array of firms, from e-tailers such as Amazon to search engines and portals (Google), transaction sites (eBay), and content sites (ESPN.com). Click-and-mortar companies operate both as existing brick-and-mortar retailers and online.

6.2 Online Marketing Domains

Figure 14.2 shows the four major online marketing domains.

- Business-to-consumer (B2C) online marketing is selling goods and services online to final consumers. U.S. consumers generate over $175 billion in online retail sales, up 22 percent in a year. Then Internet now influences 35 percent of total retail sales.

- Business-to-business (B2B) online marketing is using online resources to reach new business customers, serve current customers more effectively, and obtain buying efficiencies and better prices.

- Consumer-to-consumer (C2C) online marketing occurs on the Web between interested parties over a wide range of products and subjects. eBay's C2C online trading community of more than 275 million registered users worldwide transacted some $60 billion in trades last year.

- Consumer-to-business (C2B) online marketing occurs when consumers communicate with companies. Consumers search out sellers on the Web, learn about their offers, initiate purchases, and give feedback.

6.3 Setting Up an Online Marketing Presence

For most companies, the first step in conducting online marketing is to create a Web site.

6.3.1. Types of Websites

Corporate (or Brand) Web Sites are the most basic. These sites are designed to build customer goodwill, collect customer feedback, and supplement other sales channels.

Marketing Web sites engage consumers in an interaction that will move them closer to a direct purchase or other marketing outcome.

6.3.2. Designing Effective Web Sites

A key challenge is designing a Web site that is attractive on first view and interesting enough to encourage repeat visits. Online marketers should pay close attention to the seven Cs of effective Web site design:

Context: the site's layout and design
Content: the text, pictures, sound, and video that the Web site contains
Community: the ways that the site enables user-to-user communication
Customization: the site's ability to tailor itself to different users or to allow users to personalize the site
Communication: the ways the site enables site-to-user, user-to-site, or two-way communication
Connection: the degree that the site is linked to other sites
Commerce: the site's capabilities to enable commercial transactions

To keep customers coming back to the site, companies need to embrace yet another "C"—constant change.

6.4 Placing Ads and Promotions Online

6.4.1 Forms of Online Advertising

- Banners are banner-shaped ads found at the top, bottom, left, right, or center of a Web page.
- Interstitials are online display ads that appear between screen changes on a Web site, especially while a new screen is loading.
- Pop-ups are online ads that appear suddenly in a new window in front of the window being viewed.
- Pop-unders are online ads that appear in a new window that evades pop-up blockers by appearing behind the page you're viewing.
- Rich media display ads are online ads that incorporate animation, video, sound, and interactivity.
- Search-related ads (or Contextual advertising) is online advertising in which text-based ads and links appear alongside search engine results.

6.4.2 Other Forms of Online Promotion

- Companies gain name exposure on the Internet by sponsoring special content on various Web sites.
- Alliances and affiliate programs allow companies to promote each other.
- Viral marketing is the Internet version of word-of-mouth marketing.

6.5 Creating or Participating in Online Social Networks

Online social networks or Web communities are Web sites that give consumers online places to congregate, socialize, and exchange views and information. Marketers can engage in online communities in two ways: They can participate in existing Web communities. They can set up their own Web communities.

6.6 Using Email

U.S. companies currently spend about $1.2 billion a year on e-mail marketing, up from just $164 million in 1999. Spam is the unsolicited, unwanted commercial e-mail messages that clog up e-mailboxes.

6.7 The Promise and Challenges of Online Marketing

As it continues to grow, online marketing will prove to be a powerful direct marketing tool for improving sales, communicating company and product information, delivering products and services, and building customer relationships more efficiently and effectively.

7. PUBLIC POLICY ISSUES IN DIRECT MARKETING

7.1 Irritation, Unfairness, Deception, and Fraud

Phishing is a type of identity theft that uses deceptive emails and fraudulent Web sites to fool users into divulging their personal data. Online security issues continue to grow. Consumers fear that unscrupulous snoopers will eavesdrop on their online transactions, picking up personal information or intercepting credit and debit card numbers. Access by vulnerable or unauthorized groups is another area of concern. For example, marketers of adult-oriented materials have found it difficult to restrict access by minors.

7.2 Invasion of property

Invasion of privacy is perhaps the toughest public policy issue now confronting the direct-marketing industry. Online privacy causes special concerns. Most online marketers have become skilled at collecting and analyzing detailed consumer information.

7.3 A Need for Action

This calls for strong actions by marketers to curb privacy abuses before legislators step in to do it for them. TRUSTe, a nonprofit self-regulatory organization, works with many large corporate sponsors to audit companies' privacy and security measures and help consumers navigate the Web safely.

Student Exercises

1.   Key Term: Direct Marketing

Direct marketing is a direct connection with carefully targeted individual consumers to both obtain an immediate response and cultivate lasting customer relationships. Direct marketing communicates directly with customers, often on a one-to-one interactive basis. Take a look at Gateway's website (www.gateway.com). How do they differentiate between direct marketing and more traditional in-store marketing?

2.   Key Term: Customer Database

An organized collection of comprehensive data about individual customers or prospects, including geographic, demographic, psychographic, and behavioral data is known as a customer database. Think about your school. What type of database do you think they have created regarding their students?

3.   Key Term: Direct-Mail Marketing

Direct-mail marketing is direct marketing by sending an offer, announcement, reminder, or other item to a person at a particular address through the mail. Direct mail is by far the largest direct marketing medium. Much direct mail is considered junk mail or spam by recipients. Take a look at a direct-mail marketer such as Columbia House (www.columbiahouse.com). What can they do to keep the recipients of their direct mail offers from viewing the direct-mail piece as junk mail?

4.   Key Term: Catalog Marketing

Direct marketing through print, video, or electronic catalogs that are mailed to select customers, made available in stores or presented online is known as catalog marketing. Advances in technology, along with the move toward more personalized marketing, has resulted in dynamic changes in catalog marketing. Take a look at a catalog from Victoria's Secret (either online at www.victoriassecret.com or a hard copy). Compare the product offering in the catalogs with what is offered in their stores.

5.   Key Term: Telephone Marketing

Telephone marketing is using the telephone to sell directly to customers. Telephone marketing accounts for approximately 22 percent of all direct marketing-driven business. Telephone marketing is not just outbound marketing. Much of the growth in telephone marketing has come from inbound marketing – the 800 numbers consumers can call in on to reach a company. Take a look at Butterball Turkey (www.butterball.com). They offer consumers an 800 number (1-800-BUTTERBALL). What is the purpose of this number and what types of information can you receive?

6.   Key Term: Direct-Response Television Marketing

Direct-response television marketing is direct marketing via television, including direct-response television advertising (or infomercials) and home shopping channels. It is a huge growth business. Go to the Home Shopping Network's homepage (www.hsn.com) and log on to "Watch HSNtv Live." Explain how HSN (and other similar marketers) generate product excitement and sales.

7.   Key Term: Kiosk Marketing

As consumers become more and more comfortable with computer and digital technologies, many companies are placing information and ordering machines (kiosks) in stores, airports, and other locations. These are not the same as vending machines, which dispense actual products. Airlines are increasingly turning to kiosk marketing in an effort to more efficiently service customers and decrease overall costs. Take a look at how Delta Airlines is using kiosk marketing. Go to the following link to learn about Delta's use of kiosks. www.delta.com/traveling_checkin/itineraries_checkin/options/index.jsp

8.   Key Term: Mobile Phone Marketing

Mobile phone marketing is viewed by many marketers as the next big thing. It is believed that, in the near future, almost 90 percent of major brands will be marketed via mobile phones. Take a look at the T-Mobile website (www.t-mobile.com). How T-Mobile using mobile phone marketing?

9.   Key Term: Internet

The internet is a vast public web of computer networks that connects users of all types all around the world to each other and to an amazingly large information repository. Internet usage continues to grow at a steady rate. One of the largest "virtual" stores is Amazon. Go to Amazon (www.amazon.com) and take a tour of all the product categories from which a customer can select products and services. How does this compare to traditional "brick and mortar" retailers?

10.   Key Term: Click-and-Mortar Companies

Click-and-mortar companies are traditional brick-and-mortar companies that have added online marketing to their operations. As the internet grew, established brick-and-mortar companies realized that to compete effectively with online competitors they had to go online themselves. Sears is one such company (www.sears.com). How does Sears use its online presence to compete with the online-only companies, such as Amazon?

Marketing ADventure Exercises

1.   Ad Interpretation Challenge: Direct Marketing
      Ad: Advertising – Studio Funk

Direct marketing is a direct connection with carefully targeted individual consumers to both obtain an immediate response and cultivate lasting customer relationships. Direct marketing communicates directly with customers, often on a one-to-one interactive basis. Consider Studio Funk. How could their "attention grabbing" radio commercials incorporate direct marketing

2.   Ad Interpretation Challenge: Customer Database
      Ad: Internet – El Sitio

A customer database is an organized collection of comprehensive data about individual customers or prospects, including geographic, demographic, psychographic, and behavioral data. How would El Sitio make use of a customer database in its business?

3.   Ad Interpretation Challenge: Direct-Mail Marketing
      Ad: Auto – Audi A3

Direct-mail marketing is direct marketing by sending an offer, announcement, reminder, or other item to a person at a particular address. What would Audi have to do with this magazine ad to make it acceptable as a direct-mail piece?

4.	Ad Interpretation Challenge: Catalog Marketing
	Ad: Travel & Tourism – Travel Price

Catalog marketing is direct marketing through print, video, or electronic catalogs that are mailed to select customers, made available in stores, or presented online. Why could Travel Price be said to use catalog marketing?

5.	Ad Interpretation Challenge: Telephone Marketing
	Ad: Travel & Tourism – Imperial Hotel

Telephone marketing accounts for approximately 22 percent of all direct marketing-driven business. It is using the telephone to market directly to consumers. Telephone marketing is not just outbound marketing. Much of the growth in telephone marketing has come from inbound marketing – the 800 numbers consumers can call in on to reach a company. Look at the ads for the Imperial Hotel. Is this a form of telephone marketing?

6.	Ad Interpretation Challenge: Direct-Response Television Marketing
	Ad: Newspaper & TV – MTV

Direct-response television marketing is direct marketing via television, including direct-response television advertising (or infomercials) and home shopping channels. It is definitely a growth business. How does MTV use direct-response television marketing?

7.	Ad Interpretation Challenge: Kiosk Marketing
	Ad: Travel & Tourism – American Airlines

Information and ordering machines (kiosks) are popping up everywhere, as consumers become more comfortable with computers and new technologies. Kiosks do not dispense actual products, as do vending machines. How does American Airlines currently make use of kiosks? (For more information, you can go to www.aa.com)

8.	Ad Interpretation Challenge: Mobile Phone Marketing
	Ad: Electronics – Axiom

With almost 200 million Americans new subscribing to wireless services, many marketers view mobile phones as the next big direct marketing medium. How could Axiom make use of mobile phone marketing?

9.	Ad Interpretation Challenge: Marketing Web Site
	Ad: Electronics – Polaroid

A marketing website is a website that engages consumers in interactions that will move them closer to a direct purchase or other marketing outcome. Consider Polaroid. Go to the Polaroid web site (www.polaroid.com). Is this a marketing website?

10.   Ad Interpretation Challenge: Spam
            Ad: Travel & Transportation – Aeromexico

Spam is unsolicited and unwanted commercial e-mail messages that clog up your e-mailboxes. It is a big problem and becoming bigger. Aeromexico wants to be able to communicate with its customers via e-mail, but it does not want to be viewed as spam. How would you suggest they overcome this hurtle?

Chapter 18
Creating Competitive Advantage

Learning Objectives

1. Discuss the need to understand competitors as well as customers through competitor analysis.
2. Explain the fundamentals of competitive marketing strategies based on creating value for customers.
3. Illustrate the need for balancing customer and competitor orientations in becoming a truly market-centered organization.

Chapter Overview

This chapter pulls all of the marketing basic together. Understanding customers is an important first step in developing profitable customer relationships, but it is not enough. To gain competitive advantage, companies must use this understanding to design marketing offers that deliver more value than the offers of competitors seeking to win the same customers. This chapter looks at competitor analysis, the process companies use to identify and analyze competitors. Then, the chapter moves to competitive marketing strategies by which companies position themselves against competitors to gain the greatest possible competitive advantages.

Chapter Outline

1. INTRODUCTION

The Nike "swoosh" – it's everywhere! Through innovative marketing, Nike has built the ever-present swoosh into one of the best-known brand symbols on the planet. During the 1980s, under Phil Knight's leadership, Nike revolutionized sports marketing. To build its brand image and market share, Nike lavishly outspent its competitors on big-name endorsements, splashy promotional events, and in-you-face "Just Do It" ads. At Nike, good marketing meant consistently building strong relationships with customers based on real value. Throughout the 1980s and 1990s, still playing the role of the upstart underdog, Nike solidified its position as the dominant market leader. The company slapped its familiar swoosh logo on everything from sunglasses and soccer balls to bating gloves and golf clubs. Nike invaded a dozen new sports. In the late 1990s, however, Nike stumbled as a new bread of competitor arose and the company's sales slipped. The whole industry suffered a setback, as a "brown shoe" craze for hiking and outdoor shoe styles ate into the athletic sneaker business. Nike's biggest obstacle may have been its own incredible success. The brand appeared to suffer from big-brand backlash. Instead of being the antiestablishment, Nike was the establishment. Nike now had to grow up and act its age. And grow up it did. The company still spends heavily on very creative advertising and big-name endorsers. But behind the bright lights, Nike now focuses on the important marketing basics: customer relationships, new-product innovation, and leaving competitors in the dust. When it comes to competition, Nike is ruthless but a little paranoid. With its deep pockets, Nike can outspend most competitors on marketing by a wide margin. But where today's Nike really out-points its competitors is in its cutting-edge efforts to build deep community with customers. As a result, the modern-day Nike is once again achieving stunning results. To stay ahead of competitors, however, Nike will have to keep its marketing strategy fresh, finding new ways to deliver the kind of innovation and value that built the brand so powerfully in the past. To win in today's marketplace, companies must become adapt not just in managing products, but in managing customer relationships in the face of determined competition. Building profitable customer relationships and gaining competitive advantage requires delivering more value and satisfaction to target consumers than competitors do. Customers see competitive advantages as customer advantages. The first step is competitor analysis—the process of identifying, assessing, and selecting key competitors. The second step is developing competitive marketing strategies that strongly position the company against competitors and give it the greatest possible competitive advantage.

Opening Vignette Questions

1. What types of innovative marketing did Nike initially employ to bust onto the scene?
2. During the 1990s, Nike stumbled. What happened?
3. The modern-day Nike is very different from its past. How is Nike connecting with customers today?

2. COMPETITOR ANALYSIS

As shown in Figure 18.1, competitor analysis involves first identifying and assessing competitors and then selecting which competitors to attack or avoid.

2.1 Identifying Competitors

At the narrowest level, a company can define its competitors as other companies offering similar products and services to the same customers at similar prices. Companies actually face a much wider range of competitors. The company might define competitors as all firms making the same product or class of products. Even more broadly, competitors might include all companies making products that supply the same service. Finally, and still more broadly, competitors might include all companies that compete for the same consumer dollars. Companies must avoid "competitor myopia." A company is more likely to be "buried" by its latent competitors than its current ones. Companies can identify their competitors from the industry point of view. A company must understand the competitive patterns in its industry if it hopes to be an effective "player" in that industry. Companies can also identify competitors from a market point of view. Here they define competitors as companies that are trying to satisfy the same customer need or build relationships with the same customer group. In general, the market concept of competition opens the company's eyes to a broader set of actual and potential competitors.

2.2 Assessing Competitors

2.2.1 Determining Competitors' Objective

Each competitor has a mix of objectives. The company wants to know the relative importance that a competitor places on current profitability, market share growth, cash flow, technological leadership, service leadership, and other goals. Knowing a competitor's mix of objectives reveals whether the competitor is satisfied with its current situation and how it might react to different competitive actions. A company must also monitor its competitors' objectives for various segments.

2.2.2 Identifying Competitors' Strategies

The more that one firm's strategy resembles another firm's strategy, the more the two firms compete. A strategic group is a group of firms in an industry following the same or a similar strategy in a given target market.
- Some of the strategic groups may appeal to overlapping customer segments.
  - The customers may not see much difference in the offers of different groups.
  - Members of one strategic group might expand into new strategy segments.
The company needs to look at all of the dimensions that identify strategic groups within the industry.

2.2.3 Assessing Competitors' Strengths and Weaknesses

Marketers need to assess each competitor's strengths and weaknesses carefully in order to answer the critical question: What **can** our competitors do?
- As a first step, companies can gather data on each competitor's goals, strategies, and performance over the last few years.
- Companies normally learn about their competitors' strengths and weaknesses through secondary data, personal experience, and word of mouth.
- They can conduct primary marketing research with customers, suppliers, and dealers.
- They can benchmark themselves against other firms, comparing the company's products and processes to those of competitors or leading firms in other industries to find ways to improve quality and performance.

2.2.4 Estimating Competitors' Reactions

Next, the company wants to know: What will our competitors do?

- A competitor's objectives, strategies, and strengths and weaknesses go a long way toward explaining its likely actions. They also suggest its likely reactions to company moves such as price cuts, promotion increases, or new-product introductions.
- In addition, each competitor has a certain philosophy of doing business, a certain internal culture and guiding beliefs.
- Each competitor reacts differently.

2.3 Selecting Competitors to Attack and Avoid

2.3.1 Strong or Weak Competitors

The company can focus on one of several classes of competitors. Most companies prefer to compete against weak competitors. This requires fewer resources and less time. But in the process, the firm may gain little. A useful tool for assessing competitor strengths and weaknesses is customer value analysis. The aim of customer value analysis is to determine the benefits that target customer value and how customers rate the relative value of various competitors' offers. The key to gaining competitive advantage is to take each customer segment and examine how the company's offer compares to that of its major competitor.

2.3.2 Close or Distinct Competitors

Most companies will compete with close competitors—those that resemble them the most—rather than distant competitors. At the same time, the company may want to avoid trying to "destroy" a close competitor.

2.3.3 "Good" or "Bad" Competitors

The existence of competitors results in several strategic benefits.

- Competitors may help increase total demand.
- They may share the costs of market and product development and help to legitimize new technologies.
- They may serve less-attractive segments or lead to more product differentiation.
- They lower the antitrust risk and improve bargaining power versus labor or regulators.

However, a company may not view all of its competitors as beneficial. An industry often contains "good" competitors and "bad" competitors.

- Good competitors play by the rules of the industry.
- Bad competitors break the rules. They try to buy share rather than earn it, take large risks, and in general shake up the industry.

202

2.3.4 Finding Uncontested Market Spaces

Rather than competing head to head with established competitors, many companies seek out unoccupied positions in uncontested market spaces. They try to create products and services for which there are no direct competitors.

2.4 Designing a Competitive Intelligence System

The competitive intelligence system:
- Identifies the vital types of competitive information and the best sources of this information;
- Continuously collects information from the field and from published data;
- Checks the information for validity and reliability, interprets it, and organizes it in an appropriate way;
- Sends key information to relevant decision makers and responds to inquiries from managers about competitors.

Smaller companies that cannot afford to set up formal competitive intelligence offices can assign specific executives to watch specific competitors.

3. COMPETITIVE STRATEGIES

Having identified and evaluated its major competitors, the company now must design broad competitive marketing strategies by which it can gain competitive advantage by offering superior customer value.

3.1 Approaches to Marketing Strategy

No one strategy is best for all companies. Each company must determine what makes the most sense given its position in the industry and its objectives, opportunities, and resources. Even within a company, different strategies may be required for different businesses or products. Approaches to marketing strategy and practice often pass through three stages.

- Entrepreneurial marketing: Most companies are started by individuals who live by their wits. They visualize an opportunity, construct flexible strategies on the backs of envelopes, and knock on every door to gain attention.
- Formulated marketing: As small companies achieve success, they inevitably move toward more-formulated marketing. They develop formal marketing strategies and adhere to them closely.
- Intrepreneurial marketing: Many large and mature companies get stuck in formulated marketing. These companies sometimes lose the marketing creativity and passion that they had at the start. They need to re-establish within their companies the entrepreneurial spirit and actions that made them successful in the first place.

3.2 Basic Competitive Strategies

More than two decades ago, Michael Porter suggested four basic competitive positioning strategies that companies can follow—three winning strategies and one losing one.

Winning strategies are:
- Overall cost leadership: The company works hard to achieve the lowest production and distribution costs.
- Differentiation: The company concentrates on creating a highly differentiated product line and marketing program.
- Focus: The company focuses on serving a few market segments well rather than going after the whole market.

The losing strategy is:
- Middle-of-the-road: The company tries to be good on all strategic counts, but ends up being not very good at anything.

More recently, a new classification of competitive marketing strategies has been offered. It is suggested companies gain leadership positions by delivering superior value to their customers. Companies can pursue any of three strategies—called value disciplines—for delivering superior customer value.

- Operational excellence: The company provides superior value by leading its industry in price and convenience.
- Customer intimacy: The company provides superior value by precisely segmenting its markets and tailoring its products or services to match exactly the needs of targeted customers.
- Product leadership: The company provides superior value by offering a continuous stream of leading-edge products or services.

Some companies successfully pursue more than one value discipline at the same time. However, such companies are rare—few firms can be the best at more than one of these disciplines.

3.3 Competitive Positions

Firms competing in a given target market, at any point in time, differ in their objectives and resources. Firms can base their competitive strategies on the roles they play in the target market—market leader (40%), market challenger (30%), market follower (20%), or market nicher (10%). Table 18.1 shows specific marketing strategies that are available to market leaders, challengers, followers, and nichers. Remember, however, that these classifications often do not apply to a whole company, but only to its position in a specific industry.

3.3.1. Market Leader Strategies

Most industries contain an acknowledged market leader. Competitors focus on the leader as a company to challenge, imitate, or avoid. To remain number one, leading firms can take any of three actions.
- They can find ways to expand total demand.
- They can protect their current market share through good defensive and offensive actions.
- They can try to expand their market share further, even if market size remains constant.

3.3.2 Market Challenger Strategies

Firms that are second, third, or lower in an industry are sometimes quite large. These runner-up firms can adopt one of two competitive strategies:

- They can challenge the leader and other competitors in an aggressive bid for more market share (market challengers).
- They can play along with competitors and not rock the boat (market followers).

3.3.3. Market Follower Strategies

A follower can gain many advantages. The market leader often bears the huge expenses of developing new products and markets, expanding distribution, and educating the market. By contrast, the market follower can learn from the leader's experience. It can copy or improve on the leader's products and programs, usually with much less investment. Although the follower will probably not overtake the leader, it often can be as profitable. Following is not the same as being passive or a carbon copy of the leader. Each follower tries to bring distinctive advantages to its target market. The follower is often a major target of attack by challengers. Therefore, the market follower must keep its manufacturing costs low and its product quality and services high. It must also enter new markets as they open up.

3.3.4. Market Nicher Strategies

Almost every industry includes firms that specialize in serving market niches. Instead of pursuing the whole market, or even large segments, these firms target subsegments. Nichers are often smaller firms with limited resources. The key idea in niching is specialization. A market nicher can specialize along any of several market, customer, product, or marketing mix lines.

4. BALANCING CUSTOMER AND COMPETITOR ORIENTATIONS

Whether a company is a market leader, challenger, follower, or nicher, it must watch its competitors closely and find the competitive marketing strategy that positions it most effectively. It must continually adapt its strategies to the fast-changing competitive environment. A competitor-centered company is one that spends most of its time tracking competitors' moves and market shares and trying to find strategies to counter them. In practice, today's companies must be market-centered companies, watching both their customers and their competitors. But they must not let competitor watching blind them to customer focusing.

Figure 18.4 shows that companies have moved through four orientations over the years.
- In the first stage, they were product oriented, paying little attention to either customers or competitors.
- In the second stage, they became customer oriented and started to pay attention to customers.
- In the third stage, when they started to pay attention to competitors, they became competitor oriented.
- Today, companies need to be market oriented, paying balanced attention to both customers and competitors.

Student Exercises

1.   Key Term: Competitive Advantage

Competitive advantage is an advantage over competitors gained by offering consumers greater value than competitors offer. What is the competitive advantage enjoyed by AT&T? Go to their website (www.att.com) to learn more about the company.

2.   Key Term: Competitor Analysis

Competitor analysis is the process of identifying key competitors; assessing their objectives, strategies, strengths and weaknesses, and reaction patterns; and selecting which competitors to attack or avoid. Learn about Lenovo computers (www.lenovo.com/us/en/). Identify their key competitors.

3.   Key Term: Strategic Groups

In most industries, the competitors can be sorted into groups that pursue different strategies. A strategic group is a group of firms in an industry following the same or similar strategies. Look at Palm (www.palm.com). What is the strategic group to which they belong and who are the other members?

4.   Key Term: Benchmarking

Benchmarking is the process of comparing the company's products and processes to those of competitors or leading firms in other industries to find ways to improve quality and performance. If you were in charge of marketing Corel Paint Shop Pro photo editing software (www.corel.com), who would you benchmark?

5.   Key Term: "Bad" Competitors

There are two types of competitors that a company with which a company may have to deal—"good" competitors and "bad" competitors. "Good" competitors play by the rules of the industry. "Bad" competitors, on the other hand, break some of those rules. They try to buy share, rather than earn it, take large risks, and play by their own rules. Your text highlights iTunes as a competitor that is viewed as bad by other industry players. Find another example.

6.   Key Term: Differentiation

Differentiation is a competitive positioning strategy where the company concentrates on creating a highly differentiated product line and marketing program so that it comes across as the class leader in the industry. Consider Apple (www.apple.com). How does Apple differentiate itself from its competition?

7.   Key Term: Focus

Focus is a differentiation strategy where the company concentrates its efforts on serving only a few market segments well, rather than going after the entire market. Find a company in the transportation industry that uses a focus differentiation strategy.

8.   Key Term: Customer Intimacy

Customer-intimate companies serve customers who are willing to pay a premium to get precisely what they want. These companies will do almost anything to build long-term customer loyalty and to capture customer lifetime value. Look at how Wyndham work to develop customer intimacy (www.wyndham.com).

9.   Key Term: Market Follower

A market follower is a runner-up firm that wants to hold its share in an industry without rocking the boat or taking unnecessary risks. Market followers follow the market from a safe distance, only taking risks when the results seem clear. Research the U.S. breakfast cereal market. What is a company that you would consider a follower in this market?

10.   Key Term: Market Nicher

Almost every industry includes firms that specialize in serving small market niches. Instead of pursuing the whole market, or even large segments, these firms target subsegments. Nichers are often smaller firms with limited resources. Consider again, the U.S. breakfast cereal market. What is a company that you would consider a market nicher?

Marketing ADventure Exercises

1.   Ad Interpretation Challenge: Competitive Advantage
      Ad: Financial—MBNA

An advantage over competitors gained by offering consumers greater value than the competitors offer is known as competitive advantage. Take a look at this ad for MBNA. What is the competitive advantage MBNA has over its competition?

2.   Ad Interpretation Challenge: Identifying Competitors
      Ad: Electronics—LG

Normally, identifying competitors would seem a simple task. At the narrowest level, a company can define its competitors as other companies offering similar products and services to the same customers at similar prices. Look at this ad for LG televisions and then go to their website (http://us.lge.com) to learn more about their product offering in televisions. Who would you identify as their major competitors in television?

3.   Ad Interpretation Challenge: Strategic Groups
      Ad: Auto—Porsche

A strategic group is a group of firms in an industry following the same or similar strategies. While you will have competitors outside of the strategic group, your primary competitors are other firms within the strategic group. Consider Porsche. How would you describe the strategic group of which it is a member? What are some of the other firms that would make up its strategic group?

4.   Ad Interpretation Challenge: Benchmarking
      Ad: Cosmetics and Pharmaceuticals—Mentadent

Benchmarking is the process of comparing a company's products and processes to those of competitors or leading firms in other industries to find ways to improve quality and performance. If you were the marketing manager for Mentadent toothpaste, a toothpaste with a relatively small market share, what companies would look to benchmark?

5.   Ad Interpretation Challenge: Close Competitors
      Ad: Financial—Ameritrade

Competitors come in all sizes and strengths. Most companies will choose to compete with close competitors. Close competitors are those that most resemble your company. Close competitors are the competitors that are most like your company. What type of companies would be close competitors to Ameritrade?

6. Ad Interpretation Challenge: Entrepreneurial Marketing Strategy
   Ad: Student Choice

Entrepreneurial marketing strategies are typically those strategies employed by young companies (although not always that young) looking to stand out, be recognized, and make a name. These are strategies that may be somewhat unorthodox, but are designed to take a chance and (hopefully) make a splash. Find an ad for a product or company that you believe is employing an entrepreneurial marketing strategy.

7. Ad Interpretation Challenge: Differentiation
   Ad: Services and B2B—24 Hour Fitness

Differentiation is a competitive positioning strategy where the company concentrates on creating a highly differentiated product line and marketing program so that it comes across as the class leader in the industry. How does 24 Hour Fitness differentiate itself from its competitors?

8. Ad Interpretation Challenge: Focus
   Ad: Apparel—Polartec

Using a focus strategy, a company focuses its efforts on serving a few market segments well rather than going after the whole market. Look at this ad for Polartec. How is this company effectively using a focus strategy to compete?

9. Ad Interpretation Challenge: Product Leadership
   Ad: Student Choice

A company which employees a product leadership strategy provides superior value in its own way. It provides value to its customers by offering a continuous stream of leading-edge products or services. It aims to make its own and competing products obsolete. These companies typically serve customers who want state-of-the-art products and services, regardless of the costs in terms of price or inconvenience. Find an ad for such a company.

10. Ad Interpretation Challenge: Market Leader Strategies
    Ad: General Retail—Hallmark

Most industries contain an acknowledged market leader. The leader has the largest market share and usually leads the other firms in price changes, new-product introductions, distribution coverage, and promotion spending. Hallmark is the acknowledged market leader in the greeting card market. What must Hallmark do to stay on top?

Chapter 19
The Global Marketplace

Learning Objectives

1. Discuss how the international trade system and economic, political-legal, and cultural environments affect a company's international marketing decisions.
2. Describe three key approaches to entering international markets.
3. Explain how companies adapt their marketing mixes for international markets.
4. Identify the three major forms of international marketing organization.

Chapter Overview

Companies must do more than just create customer value. They must also use promotion to clearly and persuasively communicate that value. Promotion is not a single tool but, rather, a mix of several tools. Under the concept of integrated marketing communications, the company must carefully coordinate these promotion elements to deliver a clear, consistent, and compelling message about the organization and its brands.

The chapter begins with an introduction to the various promotion mix tools. Next, we examine the rapidly changing communications environment and the need for intergraded marketing communications. Finally, the chapter discusses the steps in developing marketing communications and the promotion budgeting process.

Chapter Outline

1. INTRODUCTION

Most Americans think of McDonald's as their very own. After all, what could be more American than burger and fries? But, as it turns out, McDonald's does more of their business abroad they at home. Nearly 65% of their sales come from outside the U.S. To realize how far McDonald's has come, consider their experiences in Russia, a country very unique and different from our own.

McDonald's first set sights on Russia in 1976. Over the next 14 years, George Cohen (head of McDonald's Canada) visited Russia over 100 times to try and gain permission for McDonald's to provide food for the Olympics and then to open restaurants. He was turned down on both requests initially. Russians had no clue what McDonald's was.

It was not until 1988 that permission was finally given. However, permission was only the beginning. Russian bureaucracy was a daunting challenge; over 200 separate signatures had to be obtained just to open one restaurant. They had to build their own facilities to supply the needed products to use in production.

Today, less than 20 years after opening their first restaurant there, McDonald's is a huge success. The Pushkin Square location is the busiest in the world. The company has 180 restaurants in 40 cities each of which averages 850,000 diners a year.

2. GLOBAL MARKETING TODAY

Since 1990, the number of multinational corporations in the world has grown from 30,000 to more than 60,000. Since 2003, total world trade has been growing at 6 to 11 percent annually, while global gross domestic product has grown at only 2.5 to 5 percent annually. Foreign firms are expanding aggressively into new international markets, and home markets are no longer as rich in opportunity. Few industries are now safe from foreign competition.

A global firm is one that, by operating in more than one country, gains marketing, production, R&D, and financial advantages that are not available to purely domestic competitors.

The global company sees the world as one market. It minimizes the importance of national boundaries and develops "transnational" brands. The rapid move toward globalization means that all companies will have to answer basic questions:

- What market position should we try to establish in our country, in our economic region, and globally?
- Who will our global competitors be and what are their strategies and resources?
- Where should we produce or source our products?
- What strategic alliances should we form with other firms around the world?

A company faces six major decisions in international marketing. (Figure 19.1)

3. LOOKING AT THE GLOBAL MARKETING ENVIRONMENT

3.1 The International Trade System

Tariffs are taxes on certain imported products designed to raise revenue or to protect domestic firms.

Quotas are limits on the amount of foreign imports that a country will accept in certain product categories.

The purpose of a quota is to conserve on foreign exchange and to protect local industry and employment.

Exchange controls are limits on the amount of foreign exchange and the exchange rate against other currencies.

Nontariff trade barriers are such things as biases against U.S. company bids, restrictive product standards, or excessive regulations.

3.2 The World Trade Organization and GATT

The General Agreement on Tariffs and Trade (GATT) is a 60-year-old treaty designed to promote world trade by reducing tariffs and other international trade barriers. Since the treaty's inception in 1947, member nations (currently numbering 152) have met in eight rounds of GATT negotiations to reassess trade barriers and set new rules for international trade.

The first seven rounds of negotiations reduced the average worldwide tariffs on manufactured goods from 45 percent to just 5 percent. The benefits of the Uruguay Round (1994) include reducing the world's remaining merchandise tariffs by 30 percent.

The Uruguay Round set up the World Trade Organization (WTO) to enforce GATT rules. The WTO acts as an umbrella organization, overseeing GATT, mediating global disputes, and imposing trade sanctions.

3.3 Regional Free Trade Zones

Free trade zones or Economic communities are groups of nations organized to work toward common goals in the regulation of international trade.

One such community is the European Union (EU). The European Union represents one of the world's single largest markets. Currently, it has 27 member countries containing close to half a billion consumers and accounts for more than 20 percent of the world's exports. As a result of increased unification, European companies have grown bigger and more competitive. Widespread adoption of the euro will decrease much of the currency risk associated with doing business in Europe, making member countries with previously weak currencies more attractive markets. However, even with the adoption of the euro, it is unlikely that the EU will ever go against 2,000 years of tradition and become the "United States of Europe."

The North American Free Trade Agreement (NAFTA) established a free trade zone among the United States, Mexico, and Canada. The agreement created a single market of 447 million people who produce and consume over $16 trillion worth of goods and services annually. NAFTA eliminates trade barriers and investment restrictions among the three countries. Trade among the NAFTA nations has risen 198 percent. U.S. merchandise exports to NAFTA partners grew 157 percent, compared with exports to the rest of the world at 108 percent. Canada and Mexico are now the nation's first and second largest trading partners.

The Central American Free Trade Agreement (CAFTA) established a free trade zone between the United States and Costa Rica, the Dominican Republic, El Salvador, Guatemala, Honduras, and Nicaragua.

Talks have been underway since 1994 to investigate establishing a Free Trade Area of the Americas (FTAA).

Mercosur links eleven Latin America and South America countries.

The Andean Community (CAN, for its Spanish initials) links four more countries.

In late 2004, Mercosur and CAN agreed to unite, creating the Union of South American Nations (Unasur).

3.4 Economic Environment

Two economic factors reflect the country's attractiveness as a market:

- Industrial structure
- Income distribution.

3.4.1   The country's industrial structure shapes its product and service needs, income levels, and employment levels.

The four types of industrial structures are as follows:

- Subsistence economies: The vast majority of people engage in simple agriculture. They consume most of their output and barter the rest for simple goods and services. They offer few market opportunities.

- Raw material exporting economies: These economies are rich in one or more natural resources but poor in other ways. These countries are good markets for large equipment, tools and supplies, and trucks.

- Industrializing economies: Manufacturing accounts for 10 to 20 percent of the country's economy. The country needs more imports of raw textile materials, steel, and heavy machinery, and fewer imports of finished textiles, paper products, and automobiles.

- Industrial economies: Major exporters of manufactured goods, services, and investment funds. They trade goods among themselves and also export them to other types of economies for raw materials and semifinished goods.

3.4.2. Income distribution is the second factor.

- Industrialized nations may have low-, medium-, and high-income households. Countries with subsistence economies may consist mostly of households with very low family incomes. Still other countries may have households with only either very low or very high incomes.

- Even poor or developing economies may be attractive markets for all kinds of goods, including luxuries.

3.5 Political-Legal Environment

Some nations are very receptive to foreign firms; others are less accommodating. Companies must consider a country's monetary regulations.

Countertrade takes several forms:

- Barter involves the direct exchange of goods or services.
- Compensation (or Buyback) is where the seller sells a plant, equipment, or technology to another country and agrees to take payment in the resulting products.
- Counterpurchase (the most common form of countertrade) is when the seller receives full payment in cash but agrees to spend some of the money in the other country.

3.6 Cultural Environment

3.6.1. The Impact of Culture on Marketing Strategy

The seller must understand the ways that consumers in different countries think about and use certain products before planning a marketing program. Business norms and behavior vary from country to country.

3.6.2. The Impact of Marketing Strategy on Cultures

Social critics contend that large American multinationals such as McDonald's, Coca-Cola, Starbucks, Nike, Microsoft, Disney, and MTV are "Americanizing" the world's cultures.

4. DECIDING WHETHER TO GO GLOBAL

Not all companies need to venture into international markets to survive.

Any of several factors might draw a company into the international arena.

- Global competitors might attack the company's home market by offering better products or lower prices.
- The company might want to counterattack these competitors in their home markets.
- The company's home market might be stagnant or shrinking.
- Foreign markets may present higher sales and profit opportunities.
- The company's customers might be expanding abroad and require international servicing.

Before going abroad, the company must weigh several risks and answer many questions about its ability to operate globally.

- Can it learn to understand the preferences and buyer behavior of consumers in other countries?
- Can it offer competitively attractive products?
- Will it be able to adapt to other countries' business cultures and deal effectively with foreign nationals?
- Do the company's managers have the necessary international experience?
- Has management considered the impact of regulations and the political environments of other countries?

5. DECIDING WHICH MARKETS TO ENTER

Before going abroad, the company should:

- Define its international marketing objectives and policies.
- Decide what volume of foreign sales it wants.
- Decide how many countries it wants to market.
- Decide on the types of countries to enter.
- Evaluate each selected country.

Possible global markets should be ranked on several factors, including:

- Market size,
- Market growth,
- Cost of doing business,
- Competitive advantage, and
- Risk level.

6. DECIDING HOW TO ENTER THE MARKET

6.1 Exporting

Exporting is the simplest way to enter a foreign market.

Indirect exporting is working through independent international marketing intermediaries. Indirect exporting involves less investment and less risk.

Direct exporting is where the company handles their own exports. The investment and risk are somewhat greater in this strategy, but so is the potential return. A company can conduct direct exporting in several ways:

- It can set up a domestic export department that carries out export activities.
- It can set up an overseas sales branch that handles sales, distribution, and

promotion.

- It can send home-based salespeople abroad at certain times in order to find business.
- It can do its exporting either through foreign-based distributors or foreign-based agents.

6.2 Joint Venturing

Joint venturing is joining with foreign companies to produce or market products or services.

There are four types of joint ventures:

1. Licensing,
2. Contract manufacturing,
3. Management contracting, and
4. Joint ownership.

6.3 Licensing

Licensing is a simple way for a manufacturer to enter international marketing. The company enters into an agreement with a licensee in the foreign market. For a fee or royalty, the licensee buys the right to use the company's manufacturing process, trademark, patent, trade secret, or other item of value.

Licensing has disadvantages:

- The firm has less control over the licensee than it would over its own operations.
- If the licensee is very successful, the firm has given up profits.
- When the contract ends, it may find it has created a competitor.

6.4 Contract Manufacturing

Contract manufacturing occurs when the company contracts with manufacturers in the foreign market to produce its product or provide its service.

The drawbacks are:

- Decreased control over the manufacturing process.
- Loss of potential profits on manufacturing.

The benefits are:

- The chance to start faster, with less risk.
- The later opportunity either to form a partnership with or to buy out the local manufacturer.

216

6.5 Management Contracting

Management contracting takes place when the domestic firm supplies management know-how to a foreign company that supplies the capital. This is a low-risk method of getting into a foreign market, and it yields income from the beginning. The arrangement is not sensible if the company can put its management talent to better uses or if it can make greater profits by undertaking the whole venture.

6.6 Joint Ownership

Joint ownership ventures consist of one company joining forces with foreign investors to create a local business in which they share joint ownership and control. A company may buy an interest in a local firm, or the two parties may form a new business venture. Joint ownership may be needed for economic or political reasons.

Joint ownership has drawbacks:

- The partners may disagree over policies.
- Whereas U.S. firms emphasize the role of marketing, local investors may rely on selling.

6.7 Direct Investment

Direct investment is the development of foreign-based assembly or manufacturing facilities.

Advantages:

- Lower costs in the form of cheaper labor or raw materials, foreign government investment incentives, and freight savings.
- The firm may improve its image in the host country.
- Development of a deeper relationship with government, customers, local suppliers, and distributors.
- The firm keeps full control over the investment.

The main disadvantage of direct investment is that the firm faces many risks.

7. DECIDING ON THE GLOBAL MARKETING PROGRAM

Standardized global marketing is using largely the same marketing strategy approaches and marketing mix worldwide.

Adapted global marketing is adjusting the marketing strategy and mix elements to each target market, bearing more costs but hoping for a larger market share and return.

Some global marketers believe that technology is making the world a smaller place and

217

that consumer needs around the world are becoming more similar. This paves the way for "global brands" and standardized global marketing. Global branding and standardization, in turn, result in greater brand power and reduced costs from economies of scale. However, because cultural differences are hard to change, most marketers adapt their products, prices, channels, and promotions to fit consumer desires in each country.

7.1 Product

Five strategies exist allow for adapting product and marketing communication strategies to a global market (Figure 19.3).

- Straight product extension means marketing a product in a foreign market without any change.
- Product adaptation involves changing the product to meet local conditions or wants.
- Product invention consists of creating something new for a specific country market. This strategy can take two forms.

  o Maintaining or reintroducing earlier product forms that happen to be well adapted to the needs of a given country.
  o Create a new product to meet a need in a given country.

7.2 Promotion

Companies can either:

- Adopt the same communication strategy they used in the home market or
- Change it for each local market.

Colors are changed sometimes to avoid taboos in other countries. Communication adaptation is fully adapting their advertising messages to local markets.

7.3 Price

Regardless of how companies go about pricing their products, their foreign prices probably will be higher than their domestic prices for comparable products.

Why? It is a price escalation problem. It must add the cost of transportation, tariffs, importer margin, wholesaler margin, and retailer margin to its factory price.
To overcome this problem when selling to less-affluent consumers in developing countries, many companies make simpler or smaller versions of their products that can be sold at lower prices. Dumping occurs when a company either charges less than its costs or less than it charges in its home market. The Internet is making global price differences more obvious.

When firms sell their wares over the Internet, customers can to see how much products sell for in different countries. This is forcing companies toward more standardized international pricing.

7.4 Distribution Channels

The whole-channel view takes into account the entire global supply chain and marketing channel. It recognizes that to compete well internationally, the company must effectively design and manage an entire global value delivery network.

Figure 19.4 shows the two major links between the seller and the final buyer.

Channels between nations move company products from points of production to the borders of countries within which they are sold.

Channels within nations move the products from their market entry points to the final consumers.

8. DECIDING ON THE GLOBAL MARKETING ORGANIZATION

A firm normally gets into international marketing by simply shipping out its goods. If its international sales expand, the company organizes an export department. Many companies get involved in several international markets and ventures. An international division may be created to handle all its international activity.

International divisions are organized in a variety of ways.

- Geographical organizations: Country managers who are responsible for salespeople, sales branches, distributors, and licensees in their respective countries.
- World product groups: each responsible for worldwide sales of different product groups.
- International subsidiaries: each responsible for its own sales and profits.

Global organizations are companies that have stopped thinking of themselves as national marketers who sell abroad and have started thinking of themselves as global marketers.

Student Exercises

1.   Key Term: Global Firm

A global firm is a firm that, by operating in more than one country, gains R&D, production, marketing, and financial advantages in its costs and reputation that are not available to purely domestic competitors. The global company sees the world as one market. Research Saab automobile (www.saab.com). Would you consider Saab to be a global firm?

2.   Key Term: GATT

The General Agreement on Tariffs and Trade (GATT) is a 59-year-old treaty designed to promote world trade by reducing tariffs and other international grade barriers. The World Trade Organization (WTO) has the primary responsibility for overseeing GATT. Read this navigational guide to the WTO and GATT.
(http://www.wto.org/english/thewto_e/whatis_e/tif_e/agrm1_e.htm).

3.   Key Term: Economic Community

An economic community is a groups of nations organized to work toward common goals in the regulation of international trade. One such community is the European Union (EU). Today, the EU represents one of the world's single largest markets. Learn more about the European Union by going to http://europa.eu/index_en.htm.

4.   Key Term: NAFTA

In 1994, the North American Free Trade Agreement (NAFTA) established a free trade zone among the United States, Mexico, and Canada. The agreement created a single market of 435 million people. Assume you are a farmer in the U.S. wishing to get into the international arena by exporting to Mexico. How should NAFTA be of benefit to you?

5.   Key Term: Subsistence Economies

In a subsistence economy, the vast majority of people engage in simple agriculture. They consume most of their output and barter the rest for simple goods and services. While these economies offer few market opportunities, they do offer some. What types of goods and services might find a market in such economies?

6.   Key Term: Income Distribution

Income distribution is the spread of low-, medium-, and high-income households throughout a society. Many industrialized nations have a wide spread of income. In contrast, countries with subsistence economies may consist mostly of household with very low family incomes. Still other countries may have income distribution at only the high and low ends of the scale. Take a look at the income distribution for Mexico (one source is: http://www.photius.com/countries/mexico/) and compare it to the United States (www.census.gov). What similarities and differences do you note?

7.   Key Term: Exporting

Exporting is entering a foreign market by selling goods produced in the company's home country, often with little modification. Exporting involves the least change in the company's product lines, organization, investments, or mission. If you were a relatively small company (such as MikWright (www.mikwright.com)) just getting into the export game, how would you most likely choose to begin?

8.   Key Term: Licensing

Licensing is a method of entering a foreign market in which the company enters into an agreement with a licensee in the foreign market. Licensing is a simple way for a manufacturer to enter international marketing. Consider a company like Nordstrom (www.nordstrom.com). If Nordstrom was considering entering into a foreign market through licensing, what would be the risk?

9.   Key Term: Standardized Marketing Mix

A standardized marketing mix is an international marketing strategy for using basically the same product, advertising, distribution channels, and other marketing mix elements in all the company's international markets. Find a company that you believe practices a standardized marketing mix.

10.   Key Term: Communication Adaptation

Communication adaptation is a global communication strategy of fully adapting advertising messages to local markets. The same advertising messages do not work equally as well globally. Adaptation is typically necessary. Take a look at the homepage of Vaseline in the United Kingdom (www.vaseline.co.uk). How might this site and its contents be adapted for the U.S. market?

Marketing ADventure Exercises

1.   Ad Interpretation Challenge: Global Firm
        Ad: Auto – Audi

A global firm is a firm that, by operating in more than one country, gains R&D, production, marketing, and financial advantages in its costs and reputation that are not available to purely domestic competitors. The global company sees the world as one market, making adaptation to the marketing mix as is necessary for each market. Is Audi a true global company?

2.   Ad Interpretation Challenge: Tariffs
        Ad: Auto – Audi

Tariffs are basically taxes a government places on imported goods to either raise revenue or protect domestic produces (or both). Consider Audi. If the United States were to place high tariffs on the importation of German automobiles (such as Audi and Mercedes) in the country, what would be the negative impact on consumers?

3.   Ad Interpretation Challenge: GATT
        Ad: Student Choice

The GATT (General Agreement on Tariffs and Trade) is a decades-old treaty designed to promote world trade by reducing and eliminating tariffs and other international trade barriers. After reviewing the information regarding GATT, find an ad for a product that may well have benefited by the GATT treaty.

4.   Ad Interpretation Challenge: European Union
        Ad: Auto – Fiat

From its beginning in 1957, the European Union (EU) set out to create a single European market by reducing barriers to the free flow of products, services, finances, and labor among member countries and to develop policies on trade with nonmember countries. Consider the Italian company Fiat. If Fiat were having difficulty filling factory positions in Italy, how might Italy being a member of the EU be of value to them?

5.   Ad Interpretation Challenge: FTAA
        Ad: Food & Beverage – Brazilian Fruit

The yet to be established Free Trade Area of the Americas (FTAA) would create a mammoth free trade zone encompassing the 34 countries of North, Central, and South America. How might this benefit Brazil and its efforts to export more fruit to the U.S.?

6.   Ad Interpretation Challenge: Raw Material Exporting Economies
        Ad: Auto – Jaguar

Raw material exporting economies are economies rich in one or more natural resources but poor in other ways. Much of their revenue comes from exporting these resources. Why might Jaguar have a market in such an economy?

7.   Ad Interpretation Challenge: Industrializing Economies
        Ad: Student Choice

In an industrializing economy, manufacturing accounts for between 10 and 20 percent of the country's economy. Industrialization typically creates a new rich class and a small buy growing middle class. Find an ad for a product or service that would likely appeal to these emerging classes.

8.   Ad Interpretation Challenge: Cultural Environment
        Ad: Apparel – Levi's New Collection Diamond Jeans

Every county has its own folkways, norms, and taboos. What is easily acceptable in one country may be completely taboo in another. When developing global marketing strategies, companies must understand these cultural differences. Think about this ad for Levi's. Why might this advertisement not be acceptable in many Muslim cultures?

9.   Ad Interpretation Challenge: "Americanizing" the World
      Ad: Student Choice

There is a growing concern that some of the global marketing strategies of the largest firms are altering individual country cultures. The iconic symbols of large American multinational companies are becoming common place objects in cultures around the world. Critics worry that countries around the globe are losing their individual country cultures. Find an ad for a product that you believe has the potential to become an iconic global symbol of American culture.

10.   Ad Interpretation Challenge: Adapted Marketing Mix
       Ad: Apparel – Levi's New Collection Diamond Jeans

An adapted marketing mix is an international marketing strategy for adjusting the marketing mix elements to each international target market, bearing more costs but hoping for a larger market share and return. Look again at this ad for Levi's Diamond Jeans. How could you vary the marketing mix to make this product more acceptable to the Muslim community?

Chapter 20
Sustainable Marketing:
Social Responsibility and Ethics

Learning Objectives

1. Define sustainable marketing and discuss its importance.
2. Identify the major social criticisms of marketing.
3. Define consumerism and environmentalism and explain how they affect marketing strategies.
4. Describe the principles of socially responsible marketing.

Chapter Overview

In this final chapter, we look at the concepts of sustainable marketing, meeting the needs of consumers, businesses, and society – now and in the future – through socially and environmentally responsible marketing actions. The chapter begins with a definition of sustainable marketing and then looks at some common criticisms of marketing as it impacts individual consumers and other businesses. Next, it covers consumerism, environmentalism, and other citizen and public actions that promote sustainable marketing. Finally, the chapter looks at how companies themselves can benefit from proactively pursuing sustainable marketing practices that bring value not just to individual customers but also to society as a whole.

Sustainable marketing actions are more than just doing the right thing; they are also good for business.

Chapter Outline

1. INTRODUCTION

Patagonia is a longtime leader in sustainability since its founding in 1973. From the start, Patagonia has pursued a passionately-help social responsibility mission.

As early as 1991, Patagonia began a comprehensive Environmental Review Process, in which it examined all of the methods and materials used in making the company's clothing. Each year, since 1985, the company has given away 10 percent of its pretax profits to support environmental causes.

In May 2007, Patagonia founder Chouinard challenged a group of 10 employees to track five products from the design studio to Patagonia's Nevada distribution center. Late that year, Patagonia launched a microsite at Patagonia.com that featured detailed footprint information and videos (hence the name Footprint Chronicles).

They vowed to share whatever they found, good or bad. Patagonia's manufacturing was found to devour more energy than thought and sometimes created eco-unfriendly by-products. In the production of one of its products, the company used PFOA, a chemical that accumulates in the bloodstream and may be toxic. But doing away with the chemical would hurt performance of the product. The footprint-chronicling process highlights the complexity of modern technology. Patagonia's footprint efforts reflect a newly refined understanding of corporate social responsibility: "You're now responsible for the impacts of your suppliers." A group of firms with progressive sustainability agendas have long informally shared best practices with each other. These companies have been working together for years to raise the environmental responsibility bar.

2. SUSTAINABLE MARKETING

Sustainable marketing calls for meeting the present needs of consumers and businesses while also preserving or enhancing the ability of future generations to meet their needs. Figure 20.1 compares the sustainable marketing concept with other marketing concepts from earlier chapters.

The marketing concept recognizes that organizations thrive from day to day by deterring the current needs and wants of target group customers and fulfilling those needs and wants more effectively and efficiently than the competition. Whereas the societal marketing concept considers the future welfare of consumers and the strategic planning concept considers future company needs, the sustainable marketing concept considers both. Sustainable marketing calls for socially and environmentally responsible actions that meet both the immediate and future needs of customers and the company.

3. SOCIAL CRITICISMS OF MARKETING

3.1 Marketing's Impact on Individual Consumers

Consumer advocates, government agencies, and other critics have accused marketing of harming consumers through high prices, deceptive practices, high-pressure selling, shoddy or unsafe products, planned obsolescence, and poor service to disadvantaged consumers.

Deceptive practices fall into three groups:

1. Pricing,
2. Promotion,
3. Packaging.

Deceptive pricing includes practices such as falsely advertising "factory" or "wholesale" prices or a large price reduction from a phony high retail list price.

Deceptive promotion includes practices such as misrepresenting the product's features or performance or luring the customers to the store for a bargain that is out of stock.

Deceptive packaging includes exaggerating package contents through subtle design, using misleading labeling, or describing size in misleading terms.

The Wheeler-Lea Act gives the Federal Trade Commission (FTC) power to regulate Äunfair or deceptive acts or practices."

"Puffery" is defined as innocent exaggeration for effect.

3.2 Marketing's Impact on Society as a Whole

Critics have charged that the marketing system urges too much interest in material possessions. Business has been accused of overselling private goods at the expense of public goods. A way must be found to restore a balance between private and public goods. Options include the following:

- Make producers bear the full social costs of their operations.
- Make consumers pay the social costs.

Critics charge the marketing system with creating cultural pollution. Marketers answer the charges of "commercial noise" with these arguments:

- Because of mass-communication channels, some ads are bound to reach people who have no interest in the product and are therefore bored or annoyed.
- Ads make much of television and radio free to users and keep down the costs of magazines and newspapers.
- Today's consumers have alternatives.

3.3 Marketing's Impact on Other Businesses

Critics charge that a company's marketing practices can harm other companies and reduce competition. Three problems are involved:

- Acquisitions of competitors,
- Marketing practices that create barriers to entry, and
- Unfair competitive marketing practices.

4.0 CITIZEN AND PUBLIC ACTIONS TO REGULATE MARKETING

4.1 Consumerism

American business firms have been the targets of organized consumer movements on three occasions.

- The first consumer movement took place in the early 1900s. It was fueled by rising prices, Upton Sinclair's writings on conditions in the meat industry, and scandals in the drug industry.
- The second consumer movement, in the mid-1930s, was sparked by an upturn in consumer prices during the Great Depression and another drug scandal.
- The third movement began in the 1960s. Consumers had become better educated, products had become more complex and potentially hazardous, and people were unhappy with American institutions.

Consumerism is an organized movement of citizens and government agencies to improve the rights and power of buyers in relation to sellers.

Traditional sellers' rights include:

- The right to introduce any product in any size and style, provided it is not hazardous to personal health or safety; or, if it is, to include proper warnings and controls.
- The right to charge any price for the product, provided no discrimination exists among similar kinds of buyers.
- The right to spend any amount to promote the product, provided it is not defined as unfair competition.
- The right to use any product message, provided it is not misleading or dishonest in content or execution.
- The right to use any buying incentive programs, provided they are not unfair or misleading.

Traditional buyers' rights include:

- The right not to buy a product that is offered for sale.
- The right to expect the product to be safe.
- The right to expect the product to perform as claimed.

Consumer advocates call for the following additional consumer rights:

- The right to be well informed about important aspects of the product.
- The right to be protected against questionable products and marketing practices.
- The right to influence products and marketing practices in ways that will improve the "quality of life."

- The right to consume now in a way that will preserve the world for future generations of consumers.

4.2 Environmentalism

Environmentalism is an organized movement of concerned citizens, businesses, and government agencies to protect and improve people's living environment. The first wave of modern environmentalism in the United States was driven by environmental groups and concerned consumers in the 1960s and 1970s. The second environmentalism wave was driven by government, which passed laws and regulations during the 1970s and 1980s governing industrial practices impacting the environment. The third environmentalism wave is a merging of the first two waves in which companies are accepting more responsibility for doing no harm to the environment. More companies are adopting policies of environmental sustainability.

Figure 20.2 shows a grid that companies can use to gauge their progress toward environmental sustainability.

Pollution prevention - Eliminating or minimizing waste before it is created.

Product stewardship - Minimizing not just pollution from production and product design but all environmental impacts throughout the full product life cycle, and all the while reducing costs.

Design for environment (DFE) and cradle-to-cradle practices are practices that involve thinking ahead to design products that are easier to recover, reuse, or recycle and developing programs to reclaim products at the end of their lives.

4.3 Public Actions to Regulate Marketing

Many of the laws that affect marketing are listed in Chapter 3. The task is to translate these laws into the language that marketing executives understand as they make decisions.

5. BUSINESS ACTIONS TOWARD SUSTAINABLE MARKETING

5.1   Sustainable Marketing Principles

The philosophy of sustainable marketing holds that a company's marketing should support the best long-run performance of the marketing system. Enlightened marketing consists of five principles:

5.1.1. Consumer-Oriented Marketin

Consumer-oriented marketing means that the company should view and organize its marketing activities from the consumer's point of view.

5.1.2. Customer-Value Marketing

Customer-value marketing means the company should put most of its resources into customer value-building marketing investments. By creating value for consumers, the company can capture value from consumers in return.

5.1.3. Innovative Marketing

Innovative marketing requires that the company continuously seek real product and marketing improvements.

5.1.4. Sense-of-Mission Marketing

Sense-of-mission marketing means that the company should define its mission in broad social terms rather than narrow product terms.

5.1.5. Societal Marketing

Societal marketing means an enlightened company makes marketing decisions by considering consumers' wants and interests, the company's requirements, and society's long-run interests.

Products can be classified according to their degree of immediate consumer satisfaction and long-run consumer benefit. (Figure 20.4)

- Deficient products have neither immediate appeal nor long-run benefits.
- Pleasing products give high immediate satisfaction but may hurt consumers in the long run.
- Salutary products have low appeal but may benefit consumers in the long run; for instance.
- Desirable products give both high immediate satisfaction and high long-run benefits.

The concepts of sustainable marketing should not be difficult to understand, however, you should go through them carefully. Consumer-oriented marketing should certainly not be new, but the term will be.

5.2 Marketing Ethics (Table 20.1)

Corporate marketing ethics policies are broad guidelines that everyone in the organization must follow. What principle should guide companies and marketing managers on issues of ethics and social responsibility? One philosophy is that such issues are decided by the free market and legal system. A second philosophy puts responsibility not on the system but in the hands of individual companies and managers. Written codes and ethics programs do not ensure ethical behavior.

5.3 The Sustainable Company

Sustainable companies are those that create value for customers through socially, environmentally, and ethically responsible actions.

Sustainable marketing provides the context in which companies can build profitable customer relationships by creating value for customers in order to capture value from customers in return, now and in the future.

Student Exercises

1.　Key Term: High Advertising Costs

Marketers are always being accused of pushing up the prices on products to finance heavy advertising. A company may spend millions of dollars to advertise a product. Why can't they just cut back on the advertising and drop the price to the consumer? If you were responsible for the marketing of Dole pineapple (www.dole.com), how would you respond to such a statement?

2.　Key Term: Planned Obsolescence

Planned obsolescence is the practice of making products obsolete before they actually should need to be replaced. Critics charge that some producers continually change consumer concepts of acceptable styles to encourage more and earlier buying. Take a few minutes look at the new season of ready-to-wear fashion from BCBG (www.bcbg.com). How is it different from what you currently see being worn by women? Is BCBG engaging in planned obsolescence? How would marketers respond to this charge?

3.　Key Term: Consumerism

Consumerism is an organized movement of citizens and government agencies to improve the rights and power of buyers in relation to sellers. Consumers have not only the right but the responsibility to protect themselves instead of leaving this function entirely to someone else. Knowledge is one of the most powerful ways that the consumer can protect themselves. Knowing from whom you are buying, their reputation and standing in the market, provides the buyer with tremendous power. Look at the website for the Better Business Bureau (www.bbb.org). The Better Business Bureau provides the consumer with a wealth of information regarding merchants all around the country and in your home town. Take some time to look up some of your favorite companies.

4.　Key Term: Environmentalism

Environmentalists are concerned with marketing's effects on the environment. Environmentalism is an organized movement of concerned citizens, businesses, and government agencies to protect and improve people's living environment.

Environmentalists want people and organizations to operate with more care and concern for the environment. Take a look at Green Globe (www.greenglobe.org). Green Globe is selling land which it will then "green." How does this benefit consumers?

5.   Key Term: Environmental Sustainability

Environmental sustainability is a management approach that involves developing strategies that both sustain the environment and produce benefits for the company. Environmental sustainability takes on many forms. Review the Environmental Sustainability Grid from this chapter. Now, think about Patagonia (www.patagonia.com). Where does Patagonia fit on this grid?

6.   Key Term: Innovative Marketing

Innovative marketing is a principle of enlightened marketing that requires a company seek real product and marketing improvements. The company that overlooks new and better ways to do things will eventually lose customers to another company that has found a better way. Find a company that you believe exemplifies innovative marketing.

7.   Key Term: Sense-of-Mission Marketing

Sense-of-mission marketing is a principle of enlightened marketing that holds a company should define its mission in broad social terms rather than narrow product terms. Brands linked with broad social missions can serve the best long-run interests of both the brand and the consumer. Take a look at Starbucks (www.starbucks.com). How is there sense-of-mission made evident to consumers?

8.   Key Term: Societal Marketing

Societal marketing is a principle of enlightened marketing that holds a company should make marketing decisions by considering consumers' wants, the company's requirement, consumers' long-run interests, and society's long-run interests. Alert companies view societal problems as opportunities. Locate a company that practices societal marketing.

9.   Key Term: Pleasing Products

Pleasing products are products that give high immediate satisfaction but may hurt consumers in the long run. From a societal marketing standpoint, companies should question their long-term commitment to such products. Your text cites cigarettes and junk food as examples. What about alcohol? Do you believe alcohol fits into this category? Take a look at some of producers' websites (www.stoli.com; www.barcardi.com; www.millerlite.com) for more information.

10.	Key Term: Desirable Products

Products (or services) that give both high immediate satisfaction and high long-run benefits to consumers are known as desirable products. Companies should try to turn all of their products into desirable products. Do you believe Hard Rock Casinos (www.hardrock.com/casinos) to be a desirable product?

Marketing ADventure Exercises

1.	Ad Interpretation Challenge: Planned Obsolescence
	Ad: Apparel – Levi's New Collection Diamond Jeans

Critics have charged that some producers follow a program of planned obsolescence, causing their products to become obsolete before they actually should need replacement. Consider this ad for Levi's. Why might some say this is an ad for a planned obsolescence product?

2.	Ad Interpretation Challenge: "Shop till You Drop"
	Ad: Apparel – Johnsons

The term "shop till you drop" seems to have characterized the go-go 1980s and 1990s, when the drive for wealth and possessions hit new highs. Critics have charged that the marketing system urges too much interest in material possessions. How might this ad for Johnsons encourage this "shop till you drop" mentality?

3.	Ad Interpretation Challenge: "Congestion Toll"
	Ad: Auto – Porsche

Business has been accused of overselling private goods at the expense of public goods. As private goods increase, they typically require more public services that are usually not forthcoming. A way must be found to restore a balance between private and public goods. Why might Porsche be subjected to a congestion toll in some cities?

4.	Ad Interpretation Challenge: Consumerism
	Ad: Food & Beverage – McDonalds

Consumerism is an organized movement of citizens and government agencies to improve the rights and power of buyers in relation to sellers. Consumers have not only the right but the responsibility to protect themselves instead of leaving this function entirely to someone else. How might McDonalds possibly find themselves on the wrong end of the consumerism movement?

5.   Ad Interpretation Challenge: Environmental Sustainability
       Ad: Apparel – Timberland

Environmental sustainability is a management approach that involves developing strategies that both sustain the environment and produce benefits for the company. Simply stated, environmental sustainability is about generating profits while helping to save the planet. Environmental sustainability takes on many forms. Go to Timberland's website (http://www.timberland.com/timberlandserve/timberlandserve_index.jsp) and learn about their belief in environmental sustainability.

6.   Ad Interpretation Challenge: Consumer-Oriented Marketing
       Ad: Student Choice

Consumer-oriented marketing means that the company should view and organize its marketing activities from the consumer's point of view. It should work hard to sense, serve, and satisfy the needs of a defined group of customers. Find an ad for a company that you believe practices consumer-oriented marketing.

7.   Ad Interpretation Challenge: Innovative Marketing
       Ad: Apparel – Polartec

The principle of innovative marketing requires that the company continuously seek real product and marketing improvements. Why does Polartec (www.polartec.com) fit here? Or does it?

8.   Ad Interpretation Challenge: Sense-of-Mission Marketing
       Ad: Travel & Tourism – Wild Drift

Sense-of-mission marketing is a principle of enlightened marketing that holds a company should define its mission in broad social terms rather than narrow product terms. Take a look at these ads for Wild Drift Adventures. How do you believe sense-of-mission marketing fits in with this company?

9.   Ad Interpretation Challenge: Pleasing Products
       Ad: Student Choice

Pleasing products are products that give high immediate satisfaction but may hurt consumers in the long run. From a societal marketing standpoint, companies should question their long-term commitment to such products. Locate an ad that is promoting a product you could consider as fitting into this category.

10.   Ad Interpretation Challenge: Marketing Ethics
       Ad: Auto – Jeep

Because not all managers have finely-tuned moral sensitivity, companies need to develop corporate marketing ethics policies. These are broad guidelines that everyone in the organization must follow. Consider Jeep. If Jeep were attempting to initiate business in another country (Saudi Arabia, for example), should they be held accountable to marketing ethics as practiced in the United States or marketing ethics as practiced in the foreign country?

Suggested Answers

Chapter 1

Student Exercises

1.   Apple: Right up front, Apple highlights "news" concerning their products—from an iPod on the international space station to praise from recent product reviews. This format helps to pull in new customers by showing Apple products as advanced, user-friendly, and "cool." Cingular: Prominently displayed on the home page is a graphic which alternates between touting the Cingular network as having the fewest dropped calls and claiming to have the best phones AND the best plans. What a great way to pull in new customers while reinforcing your present customers. American Cancer Society: The "I need information for…" link dominate on the ACS home page makes it easy for new visitors to quickly find the information they are seeking. Likewise, return guests are presented with links to take them to their personalized page.

2.   In this case, Bank of America is presenting a "market offering" designed to provide information on and possible solutions to the problems around residents' lack of grocery stores and nutritious food choices.

3.   The HD-DVD does a much better job of connecting with the customer and focusing on customer-related benefits. Blu-ray just doesn't seem to be focused on benefits to the consumer. Too much emphasis is given to the technology and how great it is, while overlooking the customer.

4.   A quick review of their websites leads you to believe that Starbucks is targeting a more "sophisticated" coffee drinker by placing emphasis on its music offerings and the lushness of its stores. Caribou, on the other hand, comes across as targeting a more "outdoorsy," fun crowd. Caribou retail locations also follow this theme by their rustic décor and furnishings.

5.   Tobacco manufacturers are in a difficult position. Their primary product is one that has been shown to be harmful to their customers, with long-term use. On the other hand, to just stop the manufacture and marketing of the product, not only divests the companies of their livelihood but also deprives their customers of a product they desire. All the companies mentioned here are trying to walk this tightrope by providing their customers with lots of easily accessible information about the dangers of smoking and where to turn to for help if they are trying to give it up.

6.   Many universities today are offering condensed classes during traditional break periods (like Christmas or Spring Break). Schools are also offering more weekend and on-line classes, in an effort to better serve their increasingly diverse population.

7.   Several examples may come readily to mind, including airline partner alliances, such as SkyTeam (www.skyteam.com), OneWorld (www.oneworld.com), and Star Alliance (www.staralliance.com). Another notable example is the Caribbean Tourism Organization (www.doitcaribbean.com).

8.   Here you are looking for local companies that you believe have done a good job of maintaining and growing customers. The most successful companies are those that are able to acquire a customer relatively early on and then "grow" that customer. "Growing" a customer refers to having that customer return for more and more additional (hopefully, higher margin) products and/or services.

9.   When looking at how globalization has impacted you directly, don't just think about whether you believe you may someday be working overseas. Look at the labels in the clothes you wear. Think about the car you drive and where either the car or its components were made. It's hard to escape the impact of globalization in our lives. It truly is everywhere.

10.   When considering companies you believe have a social responsibility mindset, you might want to think about those who place their responsibility to society right up front. For example, take a look at companies such as Newman's Own (www.newmansown.com), Starbucks coffee (www.starbucks.com), Chevron (www.chevron.com), and Syngenta (www.syngenta.com).

Marketing ADventure Exercises

1.   Ad Interpretation Challenge: New Marketing Frontiers
        Ad: Apparel—Levi's New Collection

Levi's have been negatively impacted by the move to more "fashion"-oriented jeans (for example, Citizens of Humanity and 7 for All Mankind). Levi has been viewed as a rather traditional company offering traditional products. This ad shows that the company's market offering includes the non-traditional, fashion-forward products today's consumers crave.

2.   Ad Interpretation Challenge: Insightful Segmentation
        Ad: Electronics—Compaq

Compaq is appealing to the socially conscious consumer with this ad. They are targeting the consumer who wants and expects more from the companies they do business with than just a quality product. In essence, they are saying "We know you have a choice of many computer companies with which to do business. However, we are more than just a computer company; we are also a socially conscious member of our community, working to make life better for those with need."

3. Ad Interpretation Challenge: The Production Concept
    Ad: Student Choice

You should be looking for an ad that highlights the principles of the production concept—for example, an ad that focuses on a product's wide availability and/or affordability. Ad examples may include Pepsi and/or IKEA.

4. Ad Interpretation Challenge: The Marketing Concept
    Ad: Travel and Tourism—Leisure Entertainment—Bali

This ad is appealing to the basic hedonistic need that people have to just unwind and relax. The ad is successful because it, first, recognizes the consumer need and then, second, provides the reader with an avenue of satisfying this need.

5. Ad Interpretation Challenge: The Marketing Concept
    Ad: Student Choice

Keeping in mind the marketing concept is a customer-driven concept, you may want to consider either the ad for Polartec (Apparel – Polartec) or the ad for Tabasco (Food & Beverage – Tobasco). Both of these ads highlight the benefits to consumers from the use and consumption of the products.

6. Ad Interpretation Challenge: What's Good for Society
    Ad: Auto—Hyundai Avante

The company is fulfilling its societal interests by producing and marketing a vehicle with exceptionally high fuel economy. At the same time, they are providing a product with appeal to the marketplace, thus resulting (hopefully) in increased sales.

7. Ad Interpretation Challenge: Value
    Ad: General Retail—World's Biggest Bookstore

This ad just screams "Value!" By claiming to have book prices so low that even those who do not typically read can afford them, World's Biggest Bookstore is showing how they provide the customer with exceptional value.

8. Ad Interpretation Challenge: Making the Customer Happy
    Ad: Auto—Volvo S60

This ad highlighting the Volvo S60 wears its customer loyalty (hence customer satisfaction) on its arm, literally. This is one example of an ad prominently exhibiting the central component of the ad. Other examples you might select include: Food and Beverage—Winterfresh and Autos—Mercedes.

9.   Ad Interpretation Challenge: Club Marketing Program
        Ad: Student Choice

You may want to consider the ad for MBNA (Financial—MBNA). This ad highlights a product that seeks customers with a common interest and works to create a member community—those customers loyal to Clemson University.

10.   Ad Interpretation Challenge: Increasing Lifetime Value and Customer
        Equity
        Ad: Auto—Jaguar

These ads seek to distinguish Jaguar from other competitors in the luxury automobile category by portraying Jaguars as different from the "run-of-the-mill" luxury auto. At the same time, the ads are a departure from previous Jaguar advertising by emphasizing a more youthful, playful image and deemphasizing the stogy traditional image that has for so long dominated Jaguar ads. As a result, the ads should appeal to younger consumers. The resulting hope is that these consumers will make their initial Jaguar purchase and then stay with the brand as they grow and mature in their lives.

Chapter 2

Student Exercises

1.   Recognizing the increasingly competitive global automobile environment, Ford has announced a plan to direct additional attention to worldwide markets and customers. Additionally, acknowledging the squeeze on profits, Ford has undertaken efforts to improve leverage of global assets and capabilities.

2.   All three of these mission statements emphasize putting the customer first. Starbucks, however, goes much further with their mission statement by emphasizing the relationship between the company, the environment, the customer, the supplier, and the communities in which they operate.

3.   Ford Motor Company is made up of a number of different products and businesses including: Ford, Mercury, Jaguar, Land Rover, and Ford Credit.

4.   Numerous possibilities exist that would fulfill this requirement. You might want to consider taking a look at either Waffle House (www.wafflehouse.com), which has now started accepting credit cards, or Subway (www.subway.com), which continues to rapidly open more and more locations.

5.   This is a wide-open question with multiple possible solutions. Take a look at either Monarch Beverage Company (www.monarchbeverages.com) or Quinenco S.A. (www.quinenco.cl) for two good examples.

6.   You might want to consider IBM (www.ibm.com) who recently sold its personal computer business to Levono (www.levono.com), a Chinese company. You may also wish to take a look at Alcoa (www.alcoa.com), which recently completed the sale of its specialty chemicals division.

7.   Without a doubt, Rolls Royce is targeting to the ultra-luxury car customer. They are directing themselves toward that consumer who wants the best, has the means to purchase the best, and is willing to do so. On the other hand, Chery, who is seeking to begin selling cars in the United States, is targeting the most financially cautious customer—those consumers who have very limited funds to spend on an automobile.

8.   Local restaurants can choose to position themselves in many ways. They may decide they want to be known as "home grown" and local, catering to the community and being a part of that community. Or, they may want to be known as an upscale establishment, where only the most social elite are welcome. Many other possible positioning strategies exist from which your favorite restaurant may choose.

9.   The product being offered, in the case of Southwest Airlines, is transportation. Just because it is not a physical entity does not mean it is not a product. Price is the amount of money customers have to pay in order to receive the product. In the case of airlines, this price is very volatile and changes frequently based on availability, time from departure, and a myriad of other variables. Place involves everything that Southwest does to make its product available to the consumer. Not only the airports, but the ticket counters and self-service kiosks. Finally, promotion is everything involved in communicating Southwest to the customer. This includes traditional television and billboard advertising. This also includes their easy to navigate website and their enthusiastic employees.

10.   When considering the SWOT analysis for your school, keep in mind that you need to view your school from a dispassionate or neutral point of view. Only in this manner can you truly see what challenges and problems it may be facing.

Marketing ADventure Exercises

1.   Ad Interpretation Challenge: The Mission Statement
        Ad: Apparel—Polartec

Polartec's mission statement could read something like this: "We seek to be the premier provider of high performance cold weather clothing for the extreme outdoor enthusiast."

2.   Ad Interpretation Challenge: Distinctive Competencies
        Ad: Apparel—Umbro

Football. Umbro is making the statement that they are the authority and/or leader in providing football (soccer) footwear. Their ads make very clear to the viewer that this is their distinctive competency.

3.   Ad Interpretation Challenge: Business Portfolio
        Ad: Food and Beverage—Pizza World

The new product the ad is promoting is a seafood pizza—a product not typically found in the collection of products offered by most pizza restaurants.

4.   Ad Interpretation Challenge: Stars
        Ad: Student Choice

Several examples exist. You may want to examine the ad for Sony's PlayStation (Electronics—PlayStation). Certainly, PlayStation would be considered a star in the gaming market, with its high-market share in a high-growth market.

5.   Ad Interpretation Challenge: Market Penetration
      Ad: General Retail—Drugmart

Drugmart is reaching out to its current market segment by informing them of home delivery of their drug order. In this way, they are attempting to set themselves apart from the competition and entice more of their current market segment to increase frequency of use.

6.   Ad Interpretation Challenge: Market Development
      Ad: Travel and Tourism—Turkish Airlines

With this ad, Turkish Airlines is introducing new and expanded service. The company does not appear to be reaching out to new market segments; rather, they are providing new services to their existing customers.

7.   Ad Interpretation Challenge: Value Chain
      Ad: Exhibits and Entertainment—D-Day (Melting Pot)

This ad is a great example of how a value chain actually works. In a value chain, the sum of the individual members is greater (and, thus, provides greater value) than the individual members. Through coordinated work together, the members of the D-Day forces were able to overcome incredible odds and carry the day—something none of the solo players would have been able to accomplish individually.

8.   Ad Interpretation Challenge: The Value-Delivery Network
      Ad: Internet—Shopnow

This ad shows how Shopnow acts as a clearinghouse for over 50,000 stores. This relationship allows the consumer to compare stores, products, and prices in one place. The ultimate goal is providing the customer with superior value.

9.   Ad Interpretation Challenge: Product Positioning
      Ad: Auto—Lincoln

SUVs have gotten a lot of attention lately, in part due to the ever-increasing price of gasoline and their relatively poor mileage performance. Lincoln shifts the emphasis to safety. In this ad Lincoln is positioning the Navigator as "big." Along with this large size comes occupant safety.

10.   Ad Interpretation Challenge: The Product
      Ad: Student Choice

You may want to consider the ad for Rimmel (Cosmetics and Pharmaceuticals—Rimmel) or Scholl (Cosmetics and Pharmaceuticals—Scholl). Both of these ads downplay the actual product; however, they still make certain you realize its importance.
Marketing ADventure Exercises

Chapter 3

Student Exercises

1.   While the microenvironment is going to vary from school to school, all are faced with some of the same basic microenvironmental actors, such as availability of qualified teachers and support personnel, alumni, quantity and quality of students (both current and potential), and the physical plant.

2.   From a review of Amazon.com's website, you will find that they partner with both the USPS and UPS to efficiently deliver their merchandise. Also, Amazon has partnered with and makes heavy use of banner advertising on sites such as Google.com and CNN.com in an effort to draw more customers to the Amazon site. Bebe, a moderately-pricy and trendy women's clothing store, makes exclusive use of UPS to deliver their products. Additionally, Bebe is a featured store occasionally on the Style Channel's "The Look for Less," providing the store with increased exposure and promotional opportunities.

3.   Many publics have an interest in or impact on your school. Your administrators must consider, among others, you (students), parents, the community, funding sources (private and public), alumni, and employers. This is many different people to try and take into consideration when making organizational decisions.

4.   There are so many possible answers to this question. You may want to consider taking a look at Curves Fitness (www.curves.com), a fitness center that caters to older women, and SeaRay (www.searay.com), a yacht manufacturing company whose primary clientele are baby boomer males.

5.   Just a casual look at the Scion website will let you know that this is not your typical car website or your typical car. Everything about the site screams Generation Y, from the use of language to the music played. Take the time to "build" your favorite car. This process reveals much that is geared toward the sensibilities of Gen Y.

6.   This is becoming a bit harder to do, as more and more companies recognize the changes and shifts in the American household. However, consider these two examples: Beaches Family Resorts (www.beaches.com) and McDonald's (www.mcdonalds.com). Find others.

7.   Abercrombie takes great care in the selection of their spokespersons and models to ensure they project the image of the company. That is not to say the spokespersons and models actually mirror the typical Abercrombie customer.

8.   These decisions are not contradictory to Engel's Law. All Jaguar and BMW are doing is making less expensive products available that appeal to consumers in less affluent income brackets. These customers typically spend the same percentage of their income on transportation as do consumers in higher income categories. By offering lower

priced products, these companies are making it possible for more consumers to experience their products, while still maintaining spending on transportation at the same constant rate.

9.   There are so many recent accomplishments that it is difficult to name just four. However, you might want to consider camera phones (www.nokia.com, www.samsung.com as two examples), nanites used for microsurgery (www.nanobites.com), LASIK eye surgery to correct vision (www.fda.gov/cdrh/lasik), and the cloning of animals (www.time.com/time/newsfiles/cloning). Many more recent examples exist.

10.   How do you feel about this? The products are legal, yet we are increasingly seeing it targeted for restrictive regulations. Just because we may not personally like the product, does that give us (or others) the right to "unfairly" restrict its use? It's a debate that will continue for the foreseeable future.

Marketing ADventure Exercises

1.   Ad Interpretation Challenge: The Macroenvironment
        Ad: Auto—Hyundai Avante

Hyundai is positioning the Avante as a very fuel-efficient vehicle. Fuel efficiency today is about more than just saving a few dollars at the gas station (although that is certainly of great importance!). Fuel efficiency today (and Hyundai's lean burn technology) is also about saving the environment from undue emissions and, at the same time, helping to conserve a dwindling natural resource (petroleum).

2.   Ad Interpretation Challenge: The Macroenvironment
        Ad: Food and Beverage—McDonald's

Healthy living and healthy eating are two current cultural trends that can cause some difficulties for fast food companies known for producing and marketing calorie- and fat-intensive products. McDonald's is addressing these cultural issues partially by affiliating themselves with the Olympic games of Sydney.

3.   Ad Interpretation Challenge: Marketing Intermediaries
        Ad: Student Choice

Although several examples exist, you may want to take a look at the ad for Sedex (Services and B2B—Sedex) or the ads for the Italian postal system (Services and B2B—Posta).

4.   Ad Interpretation Challenge: Competition
      Ad: Student Choice

Consider the following as possible solutions to this question: Fiat's air conditioning (Auto—Fiat); Honda's claim of having the sportiest sedan (Auto—Honda); or LG's ad for its televisions (Electronics—LG).

5.   Ad Interpretation Challenge: Publics
      Ad: Auto—Cadillac Escalade

Although this ad is obviously appealing to the SUV owner (or potential owner) looking for more power and performance, Cadillac might also pay attention to Media Publics (as more and more negativity is written about gas-guzzling SUVs) and General Publics (as the public, in general, reexamines its love affair with high-performance vehicles).

6.   Ad Interpretation Challenge: Demography
      Ad: Travel and Tourism—Leisure Entertainment

The general aging of the U.S. population is the basis of this ad—from a standpoint of demography. As the baby boom generation continues to gray and reach retirement age, we are witnessing a large increase in expenditures on leisure activities, with "exotic" travel at the front of the list.

7.   Ad Interpretation Challenge: Baby Boomers
      Ad: Student Choice

Take a look at either the ad for Schwab (Financial—Schwab) that is using Ringo Starr of the Beatles fame as spokesperson or one of the two Jaguar ads (Auto—Jaguar) that are touting the understated elegance of this brand.

8.   Ad Interpretation Challenge: Generation Y
      Ad: Apparel—Levis New Collection

Generation Y (a.k.a., echo boomers) are those 72 million people born between 1977 and 2000. After several years of decline, this generation has given a new boom to the market for fashion clothing. They also have the money to spend on such items. Levi's has tailored their product offering to reach this generation by designing or redesigning much of their clothing to reflect a more "modern" time.

9.   Ad Interpretation Challenge: The "Traditional Family"
      Ad: Auto—Toyota

This ad is for a Toyota minivan—a family icon. The ad is stressing safety, surely an important factor to consider in the purchase of a family vehicle in which to carry the children.

10.   Ad Interpretation Challenge: Diversity
       Ad: Nonprofit Corporate Images—Nike

These three ads for Nike are all dealing with people with disabilities. Nike is saying "Yes, these people are different. But why are they REALLY different? They are different because they are achievers."

Chapter 4

Student Exercises

1.   Today, colleges and universities are continually reviewing course offerings—taking a look at what classes they are offering, when they are offered, and who is enrolling in them. From this and other information they are able to change or modify what and when courses are offered in an effort to better meet the needs of today's busy students.

2.   You would want to have available to you both secondary information (information that already exists somewhere) and primary information (information that is collected for the specific purpose at hand).

3.   The magazine presents secondary statistics in its media kit. Here you will find all kinds of results derived from secondary research, including retail sales figures and sales tax estimates.

4.   There is so much information available here that it would be easy to end up with a case of information overload. Here you can find information pertaining to household composition, size, income, and health insurance—among much more. The government makes readily available a wealth of information that may be of great importance and use to marketers. All we have to do is take the time to look.

5.   It is truly amazing the capabilities of Zoomerang – and there are several other online survey houses that operate in a similar manner. You will have noticed the ease with which you were able to create your own online survey. Think how easy it can be to now conduct online survey research

6.   There are many ways to answer this question. You could, for example, make use of a focus group of children to delve into what kids like and dislike about the pizza-eating experience—maybe the chairs are too big for them or maybe the pizza slices are too large for their smaller mouths. Alternatively, you might employ a focus group to find in-depth insight into how your current customers view CiCi's relative to your primary competition.

7.   Keep in mind that you can not survey everyone. In determining who to sample, you must think of who would be most impacted if your school moved totally online—current students, prospective students? When considering how many people to sample, remember that the more people you sample the more it costs. However, typically speaking, the more you sample the better the information. Sample selection comes down to either probability or nonprobability sampling. Be sure to look at the advantages and disadvantages of each.

8.   You can pretty much look anywhere to fulfill this question. For many websites, when you initially sign up or register, you are required to fill out a registration and/or personal interest form. These are examples of online questionnaires.

9.   Harrah's Entertainment (highlighted in your text) uses data mining to manage day-to-day relationships with important customers at its properties around the world (see Real Marketing 4.1).

10.   You can use many of the techniques of marketing research in a less formal manner and with little or no expense. Among the many possibilities for informal and inexpensive research are just driving around the area to see what other coffee shops are around. While you are doing this, you can also get a feel for how much business they have and the type of customers that frequent them. Additionally, through observing the shops over time, you can get a feel for both busy and slack times.

Marketing ADventure Exercises

1.   Ad Interpretation Challenge: Marketing Information System
       Ad: Services and B2B—24 Hour Fitness

This is a company that is catering to the need of its customers to have access to a health club at any time of the day or night. You might want to check out their website for more information about them—www.24hourfitness.com. Through the use of a marketing information system, this company may have been able to pinpoint a weakness in the existing market for fitness clubs. They filled that niche by providing a club to which members have 24-hour access.

2.   Ad Interpretation Challenge: Internal Data
       Ad: Apparel—Puma

Puma and its customers are widely believed to be fanatics of football (soccer). A review of Puma's internal database would likely confirm this belief. Based on this, ads could be created which serve to highlight this passion, thereby helping to reinforce the image and draw others with like beliefs to the brand.

3.   Ad Interpretation Challenge: Internal Data
       Ad: Services and B2B—University of Toronto

As a routine matter, colleges and universities gather information about their graduates, compiling information such as for whom they work, where they are located, and how much they make. This information is useful for all kinds of things, such as staying in touch with you after you graduate and encouraging you to be active in your university's alumni association. Also, if you happen to have some graduates who have gone on to truly distinguish themselves, it can serve as a good way to entice future students.

4.   Ad Interpretation Challenge: Causal Research
        Ad: Student Choice

You might want to consider the ad for Advil (Cosmetics and Pharmaceuticals—Advil), which suggests that by taking Advil your splitting headache will go away. Also, take a look at the ad for Virgin Atlantic (Travel and Tourism—Virgin Atlantic). This ad leaves you with the idea that travel on Virgin will result in pleasure (hence, the smile).

5.   Ad Interpretation Challenge: Secondary Data
        Ad: Auto—Cadillac Escalade

This ad for Cadillac is promoting the new Escalade as the most powerful SUV in the world. Cadillac did not go out and actually measure the horsepower of every other available SUV in the world. Cadillac relied on previously published information to arrive at their conclusion. This previously published information is secondary data.

6.   Ad Interpretation Challenge: Primary Data
        Ad: Autos—Dunlop

Dunlop is saying that this particular advertised tire is an extremely quite tire. This is an example of findings from the company's primary research. The results of the research pertain to only this product. They are not making comparisons to any other company and/or product, which would most likely require the use of secondary data sources.

7.   Ad Interpretation Challenge: Ethnographic Research
        Ad: Student Choice

Consider the advertisements for the Audi A2 (Auto—Audi). These ads highlight the way the younger target market lives and spends time—areas in which ethnographic research excels.

8.   Ad Interpretation Challenge: Contact Methods—Personal
        Ad: Financial—Alliance

In this ad Lucy is questioning Snoopy about his financial affairs. This is a great example of using the personal contact method to collect information.

9.   Ad Interpretation Challenge: Data Mining
        Ad: Internet—EPage

EPage, a marketing research company, uses data mining to put its clients on "the same page" as their customers. Data mining has the potential to uncover information about the wants, desires, and dislikes of your customers that you may have easily overlooked.

10.   Ad Interpretation Challenge: Public Policy
       Ad: Nonprofit Corporate Images—Labatt

Labatt is addressing the issue of alcohol overindulgence. Alcoholic beverages are enjoyed by millions every day; however, a significant percentage has a problem in knowing when to stop. Labatt, along with alcoholic beverage producers everywhere, are facing this issue head-on and attempting to help the problem drinker by encouraging them to consume in moderation.

Chapter 5

Student Exercises

1.   RJR presents their products to adults only. They provide information about the disadvantages of consuming their product and they provide information for those who are currently smoking but wish to cease. In so doing, RJR is acting as a good corporate citizen by making their product available to those who desire it, while, at the same time, assisting those who wish to give it up.

2.   All schools are scrambling to adequately serve a number of diverse markets. For example, the nontraditional student now makes up a sizable portion of most college enrollments. Just a few years ago this was not the case. As a result, colleges and universities are offering more night and weekend classes to reach this important subculture. Nights and weekends allow the members of this group to continue their full-time employment while attending classes.

3.   A quick review of their website makes it apparent that Chevrolet takes the Hispanic market very seriously. Right up front on the site is an option to have the entire site presented in Spanish. This is one of the easiest, yet most effective, methods for appealing to this submarket.

4.   The mature market can be a very lucrative market for companies to tap into. The U.S. population of mature consumers will more than double in the next 25 years, to over 130 million. Many companies have found it very profitable to cater exclusively to this group. Possibly the most prominent company devoted to this important subsegment is AARP (www.aarp.com).

5.   Bentleys are exclusive, high-priced automobiles. They definitely appeal to the Upper Class. Within the Upper Class, there are two subdivisions, Upper Uppers and Lower Uppers. You could make the argument that Bentleys appeal equally well to either.

6.   Early on, Scion made a name by positioning their vehicles as young, exciting, and energetic alternatives to traditional automotive alternatives. On their homepage you will find many references to and photos of attractive, trendy young people—just the type person that Scion used to get the word out about the brand.

7.   More and more companies today are using children as a conduit to reach parents. Take a look at some children's magazines, such as Nickelodeon Magazine (www.nick.com) or National Geographic Kids (www.nationalgeographic.com). Consider how some of the ads in these kid's magazines are actually there to sell products to adults—through influencing their kids.

8.   Whether your lifestyle is active, sedentary, flamboyant, or demure, the way you live and spend money helps define who you really are.

9.   Safety and security are big business today. Companies that specialize in this lower level need have seen their business increase over the past years. Log on the ADT (www.adt.com) or Brinks (www.brinkshomesecurity.com) and take a look at what these companies (and this is only two of many) have to offer in the way of home security.

10.   L.L. Bean makes a big deal out of their guarantee. They guarantee everything purchased from them will be 100% satisfactory or they will give you your money back. While many merchants make similar claims, L.L. Bean goes further than most. Their customers have the opportunity to return anything to them AT ANY TIME for a replacement or a refund.

Marketing ADventure Exercises

1.   Ad Interpretation Challenge: Cultural Shifts
        Ad: Apparel—Levi's New Collection

Many people believed that Levi's missed the boat in the current trend of fashion jeans. New competitors entered the marketplace and took away some of Levi's fashion-conscious customers. Now they are fighting back. Their new line of rhinestone-studded jeans raises the bar for fashion-conscious customers.

2.   Ad Interpretation Challenge: Subcultures
        Ad: Autos—Chevy S10 Truck

The easiest way to see that this ad is geared to the Hispanic submarket is through language. The ad is presented in Spanish. If a company is serious about servicing this group, this is a minimum requirement.

3.   Ad Interpretation Challenge: Mature Consumers
        Ad: Student Choice

You need to look for products that seem to "fit" with this submarket of the population. Remember, they have the money to spend and the time to enjoy spending it. You might want to take a look at the ads for either Cadillac (Autos—Cadillac) or Leisure Entertainment (Bali) (Travel and Tourism—Leisure Entertainment).

4.   Ad Interpretation Challenge: Social Class
        Ad: Autos—Jaguar

It seems as though Jaguar has always had a bit of mystique here in the United States. By looking at these ads and reading the copy, it appears Jaguar is reaching out to the Upper Class. Within that class, there are two subclasses—the Upper Uppers and the Lower Uppers. Through a review of the definitions for these two subclasses, one can conclude Jaguar is directing their advertising to the Lower Uppers.

5.   Ad Interpretation Challenge: Opinion Leader
      Ad: Internet—Leaping Salmon

By providing early adopters of its products with additional incentives (such as discounts, free products, or cash), Leaping Salmon is encouraging these individuals to get out and tell others about the product. Keep in mind that early adopters are the opinion leaders.

6.   Ad Interpretation Challenge: Family
      Ad: Food and Beverage—McDonald's Happy Meal

This ad targets at least two members of the family buying organization—the parent and the child.

7.   Ad Interpretation Challenge: Life-Cycle
      Ad: Financial—MasterCard Home Alone

This ad is targeted toward younger, singles still living at home. To target a different stage of the life-cycle it would only be necessary to change to prop contained in the ad and the associated wording.

8.   Ad Interpretation Challenge: Brand Personality
      Ad: Student Choice

The brand personality trait of "sophistication" is characterized as "upper class and charming." For examples, look at the ads for Jaguar and Imperial hotel. The ads for Jaguar (Autos—Jaguar) and Imperial Hotel (Travel and Leisure—Imperial Hotel) both display the characteristics of sophistication.

9.   Ad Interpretation Challenge: Selective Attention
      Ad: Cosmetics and Pharmaceuticals—Schick

When you initially look at this ad for Schick, you may notice the woman in the swimsuit. Only when you take a closer look at the ad are you likely to see the Schick razor placed in the lower left-hand corner. This is the problem. Many times when we first see an ad, we do not pick up all of the information the marketers wants (and needs) us to.

10.   Ad Interpretation Challenge: Information Search
      Ad: Student Choice

Many of the ads will easily satisfy the requirements of this question. Differences primarily lie in the amount of information provided to the reader. At the minimal information end of the spectrum is the ad for Buenos Aires traffic laws (Nonprofit Corporate Image—Buenos Aires). The ad is not designed to give the viewer information with which to compare products. This ad is designed to provide the viewer with minimal crucial information. On the other hand, consider the ad for Fiat's air-conditioning (Autos—Fiat). This ad provides the reader with a quantity of information with which to make a direct comparison to other brands.

Chapter 6

Student Exercises

1.   Keep in mind that B2B marketers sell to other organizations—not the final consumer. Folgers Coffee is available through retail stores (e.g., Albertson's, Kroger, and Wal-Mart). You can't buy it directly from the company.

2.   Almost everything about this company operates as a result of derived demand. All of their products are used as components in further manufacturing or production. As a result of this, their business is driven by derived demand.

3.   Multiple organizations exist that can be used here. You may want to consider taking a look at either Target Stores (www.target.com) or Ocean Yachts (www.oceanyachtsinc.com) for ideas. Ocean Yachts takes a unique approach to supplier-partner development by providing public information about many of its primary suppliers.

4.   Most of the items established restaurants reorder would probably be on a straight rebuy basis. So, almost any of the products they use could fall into this category.

5.   Systems selling is one of major methods companies employ to gain and keep accounts. Companies that effectively use this technique are much more successful in maintaining long-term profitable relationships with their clients. One good example of systems selling is IBM (www.ibm.com).

6.   The answer to this exercise is unique to each individual. Within your family, the member who carries the most influence at the various stages of the buying process may be totally different from how influence is distributed in your classmate's family.

7.   The continually evolving regulatory environment surrounding the sell and consumption of cigarettes is having a significant impact on RJR buyers. More restrictions are being placed on public smoking. A smaller percentage of American adults smoke cigarettes on a regular basis. The RJR buyers must watch these factors (among others), determine the impact on the company and its customers, and try to turn these challenges into opportunities.

8.   Locating a company that is currently seeking proposals from qualified suppliers may require some searching on your part. You can look for such companies either in your home community, state, university town, or on the internet.

9.   You do not need a login name and password to address this question. Just take a look along the right-hand side of the page. Here, Office Depot outlines online purchasing for many different types of organizations.

10.   School cafeterias are not necessarily looking to make a profit. Typically they may be happy to just not loose too much money! School cafeterias want to provide good quality food to a large number of students in a short period of time. As a result, they seek to purchase large quantities of quality product at the lowest reasonable price to process and pass on to their customers (you, the student). The selections may not always seem that exciting, but they are economical.

Marketing ADventure Exercises

1.   Ad Interpretation Challenge: Business Markets
        Ad: Service and B2B—SpeedStart

The ad is letting the viewer know that SpeedStart can help you cut through your problems and get to profits quicker. Appealing to profits is one of the principal methods of communicating to business markets.

2.   Ad Interpretation Challenge: Derived Demand
        Ad: Electronics—Axiom

The demand for Nokia cell phones is, in part, derived from the demand for Axiom services. Axiom, as a telecommunications company, uses Nokia as its cell phone provider. As demand for Axiom services increase, so does the demand for Nokia phones. If demand for Axiom services were to decrease, so to would demand for Nokia handsets.

3.   Ad Interpretation Challenge: Inelastic Demand
        Ad: Autos—Dunlop

Probably the most important component which goes into the creation of their product is rubber. A change in the cost of rubber is not going to cause Dunlop to buy less rubber, at least not in the short run.

4.   Ad Interpretation Challenge: Straight Rebuy
        Ad: Services and B2B—EMS

Keep in mind that a straight rebuy happens when a company reorders and uses the same product or service. If a company had experienced good results from the use of EMS, they may well turn to EMS in the future for the exact same services again. This would be a straight rebuy.

5.   Ad Interpretation Challenge: Systems Selling
        Ad: Services and B2B—Springbow

Springbow is offering a "one stop" shopping experience for the corporate buyer who is faced with challenges in the new digital world. From this ad, you can see that Springbow is positioning their company as a solution to any problem or series of problems that a company may have operating in this digital world.

6.   Ad Interpretation Challenge: Environmental Factors
      Ad: Services and B2B—Posta

The ads for Posta Prioritaria are addressing two environmental factors—competition and economic. Through the use of priority mail, the ad is suggesting you will have your letter delivered faster than your competition that is not using the service. Associatively, you can have your letter delivered fast for a very reasonable cost.

7.   Ad Interpretation Challenge: Problem Recognition
      Ad: Services and B2B—Varig

At times, delays in cargo shipments may be inevitable. However, when these delays become frequent, then a company may be faced with a serious delivery problem. Through this ad, Varig is highlighting this issue.

8.   Ad Interpretation Challenge: E-Procurement
      Ad: Student Choice

There are many companies whose products or services would satisfy this exercise. For just two examples, take a look at Energizer batteries (Electronics—Energizer) and Heinz ketchup (Food and Beverage—Heinz). Both of these products could easily be purchased through an online procurement system.

9.   Ad Interpretation Challenge: Institutional Markets
      Ad: Student Choice

You may want to consider the advertisements for either Aeromexico (Travel and Tourism—Aeromexico) or Virgin Atlantic (Travel and Tourism—Virgin). Both of these companies may serve as institutional markets for some products, for example food services.

10.   Ad Interpretation Challenge: Government Markets
      Ad: Electronics—Energizer

Take a look at the Energizer ad. They are positioning themselves as longer lasting than any other battery. That is the key. Energizer may be able to persuade the government buyer to accept the higher bid because they are providing a superior, longer lasting product.

Chapter 7

Student Exercises

1.   Bebe has keyed in on a very specific of the women's clothing market. They are reaching out to trendy, fashion conscious, moderately upscale, younger women. Their clothing line is very specific and typically appeals only to this market segment. They have wisely chosen to not try and be all things to all people.

2.   While Polaris would be very happy to sell snowmobiles to consumers living in Mobile, Alabama, it probably is not going to happen. Likewise, customers from Flint, Michigan are not the best prospects to purchase ATVs. Polaris Industries has made the wise (and obvious) decision to concentrate marketing efforts for snowmobiles in northern states of the U.S. At the same time, you would find the primary market for ATVs among southern and southwestern states, where the warm weather persists until late in the year.

3.   Cosmetic companies have begun to realize that there are a growing number of men who desire skin care products. While desiring quality skincare products, this newly emerging segment are not willing to just pick up a "women's" product to use. They have demanded products targeted specifically to them. Clinique (and other traditional cosmetic companies) have responded by launching lines of skincare products with a decidedly "male" look.

4.   On their website, Pottery Barn makes heavy use of lifestyle segmentation. One of the primary competitive features of their site is the ability of a customer to select the "room lifestyle" which most closely matches their own. Pottery Barn allows you to shop completed rooms to match your own personal style. In this manner, Pottery Barn is letting the consumer self-select their merchandise on the basis of their lifestyle.

5.   You can probably think of many products here. Two you might want to consider are pumpkins (you see a lot of usage around Thanksgiving and Halloween) and turkeys (again, for Thanksgiving). While not wanting to decrease demand during their traditional sales or consumption periods, marketers would like to increase consumption of their products during other, slack periods. That is why you now see ads promoting the consumption of orange juice at times other than breakfast and turkey for more than Thanksgiving. Take a look at the National Turkey Federation's website for an example of promoting consumption of your product at "non-peak" times (www.eatturkey.com).

6.   Wyndham offers their customers many benefits and perks in an effort to maintain their loyalty. Chief among these is their frequent guest's club, Wyndham by Request. Wyndham takes great pains to be certain that their loyal customer is shown appreciation for that loyalty. This is the type of service that keeps customers coming back—again and again.

7.   A review of some of EBay's international sites shows that they have been adapted to meet local market requirements in several ways. First, the default language has been changed to the local language. Even for those countries which speak English, you will notice that the language has been adjusted to meet local dialects, word usages, and spellings. Also, in keeping with local customs and regulations, some items you may find for sell on the U.S. site are not available on the foreign site.

8.   Nielsen Media Research has a multitude of research reports available to cover all facets of the media. The type, quality, and quantity of segmentation data available from just this one source are most impressive. Keep in mind, while Nielsen may be the best known in the business, several others competing companies exist offering similar information.

9.   You might begin your search by looking at Putumayo Music (www.putumayo.com). Putumayo is the leading producer of World Music in the U.S. World Music makes up a very small portion of the overall recorded music industry. Instead of trying to compete in that larger music world, Putumayo has chosen to become a leader in a very small niche.

10.   On the Audi website, you have the option to "Build Your Audi." This technology allows you to "design" your ultimate Audi experience and then order it. In essence, you are able to design an automobile just to your specifications.

Marketing ADventure Exercises

1.   Ad Interpretation Challenge: Market Segmentation
        Ad: Apparel—Levi's Diamond Jeans

Based on this ad, you would have to say that Levi's Diamond Jeans are targeting a market segmented on the basis of demographics and psychographics. Specific demographic variables that seem to come into play here would be age (young women) and income (significant discretionary income). Likewise, lifestyle and personality traits would anchor the psychographic variables.

2.   Ad Interpretation Challenge: Geographic Segmentation
        Ad: Student Choice

Keep in mind that many companies are localizing their products, advertising, and promotions to the needs of individual regions of the country. Based on this, the ad for Fiat (Autos—Fiat) would be a good example of regional segmentation. The ad is highlighting the strength of the Fiat's air-conditioning. This is a product attribute especially salient to those consumers living in warmer climate regions.

3.   Ad Interpretation Challenge: Demographic Segmentation
        Ad: Services and B2B—University of Toronto

Obviously, age is the demographic segmentation variable in use in these ads. However, as the student population of colleges and universities continues to age, consideration must be given to using segmentation variables besides strictly age to divide the market.

4.   Ad Interpretation Challenge: Gender Segmentation
        Ad: Student Choice

Think along the stereotypes of men and women. Men have traditionally been viewed as aggressive, seeking power and prestige. The traditional view of women has been one of nurturing, caring, and peace maker. Based on these views, you might want to consider the ad for Nissan's Altima (Autos—Nissan Altima). This ad highlights the power and acceleration features of the new Altima—both features geared to appeal to the male market. To make this ad possibly more appealing to women, we could highlight features of safety and security.

5.   Ad Interpretation Challenge: Income Segmentation
        Ad: Autos—Hyundai

What Hyundai might want to do would be to focus their promotions on price, durability, and dependability

6.   Ad Interpretation Challenge: Psychographic Segmentation
        Ad: Apparel—Umbro

Umbro is appealing to the sports-minded individual. In doing so, Umbro is using basic lifestyle segmentation. Remember that a consumer's lifestyle is comprised of their activities, interests, and opinions. For Umbro, the activities in which consumer's engage are of primary importance—specifically football.

7.   Ad Interpretation Challenge: Occasions Based Segmentation
        Ad: Services and B2B: 24 Hour Fitness

By its name, you would expect 24 Hour Fitness to be open 24 hours a day. Most gyms and health clubs operate on a more limited schedule. Most of us are comfortable with such schedules. However, by offering a facility which operates 24 hours a day, 24 Hour Fitness is promoting the use of its facilities at times other than the traditionally accepted times. The hope would be greater enrollment and facility usage.

8.	Ad Interpretation Challenge: Undifferentiated Marketing
	Ad: Student Choice

You can't do it. None of ads here use this approach. Most modern marketers have strong reservations about this strategy. Mass marketers have a tough time competing with more focused firms that do a better job of satisfying the needs of specific market segments.

9.	Ad Interpretation Challenge: Niche Marketing
	Ad: Newspapers and TV—Football Channel

To be a player in the mainstream television market today would be a very difficult and expensive proposition. The number of competitors all offering basically the same programming is immense. It would be tough to find a way to stand out, be recognized, and make even a small profit. On the other hand, by concentrating all of your efforts in one category—in this case football—you have the unique opportunity to become the dominant competitor in a small field of competitors.

10.	Ad Interpretation Challenge: Individual Marketing
	Ad: Student Choice

One possible example you may look at is DBS (Financial—DBS). DBS, an early marketer of the debit card, is positioning the card as fulfilling the needs of each individual, regardless of what those needs may be or how they may differ from your neighbor's. Keep in mind that one of the characteristics of individual marketing is the tailoring of the product to the needs of the individual customer.

Chapter 8

Student Exercises

1.   How you answer this question depends on how you define your school's market. If the market your school is appealing to be the student, then the product is education. This educational product is manifested in the course offerings, times, and faculty. On the other hand, if you consider the market to be the organizations that hire the students upon graduation, then the product becomes the student themselves.

2.   Digital photography has become increasingly popular for many reasons. One reason is that it allows the photographer to experience something much closer to instant gratification, when compared to conventional film photography. With digital photography, you have the ability to take a photograph and almost instantly see the results of your creative work and to share this work with others.

3.   By clicking on the Products tab, you are shown all products and brands the company offers for general consumption. Keep in mind that convenience products are typically low in price, have widespread distribution, and benefit from mass promotion by the producer. Based on this, you might conclude that the vast majority of P&G products fall into this category—particularly products such as laundry, dish care, paper products, and oral care.

4.   Windmill power has been around for centuries, but has had only limited application in the modern world. The availability of units appropriate for single family homes represents a step forward in technology. The challenge facing manufacturers is letting people know of the viability of the product and technology and its appropriateness for home use. This will require a substantial commitment in advertising and personal selling to potential home owners and home builders. It's not an easy sell.

5.   Both are "Open for business!" That is the key message. New Orleans and the gulf coast region are encouraging visitors to come back and enjoy the many pleasures that made the regions so popular before. Neither is saying that everything is back to normal. However, they are saying that, as they continue the rebuilding process, now is the perfect time for the visitor to come see the progress and enjoy the area.

6.   To effectively rate the quality of your school's "products," you need to keep an open and unbiased mind. How well do you really believe your school is doing in creating good, qualified, competent graduates ready to enter the work force?

7.   How brands "speak" to you is a personal and individual experience. Marketers hope that their brands speak to you in the manner they intend! For example, Toyota – reliability, Kia – economy, Volvo – safety.

8.   While this is a completely individual decision, you will want to focus on products for which the packaging says something significant about its contents or the delivery of those contents. For example, Mentadent toothpaste (www.youareteethpeople.com) uses its packaging as a primary product attribute. For most consumers, one of the main motivations behind the purchase of this product is its unique form of product delivery.

9.   At a minimum, you can say that J. Peterman offers product lines comprised of men's clothing (shirts, pants, hats, etc.), women's clothing (dresses, skirts, shirts, pants), and items for the home (furniture, bar signs).

10.   In a brand extension it is important to always keep your primary brand and product in mind. Any extension you enter into to must maintain the credibility of that main brand. In Sea Ray's instance, they would probably want to remain with products connected in some manner to the marine industry, as that is where their strengths lie. Possibilities could include a line of Sea Ray branded marine instruments or Sea Ray branded dishes for use in your boat.

Marketing ADventure Exercises

1.   Ad Interpretation Challenge: Product
        Ad: Services and B2B—Leo's

The answer to the question is "yes." Leo's Sports Club is a product. Products include more than just tangible goods. Broadly defined, products include physical objects, services, events, people, places, organizations, ideas, or a mix of these entities. Thus, although Leo's is certainly providing a service, it is a product.

2.   Ad Interpretation Challenge: Core Benefit
        Ad: Electronics—Fujifilm

Fuji is offering the consumer a product with which to capture images. However, this is not the base, or core benefit. People buying Fuji film are buying memories. They are buying a product that will allow them to faithfully preserve their memories for a lifetime.

3.   Ad Interpretation Challenge: Convenience Products
        Ad: Student Choice

There are many ads which fulfill the requirements of this question. Take a look at Kit Kat (Food and Beverage—Kit Kat) and Pepsi (Food and Beverage—Pepsi) for two examples. Marketers of convenience goods work to keep the image of the product fresh in the consumer's mind. As such, many of the advertisements for products of this type are heavy with imagery without delving too deeply into the specifics of the product.

4.   Ad Interpretation Challenge: Organization Marketing
        Ad: Nonprofit Corporate Images—The Archdiocese

In essence, the marketing of the Archdiocese (an organization) and the marketing of a Nissan (a product) are exactly the same. The organization is interested in attracting new members. Nissan, on the other hand, is interested in selling more cars. The basic similarities in accomplishing these tasks are many.

5.   Ad Interpretation Challenge: Social Marketing
        Ad: Student Choice

Promoting products and services that are good for the person and good for society is social marketing. There are numerous ads which are promoting such social concepts. Take a look at, for example, the ad for ABC Canada (Nonprofit Corporate Images—ABC Canada). ABC Canada is a nonprofit organization whose primary goal is to teach adults how to read and write. This is certainly an example of an organization whose goal is both to improve the well-being of the individual and of society.

6.   Ad Interpretation Challenge: Product Features
        Ad: Food and Beverage—Tabasco

Look at the Tabasco ad. That is a burned toothpick in the upper portion of the ad. Tabasco is using this to symbolize the heat strength of its product. One of the most desirable features of a hot sauce is the intensity of its heat. Tabasco is telling consumers it has that feature covered.

7.   Ad Interpretation Challenge: Packaging
        Ad: Student Choice

For this exercise, you will want to focus on ads for which the packaging says something significant about its contents or the delivery of those contents. In today's highly competitive marketplace, packaging can be just as important as the product it holds. As an example, take a look at the ad for Altoids (Food and Beverage—Altoids). The metal container used to hold the mint is as much an integral part of this product as is the mint itself.

8.   Ad Interpretation Challenge: Product Line
        Ad: Autos—Jaguar

Jaguar faces the most danger in moving its product line downward through the introduction of less expensive models. Prestige products are always at risk when a less-expensive version of the item is introduced.

9. Ad Interpretation Challenge: Product Mix
    Ad: Apparel—Levi's

If you look at all the different product lines and items within those lines, you begin to understand the complexity of projecting a consistent corporate image. Ideally, a company desires for all of its products and product variations to act in concert in the projection of a single image. Levi's does a nice job of this.

10. Ad Interpretation Challenge: Brand Extensions
    Ad: Autos—Honda

Honda has been very careful when considering brand extensions. Before moving to additional transportation forms, they made certain they were strong and well regarded by consumers in the current market. Only at that time, did they extend their brand to other forms of transportation. Also, Honda has been careful to remain primarily within the transportation category with its brand extensions, therefore, keeping brand dilution to a minimum.

Chapter 9

Student Exercises

1.   It is hard to say whether the iPhone will "revolutionize" the use of cell phones. While it certainly provides the consumer with several new and somewhat novel features – such as the ability to see album covers – one can question whether these features are "revolutionary" or "evolutionary."

2.   Frog Design would have used both internal and external idea sources in the course of this project. Internally, Frog would likely have turned to company executives and on-the-floor salespeople for insights into the mind of the Victoria's Secret customer. Good new product ideas also come from customers. So it would be safe to assume Frog turned to these customers for additional suggestions and ideas.

3.   There is no truly correct answer to this exercise. Just use your imagine to come up with other uses and/or features for the iPhone. For example,

Concept 1: A low-priced phone, offered in only one version, available through all service providers, that combines standard cell phone features (such as a camera, texting, and music capabilities), but using Apple technology.

Concept 2: A moderately-priced phone, offered with limited variations, available through only one or two service providers, which offers (in addition to the features of Concept 1) the ability to perform limited word processing and spreadsheet functions and interface with your home computer.

Concept 3: A high-end device that is infinitely customizable and is "built-to-order." This device would include everything from Concept 2, with the additions of GPS, directions on demand, locator beacon, and automatic phone book updates.

4.   Given the nature of the product, you would want to concentrate your test marketing to regions or cities known for their "fashion-forward" style. Markets such as Los Angeles, Miami, and New York come readily to mind. Having settled on your test market cities, you would turn your attention to retail outlets within those markets most frequented by your potential clientele. These areas then become the focus of your test market.

5.   Finding a product for the first stage – product development – may be the most challenging. Here you are dealing with a product that is not yet released to the market. For an example of a product in this stage, consider the Chevrolet Camaro – a car not yet introduced (www.chevrolet.com/performance).

6. The Morton salt girl's dress has followed the trend of American women's fashion clothing. When dresses where longer, the Morton girl's dress was longer. When the fashion of dresses was shorter, the Morton girl's dress was shorter. The fashion forecast for women's dresses for the next couple of years is shorter, so we may see the dress on the Morton salt girl inch up.

7. A review of their product offering draws your attention to the cassette players. Pioneer currently offers a couple of cassette players for the audio buff that still maintains a large collection of cassette tapes.

8. Fads may be kind of hard to spot, because so many times they simply do not remain around that long. However, today, one may consider the military-inspired (camouflage) look so evident in women's clothing.

9. Blu-ray technology is going to have to be adopted by more electronics manufacturing companies so that more players will be available in the marketplace to consumers – at lower prices. Also, consumers – the ultimate deciders of new product fate – must be convinced of the clear superiority of this product over existing DVDs and the new competing HD-DVD format.

10. Miller produces a number of information packages designed to assist in helping parents to continue the dialogue with their teens about making responsible and healthy decisions about illegal underage drinking. Also, Miller Brewing provides signage to all merchants alerting patrons that proper I.D. will be required of them to purchase alcoholic beverages.

Marketing ADventure Exercises

1. Ad Interpretation Challenge: Idea Generation
  Ad: Food and Beverage—Altoids

This becomes an imagination game. Through the use of brainstorming, you may come up with any number of potential product ideas. Some of your ideas may be as far fetched as a breath mint that lasts for 24 hours. On the other hand, you may generate relatively minor extensions of the current product mix. Maybe, a mint that immediately dissolves in your mouth, but is effective for a couple of hours.

2. Ad Interpretation Challenge: Idea Screening
  Ad: Food and Beverage—Heinz

When looking at all of the products Heinz offers, it is probably easy to see some that you believe should never have made it into production. Keep in mind, though, that you need to look at these items on a larger scale, considering their potential regardless of your own personal likes and dislikes.

3.   Ad Interpretation Challenge: Concept Testing
        Ad: Food and Beverage—Gatorade

You might want to say something along the lines of: "An easy to swallow capsule, designed to be swallowed without water. When ingested, the capsule immediately disintegrates, releasing thirst-quenching nourishment throughout the body."

4.   Ad Interpretation Challenge: Test Marketing
        Ad: Electronics—Motorola

Motorola may have considered introducing this product through only one cell service provider. This would have allowed them the opportunity to experiment with pricing and promotion strategies before making the (expensive) decision to provide the phone to all service providers nationwide.

5.   Ad Interpretation Challenge: Commercialization
        Ad: Student Choice

If you are having trouble coming up with any ads for this exercise, you may want to take a look at the ad for Sony's projection television (Electronics—Sony) or the ad for Advantage card (Financial—Advantage Card). Read the copy on both of these ads. Both of these ads serve the purpose of introducing a new product to the market.

6.   Ad Interpretation Challenge: Fashion
        Ad: Apparel—Student Choice

Of the available ads, you would most likely settle on the ad for Levi's New Collection jeans. Here, Levi's has introduced a new variation on the traditional jean; they have added the currently fashionable rhinestone.

7.   Ad Interpretation Challenge: Introduction Stage
        Ad: Student Choice

There are several ads that you might select to fulfill the requirements of this question. Remember, you are looking for an ad that is designed to introduce the product to the market and to entice consumers to give it a try. For an example, take a look at Freedomland (Newspaper and TV—Freedomland).

8.   Ad Interpretation Challenge: Growth Stage
        Ad: Electronics—LG

If this were an ad for a LCD or plasma TV, the ad would be directed more toward the early adopter and not the middle majority. The ad would be designed to help build demand in the mass market, while still emphasizing the LG brand.

9.   Ad Interpretation Challenge: Decline Stage
        Ad: Electronics—Fujifilm

Products in the decline stage of the product life cycle are characterized by declining sales and as appealing to laggards. In this phase, you want to phase out weak versions of the product and only concentrate on the core product. Additionally, you may consider a price cut in an effort to keep sales high. Also, typically, advertising and sales promotions are reduced to minimal levels.

10.   Ad Interpretation Challenge: Social Responsibility
        Ad: Student Choice

As a possible example, look at Autos—Nissan. Specifically, take a look at the ad dealing highlighting the Nissan Primira—recognized as the most ecological vehicle on the market.

Chapter 10

Student Exercises

1.   After spending some time on the Hewlett-Packard home page (www.hp.com) and building the ultimate laptop computer, you have probably realized that the opinions are staggering. Build-to-order companies, such as HP, offer the demanding consumer a multitude of options and configurations to meet any need. In this way, HP (and others) is building greater customer loyalty and satisfaction.

2.   When making the decision to come to school, you paid a monetary price—and you continue to pay that every term. But, you have also paid a price in regards to income lost or deferred. You could have gone to work and earned an income straight out of high school, but you chose to not do that (in essence, paying a price) to continue your education.

3.   You need to be looking for products whose price may seem a bit out-of-line with the actual product. In such an instance, there must be more at work to add to the image of the product. Possible examples you may consider are Rolex watches (www.rolex.com) and Monolo Blahnik shoes (www.manoloblahnik.com).

4.   You should be able to find a multitude of products to fulfill the requirement of this exercise. Two examples you might consider are Levi Strauss Signature jeans (a less expensive version of the traditional Levi's jean) and eMachines computers (a less expensive brand of Gateway).

5.   By reviewing the website for Lexus, you will notice several value-added services for customers. For example, they have established a partnership with a collection of luxury hotels. These hotels offer special services or amenities exclusively to Lexus owners.

6.   Fixed costs (also known as overhead) do not vary with production or sales level. Examples with which Tomasini are faced include rent on the manufacturing facilities and offices, payments on equipment, utilities, insurance, and salaries. They have to pay these items no matter how much they sell.

7.   Remember, variable costs fluctuate with the quantity produced. Costs associated with materials used in production would be the primary variable costs for Tomasini. These materials would include the fabrics used to make to bedding and the pillow forms from which the final pillows are produced.

8.   No. Hot Springs Portable Spas would be wiser to use an alternative form of pricing their spas. Hot Springs spas are the number one selling brand of portable spas and hot tubs. From a review of their website, you will see they have a long history, loyal clients, and have consistently received good press. These factors push for a form of pricing other than cost-based.

9.   One good example you might consider is the oil industry. There are only a few major manufacturers and sellers in this industry. Their pricing always seems to be pretty consistent. It would be prohibitively expensive for new competitors to enter the marketplace.

10.   You will not find many large nonregulated monopolies around today. There is too much concern over consumer welfare to allow most truly monopolistic situations to continue for long periods of time. Given that they manufacture the vast majority of computer operating systems, many people consider Microsoft (www.microsoft.com) to be a nonregulated monopoly. However, others (including Microsoft) would argue they are not a monopoly. While they still sell the vast majority of PC operating systems, other competitors such as Linux (www.linux.com) and Apple (www.apple.com) are slowing making inroads.

Marketing ADventure Exercises

1.   Ad Interpretation Challenge: Price
        Ad: Services and B2B—University of Toronto

Remember, price includes more than just a monetary exchange. In this case, price encompasses loss of time to attend classes and potential loss of income, if you were working. Price is everything you give up in exchange for the product or service.

2.   Ad Interpretation Challenge: Value-based Pricing
        Ad: Autos—Jaguar

By reviewing the ad, you see that Jaguar is positioning itself as a sophisticated product, unlike the competing BMW (which would be considered simply a "grown up" product). Along with this level of sophistication comes a certain respect. Jaguar knows that this perceived respect is worth money, in the eyes of its customers. Based on this, Jaguar customers are willing to pay a premium for their cars while still maintaining they are receiving value.

3.   Ad Interpretation Challenge: Good-Value Pricing
        Ad: General Retail—Target

Target has been able to effectively compete with Wal-Mart in the battle of good-value pricing by offering its customers a different mix from Wal-Mart of quality, service, and fair prices. Knowing that they cannot compete solely on the basis of price, Target has made the decision to offer customers good-value pricing by having quality products, with enhanced levels of customer service, at prices that are close to those offered by Wal-Mart.

4.   Ad Interpretation Challenge: Cost-based Pricing
        Ad: Autos—Mercedes

The answer is probably not. Although Mercedes operates in the highly competitive luxury automobile market, they have established a long-standing reputation for quality, dependability, and engineering excellence. These are all product attributes for which the customer is willing to pay a premium.

5.   Ad Interpretation Challenge: Fixed Costs
        Ad: Travel and Tourism—American Airlines

American Airlines, like all airlines in the United States, is faced with severe fixed costs. Some of the fixed costs confronting AA are payments for airplanes, wages and salaries of pilots, flight attendants, and ground personnel, fuel, and landing fees to airports. These costs remain relatively set regardless of how full their planes fly.

6.   Ad Interpretation Challenge: Variable Costs
        Ad: Travel and Tourism—American Airlines

Here we are looking for costs that change, or vary with how full they fly their planes. They do not have a tremendous number of variable costs. Some of the variable costs they do incur include food and drinks. Only if the volume of passengers increases dramatically would you see an increase in expenses for items such as fuel or personnel.

7.   Ad Interpretation Challenge: Cost-Plus Pricing
        Ad: Student Choice

Some of the best examples can be found in the section for financial services. You might want to look at RKMC or Bank of Montreal for examples.

8.   Ad Interpretation Challenge: Monopolistic Competition
        Ad: Food and Beverage—Heinz

Heinz is producing a basic commodity: ketchup. However, they have worked tirelessly to differentiate their version of ketchup from all other competitors. As a result, they have established a unique brand in the crowded ketchup market and can command higher prices from consumers.

9.   Ad Interpretation Challenge: Inelastic Demand
        Ad: Student Choice

You are looking for products that are unique or perceived as being high in quality. For one example, take a look at Altoids (Food and Beverage—Altoids). Altoids has long held a unique position in the breath mint market. Its "Curiously Strong Mints" stand out in a crowded breath mint market, as does its unique use of packaging.

10. Ad Interpretation Challenge: Elastic Demand
     Ad: Student Choice

One that jumps out is for World's Biggest Bookstore (General Retail—World's Biggest Bookstore). The ad states that its prices are so low even people who do not read overly well buy from them. This store has based its existence on elastic demand.

Chapter 11

Student Exercises

1.   A lot of new technology-driven products employ a market-skimming pricing strategy. For example, take a look at the newest professionally-oriented EOS digital cameras from Canon (www.usa.canon.com) or look at the newest version of Apple's iPod (www.apple.com).

2.   Keep in mind that several conditions have to be met for market-penetration pricing to really work. The market must be highly price sensitive so that a low price produces more sales. Also, the low cost must help to keep out the competition. By pricing their products so low, JR Cigar has been able to greatly increase the volume of their business, resulting in greater overall sales and increased profits. Additionally, it has been difficult for competitors to effectively work against them due, in part, to the great volumes necessary to push the low prices.

3.   Apple offers different versions of its widely successful iPod. Within each category, it typically offer at least two varying units. Look at the website and you will see well-defined prices that range from around $80 to over $350.

4.   Cars are a great example of optional-product pricing. You start off with the base car and then add on everything you want to make it uniquely yours. After adding on everything you want to your unique SAAB, you will most probably see the price rise dramatically. Does this make the car less attractive to you?

5.   One item that seems to always crop up in the purchase of a new computer and monitor is the cable to hook the monitor to the computer. It's the kind of necessary accessory item you would expect to be included as standard equipment, but it's not.

6.   One example of a successful by-product is chicken wings. For years chicken wings were all but an unwanted by-product of production. Everyone was interested in breasts and legs. Chicken wings were viewed as a food of the lower classes. Today, "buffalo wings" of all kinds are extremely popular and profitable. Think about how much you paid for your last serving.

7.   Expedia offers the traveler the option of booking just a flight, a hotel, rental car, or any and all combinations of these services. Typically, the more services you allow them to handle for you, the greater your savings. Additionally, once you select a location, they will offer you a multitude of area attraction for which you can prepay your entrance fees and save. In these ways, Expedia is practicing product bundle pricing.

8.   By looking at the multitude of products offered, it is easy to become overwhelmed by the choices for a simple white dress shirt. Most of us, barring other knowledge, would select one of the shirts in the $85-$110 range as the highest quality. In reality, many of the less expensive shirts may be of close, if not equal quality.

9.   Overstock makes great use of "list prices." On every item for sell, they prominently provide the consumer with a reference price. This information is of great value to the shopper who may not be totally familiar with some of the brands offered.

10.   Many possibilities exist here. One of the best merchants at using promotional pricing is Best Buy (www.bestbuy.com). They do a great job of placing just enough items at a temporarily reduced price to keep the same customers coming back time after time.

Marketing ADventure Exercises

1.   Ad Interpretation Challenge: Market-Skimming Pricing
         Ad: Electronics—Sony HS Series

Yes. This product, when introduced, was one of the most technically advanced televisions on the market. Technology products will many times employ market-skimming pricing in an effort to recoup some of their massive financial outlays for research and development.

2.   Ad Interpretation Challenge: Market-Penetration Pricing
         Ad: Student Choice

One of the first responses that may come to mind is for Hyundai automobiles (Autos—Hyundai). Hyundai, a new automobile into the marketplace, is looking to become established rapidly and gain as much name recognition and market share as possible. Market-penetration pricing is the perfect avenue for them to pursue.

3.   Ad Interpretation Challenge: Product Line Pricing
         Ad: Apparel—Levi's

One of the first responses that may come to mind is for Hyundai automobiles (Autos—Hyundai). Hyundai, a new automobile into the marketplace, is looking to become established rapidly and gain as much name recognition and market share as possible. Market-penetration pricing is the perfect avenue for them to pursue.

4.   Ad Interpretation Challenge: Optional-Product Pricing
         Ad: Autos—Ford

Take a look at just about any car ad. When you read the fine print, you will notice something along the line of "possibly shown with optional equipment." This is the carmakers way of letting the consumer know that the auto they see may not be the base model. It may, in fact, be a vehicle with optional equipment and is priced accordingly.

5.   Ad Interpretation Challenge: Captive-Product Pricing
        Ad: Student Choice

One of the most obvious solutions to the exercise would be the ad for Schick razors (Cosmetics and Pharmaceuticals—Schick). Razors are typically sold independently, but are useless without the accessory blade cartridges, which are sold separately.

6.   Ad Interpretation Challenge: Product Bundle Pricing
        Ad: Cosmetics and Pharmaceuticals—Edge

One possibility would be to combine the Edge shaving gel with a razor and razor blade cartridges. This bundle would present to the consumer all that was needed for a clean, close shave in one convenient to purchase bundle.

7.   Ad Interpretation Challenge: Psychological Pricing
        Ad: Cosmetics and Pharmaceuticals—Edge

Edge shaving gel is typically priced at a premium to most other shaving creams and gels. For many consumers, there is a strong relationship between the price of a product and the perceived quality of that product. All other factors being equal, the consumer will typically consider the higher priced product to be of superior quality to the lower priced product.

8.   Ad Interpretation Challenge: Reference Prices
        Ad: General Retail—World's Biggest Bookstore

Their ads state that they have "Great books. Fantastic prices." This is giving the consumer a reference price cue. World's Biggest Bookstore is telling the consumer that their prices are great—much better than the typical retail price of a book.

9.   Ad Interpretation Challenge: Promotional Pricing
        Ad: Student Choice

Many of the products or businesses featured could be used to fulfill the requirement of this question. One example would be Pizza World (Food and Beverage—Pizza World). Pizza World could simply run their pizzas at a discount (for example, 20 percent off!) for the purpose of creating excitement, getting more customers into their store, and selling more pizzas.

10.   Ad Interpretation Challenge: Dynamic Pricing
        Ad: Travel and Tourism—Aeromexico

Airlines are heavy users of dynamic pricing strategies. Through a sophisticated system, they constantly monitor the sells activity for any given flight. If the flight is not filling up fast enough, the airline may temporarily reduce the price of tickets to stimulate traffic. If ticket sales are brisk, the airline may decide to raise prices in an effort to gain more revenue from each ticket sold.

Chapter 12

Student Exercises

1.   Members of the partner community must work effectively together to bring superior value to Mountain Valley's customers. These members include manufacturers and suppliers of the components used in production of their water and accessory products—bottle producers (plastic and glass), clothing suppliers, distributors nationwide, and (of course) their customers.

2.   Gateway gets their computers to the consumer through a variety of marketing channels. They sell directly through their website or through their retail stores. They sell through third party intermediaries—other retail establishments (such as Best Buy), and they sell through other online merchants such as Amazon.

3.   Two examples you might consider are Dell computers (www.dell.com) and Canon cameras and printers (www.canonusa.com). Both of these companies produce their products and then sell them directly to the final consumers.

4.   While the majority of Starbucks coffee is sold through its company owned stores, other indirect methods are in use. Starbucks sells much of its product through the indirect channel of supermarkets. Now, you can find many of your favorite Starbucks flavors at your local market.

5.   The easiest way for conflict to occur would be for one of the stations to lower the price of its gas. Drives do not seem to be overly loyal to particular gas stations. If one were to lower their price significantly, chances are you may migrate to them, leaving your "standard" station for the better price. In such a situation, horizontal channel conflict could occur.

6.   One thing that Subway might consider doing is to offer its products as additions to the delis of local supermarkets. Subway might also consider overnight delivery of their sandwiches from national corporate-owned stores directly to consumers nationwide. Both of these would likely generate vertical channel conflict.

7.   Green Giant does not use a conventional distribution channel. However, if Green Giant were to use a conventional distribution channel, they would sell their products to an independent wholesaler for the highest price they could get. This wholesaler would have only its own best interests in mind as it sought out the best deal it could make with a retail merchant to buy the product. This retailer (grocery store) would, in turn, price the product as high as possible in an effort to maximize their profit, with little regard for the consumer. The independent layers of the channel do not work together. In fact, many times they work at odds with one another in an effort to maximize their individual profits.

8.   Goodyear has two primary outlets for its tires: its own franchised outlets and mass-merchandisers (such as Wal-Mart). In both instances, the VMS is composed of only

Goodyear and the retail merchant. In both instances, the level of communication and corporation between Goodyear and the retailer is very good, with the result being smooth product delivery and fair prices to channel members and consumers.

9.   You can think of almost any major manufacturer or retailer to answer this exercise. Examples may include Gibson Guitars (www.gibson.com), PetSmart (www.petsmart.com), and Lowes (www.lowes.com).

10.   The easiest thing to do is to think of products that are expensive. One that comes readily to mind is the Rolex watch (www.rolex.com). Rolex is very selective when it comes to awarding dealership rights. Part of the allure of the product is that it can not be found in too many places. If you are in the market for a Rolex watch, you are forced to seek out one of the limited number of retailers licensed to carry the product. Such limited distribution contributes to the feeling of exclusivity of owning a Rolex.

Marketing ADventure Exercises

1.   Ad Interpretation Challenge: Value Delivery Network
        Ad: Apparel—Puma

In order to cover everyone, there are a lot of companies that you can add to this list. The value delivery network is composed of Puma, its suppliers of footwear, possibly wholesalers, retailers of its products, and finally the customer.

2.   Ad Interpretation Challenge: Direct Marketing Channel
        Ad: Student Choice

You are looking for a product that would be sold by the company directly to the consumer. Possible answers are American Airlines (Travel and Tourism—American Airlines) and Samsung (Electronics—Samsung). Many travelers buy their airline tickets directly from the airline, cutting out or bypassing the traditional intermediary of the travel agent. Likewise, a popular trend is to purchase your electronic equipment, particularly computers and accessories directly from the company.

3.   Ad Interpretation Challenge: Channel Conflict
        Ad: Food and Beverage—Cool Drinking Water

There are all kinds of potential conflicts with this product, as there are with most. For example, this product is likely shipped from the producer to a wholesaler. This wholesaler then, in turn, ships cases of the water to the retailer. At this point, the retailer, will uncase the water and make individual units available to the consumer. At any stage of this process, disagreements are likely to emerge between different levels of the channel over timing, costs, rewards, or other issues.

4.   Ad Interpretation Challenge: Vertical Channel Conflict
        Ad: Electronics—LG

LG sells through retailers. Thus, the channel goes from LG to the retailer and then on to the final consumer. If LG were to make the decision to sell directly to the consumer, the potential for çonflict would occur. Now, no longer would customers have to deal with a retailer (and pay the retailer's profit), they could go directly to the source and buy.

5.   Ad Interpretation Challenge: Horizontal Channel Conflict
        Ad: Autos—Ford

The most likely scenario in which this would occur would be if Ford were to allow another dealership to open close by the original dealer. In such a situation, you would have two dealers going (potentially) after the same clients.

6.   Ad Interpretation Challenge: Vertical Marketing System
        Ad: Student Choice

One good example of a company that would use a VMS is S. C. Johnson and Son, the makers of Edge shave gel (Cosmetics and Pharmaceuticals—Edge). S. C. Johnson and Son (www.edgeadvanced.com) is so large and has so much power they would have great influence over the downstream channel members.

7.   Ad Interpretation Challenge: Vertical Marketing System—Student Decision
        Ad: General Retail—Hallmark

Hallmark is using a variation of the contractual VMS known as the franchise organization. Specifically, Hallmark is engaging in a manufacturer-sponsored retailer franchise system.

8.   Ad Interpretation Challenge: Administered VMS
        Ad: General Retail—Target

Target, the second largest discount chain, has tremendous power in a VMS. Target purchases vast quantities of merchandise for sale in its stores. The company is so large that it is able to dictate channel terms to members further up the channel, many times back to the company, which manufactures the products.

9.   Ad Interpretation Challenge: Multichannel Distribution Systems
        Ad: General Retail—Hallmark

Hallmark utilizes three marketing channels to make up its multichannel distribution system. First, Hallmark products may be found in independent Hallmark stores. These are independent merchants partnering with Hallmark through a manufacturer-sponsored retail franchise system. Second, Hallmark products may be found in other retail locations (discount stores, grocery stores, etc.). Finally, the consumer may purchase Hallmark products directly from Hallmark, via the Web. This would be a direct marketing channel.

10.   Ad Interpretation Challenge: Intensive Distribution
        Ad: Student Choice

Intensive distribution is ideally suited for products of low value, which the consumer may purchase on a relatively frequent basis. Examples include Heinz ketchup (Food and Beverage—Heinz) and Listerine (Cosmetics and Pharmaceuticals—Listerine).

Chapter 13

Student Exercises

1.   No. Certainly, Amazon fulfills the requirements of engaging in retailing. However, National Cap and Set Screw Company does not engage in retailing. Remember, retailing is involved with getting the products or services to the final consumer for their personal, nonbusiness use. National Cap and Set Screw Company sell primarily to other manufacturers or organizations that use the products in creation of their own products.

2.   Yes. Even though the typical Whole Foods store has a greater level of customer service than the traditional grocery store, it is still primarily up to the customer to "locate-compare-select" the products they purchase.

3.   There are many chains you can select from to successfully complete this exercise. For examples, consider Victoria's Secret (www.victoriassecret.com) and Aloha Shirt Shop (www.alohashirtshop.com). Both of these companies carry only a very narrow product line. But, their assortment within that line is extensive.

4.   Category killers have really done great in recent years and there seems to be no stopping them. However, they are not invincible. One example is Toys R Us (www.toysrus.com). This category killer once dominated the toy market and was the largest seller of toys and games. Poor strategy execution left them vulnerable to the major superstores (e.g., Wal-Mart) which now control the majority of the toy market.

5.   Many people would say they have no weaknesses. But, for some, the sheer size of these stores is a turn off. Wal-Mart has recognized this issue and has attempted to counter it with the opening of the Wal-Mart Neighborhood Markets, miniature versions of Wal-Mart Supercenters appropriately sized for small neighborhoods.

6.   A brief review of Wal-Mart history will show that they began as a discount merchant in smaller towns, offering quality merchandise at significantly lower prices than the competition. Over the years, we have seen their stores locate in ever higher rent areas. Their merchandise mix has shifted to offer more higher-priced, designer-like products. This has been a conscious move to try and capture a somewhat higher level clientele.

7.   A review of Prime Outlets website will show you that the typical factory outlet mall is populated with company-owned stores selling merchandise at a substantial discount off the "regular" retail price. Physically, factory outlets are generally starker in appearance and offer the shopper fewer ancillary amenities—for example, smaller food courts.

8.   Power centers have grown in popularity as an alternative to the traditional enclosed shopping mall. Shoppers have become bored and are seeking variation and excitement in the shopping experience. Power centers have appeared to fill this void.

9.   The discount store is one example you might consider. Initially, discount stores entered the market as low-price, low-status, low-margin retailers. They were located in less than desirable locations and offered lower-quality merchandise. As time has progressed, they have moved into better locations (and are paying much higher rents). Now, they are operating as somewhat higher-status merchants, faced with higher costs, and, as a result, higher prices.

10.   Retailers moving into the international arena may be faced with a multitude of challenges, including language barriers and unknown cultures. Just these two issues may prove to be daunting challenges for the unprepared retailer.

Marketing ADventure Exercises

1.   Ad Interpretation Challenge: Self-Service Retailer
        Ad: Cosmetics and Pharmaceuticals—Edge

Consumers need information with which to make decisions. To be helpful, the Edge packaging should include very visible information about the product and its positive features.

2.   Ad Interpretation Challenge: Specialty Store
        Ad: Student Choice

The most obvious choice here would probably be Hallmark (General Retail—Hallmark). This is a retailer that specializes in greeting cards. Hallmark carries primarily greeting cards (with a few ancillary and related items) and has very deep assortment of cards from which the consumer may choose.

3.   Ad Interpretation Challenge: Department Store
        Ad: Electronics—LG

Department stores carry a wide range of merchandise. However, one of the differentiating factors of department stores is service. Department stores have long used service to customers to set themselves apart from other forms of retailing. For many consumers, customer information and help in making the best selection is a vital part of the shopping experience, particularly for big-ticket items such as televisions.

4.   Ad Interpretation Challenge: Supermarket
        Ad: Food and Beverage—Heinz

Heinz (and other convenience goods manufacturers) relies almost exclusively on supermarkets to make their products available to consumers. Heinz ketchup is a low-cost item, which provides only a low-margin to the merchant. This is a classic example of the type of products that need supermarkets to survive.

5.   Ad Interpretation Challenge: Category Killer
        Ad: General Retail—World's Biggest Bookstore

Category killers, such as World's Biggest Bookstore, offer the customer much greater selection within a particular product line—in this case books. Along with the deeper product line, comes knowledgeable employees who are there to answer the customer's detailed questions and to offer advice on products.

6.   Ad Interpretation Challenge: Discount Stores
        Ad: Student Choice

There is only one possibility here. Target (General Retail—Target) is a typical discount chain, albeit an upscale one.

7.   Ad Interpretation Challenge: Off-Price Retailers
        Ad: Apparel—Levi's

Off-price retailers typically stock last season's styles or factory overruns. Therefore, if Levi's New Collection Diamond Jeans did not sell during the season, they may very well find themselves at an off-price retailer come the beginning of the next fashion season.

8.   Ad Interpretation Challenge: Franchise
        Ad: Student Choice

There are several ads you can select to fulfill the requirements of this exercise. Two you might consider are McDonald's (Food and Beverage—McDonald's) and 24 Hour Fitness (Services and B2B—24 Hour Fitness).

9.   Ad Interpretation Challenge: Retail Positioning
        Ad: General Retail—Target

Target has done a very good job of competing with Wal-Mart, not by going head-to-head, but by positioning itself as an upscale alternative to the mass merchandiser of Wal-Mart. Now, the two discount behemoths are targeting very different markets and have distinctly different positions in the marketplace.

10.   Ad Interpretation Challenge: The Wheel-of-Retailing Concept
        Ad: General Retail—Worlds Biggest Bookstore

In the introductory stage of the wheel-of-retailing the merchant is a low-price, low-status operator. As time goes by and they become successful, there is a tendency for them to move into higher-priced goods, with higher-priced operations, losing some of the competitive tenacity that made them so successful early on.

Chapter 14

Student Exercises

1.   The promotion mix for your university is most likely a mix of several promotional tools. You may see that your school uses traditional advertising (such as billboards or newspaper ads). Along with this, they will likely have a "salesforce" (although they would never call them that). This salesforce are the recruiters for your school that go out to the high schools and community colleges to provide information about your school's course offerings.

2.   IMC ties together all of the company's messages and images. Apple could use IMC to help get the message out regarding the iPhone. Under IMC, they need to be certain that their television and print ads communicate the same basic message and that they do so with the same look and feel as other components of the program. Likewise, they would want their public relations materials to project the same image as their website.

3.   Noise is anything that interferes with the correct reception of the sender's message. In this example, the noise could come from many places. For example, local television ads are notorious for poor production quality. If there were the case for our favorite local Mexican restaurant, this poor production could overwhelm the intended message.

4.   BCBG is a marketer of high fashion women's clothing. They have products that cover the price scale from moderately priced to expensive. A quick review of their website might lead the viewer to believe that they only market to consumers at the upper ends of the socioeconomic scale and that they have nothing for the average or slightly-above average consumer. This would not be their intention and would not be the message they were intending to transmit.

5.   Remember, in a rational appeal, the messages typically show a product's quality, economy, value, or performance. Audi could key in on any of these attributes with their message.

6.   Rogaine appeals directly to consumer emotions by showing the happiness of a couple when the man has a full head of hair. Much of the content of this site is geared toward showing the reader how much better than can feel about themselves and how much happier they can be in relationships with a full head of newly grown hair.

7.   Keep in mind that a personal communication channel may be company controlled. With this in mind, the most common personal communication channel that would likely be employed is face-to-face. Best Buy is widely regarded as offering the consumer good in-store service. They make an effort to have highly trained salespeople and to make those salespeople easily accessible to the customer.

8.   Sites such as Trip Advisor provide the consumer with independent customer information, not controlled by the company. After reading a few of their customer reviews, you may realize that fabulous vacation destination you had always wanted to visit really may not be that grand.

9.   This product, one of a growing number of smartphone products, could do well through buzz marketing. To utilize buzz marketing, Palm would want to get a number of the units into the hands of influential members of its target market. These individuals would then serve as a primary information source for others of their cohort—providing them with seemingly unbiased word-of-mouth information.

10.   There are many possible nonpersonal communication channels Palm could consider. Primary in their consideration should be the use of media (magazines, e-mail, and websites). Also, possibly Palm may want to consider sponsoring events as another method of introducing Treo to the marketplace.

Marketing ADventure Exercises

1.   Ad Interpretation Challenge: The Promotion Mix
       Ad: Advertising—Universal McCann

From a review of this particular ad, Universal McCann appears to be concentrating solely on paid media forms of advertising. If this is in fact the case, then Universal McCann may be omitting many other portions of the promotion mix from their repertoire.

2.   Ad Interpretation Challenge: Narrowcasting
       Ad: Auto—Audi

The new A2 is targeted to a younger profile than the typical Audi automobile. Because of this, Audi might consider moving away from traditional television advertising and instead use product placements in television shows, movies, or video games.

3.   Ad Interpretation Challenge: Mass-Media Communication
       Ad: Student Choice

Many products, particularly convenience goods products, make good use of a mass-media communication strategy. You may want to take a look at Snickers (Food and Beverage—Snickers) and Energizer (Electronics—Energizer) for two examples. Both of these examples are for convenience goods products that appeal to a wide range of consumers across socioeconomic categories.

4.   Ad Interpretation Challenge: Integrated Marketing Communications (IMC)
       Ad: Auto—Chrysler

This ad is promoting the idea of Chrysler as a "bright idea." Utilizing IMC, company marketers would make certain that every communication channel used would convey the exact same idea in much the same manner. Consistency of image and consistency of delivery are important concepts of IMC.

5.   Ad Interpretation Challenge: Noise
       Ad: Newspaper and TV—Cartoon Network

Ad placement could be an issue here. One of the possible causes of noise in magazine advertising is the content surrounding the advertisement. If the content is unusually appealing or interesting, there may be a tendency for the reader to overlook the ad in an effort to continue the reading of the primary article.

6.   Ad Interpretation Challenge: Receiver
       Ad: Auto—Audi A2

Cearly, Audi is targeting younger consumers with this series of A2 ads. The style of the ads, from the models used to the wording used, indicates the intended receiver to be an early-20s individual.

7.   Ad Interpretation Challenge: Buyer-Readiness Stages
       Ad: Auto—Mercedes C Class

This is an ad for a new product—the C Class Mercedes. Based on this, and on the fact that the ad is not providing the consumer with much solid information, you would have to say the ad is targeting consumers in the awareness stage of the buyer-readiness continuum.

8.   Ad Interpretation Challenge: Emotional Appeal
       Ad: Student Choice

One good choice here is the ad for Hallmark cards (General Retail—Hallmark). This is an ad that uses the emotional appeal of love and belongingness to get its point across.

9.   Ad Interpretation Challenge: Humorous Appeal
       Ad: Financial—Fame

This ad relies on humor to make its point. Although everyone would like to be in show business, it is not a realistic goal for most of us. F.A.M.E. allows us to still feel like a part of the biz through investing in entertainment-oriented stocks. This ad makes light of this unrealistic goal many of us have.

10. Ad Interpretation Challenge: Word-of-Mouth Influence
     Ad: Auto—Ford

If you were considering the purchase of a new Ford vehicle, word-of-mouth would likely play a large role in your search for information. You might turn to friends, colleagues, and family for their opinions regarding this brand.

Chapter 15

Student Exercises

1.   Yes. The purpose of their website is to present information and promote their property. These are the basic tenants of advertising.

2.   If you take the time to thoroughly review the information contained on the SuperClubs website, you will realize that the principle objective of the site is to inform, with a secondary objective being to persuade. The website takes great pains to explain the concept of "all-inclusive" and how SuperClubs competes in that arena.

3.   Just think of any mature product—a product whose growth rate has slowed substantially and is competing in a market that is experiencing low (in any) growth. Examples may include shaving creams (such as Edge shaving gel [www.edgeadvanced.com]) and breakfast cereals (such as Kellogg's Frosted Flakes [www.frostedflakes.com]).

4.   To many vacationers, a Caribbean island is a Caribbean island. They are all pretty much alike. As the marketing executive in charge of advertising Jamaica, you must make your product stand out from the pack. (Take a look at www.visitjamaica.com for some background and ideas.) You must make Jamaica seem different and unique from other sun and sand Caribbean destinations. Maybe you do this through concentrating on potential interactions between the visiting tourists and locals. Maybe you do this by concentrating on the cultural aspects of what Jamaica has to offer the visitor—such as reggae.

5.   The creative concept ("big idea") of the new Australia tourism campaign is "So where the bloody hell are you?" With this one sentence, Australia tourism has put forth an advertising message that, not only cuts through the advertising clutter, but is also memorable.

6.   Couples Resorts is selling romance. This is an island resort that is devoted to couples-only holidays. Knowing this and by reviewing their website, it is easy to see that Couples Resorts is using Mood or Image as the execution style of choice. This style builds a mood or image around the product or service. Few claims are made about the product, except through suggestion.

7.   Scion (a brand of Toyota Motors) is geared toward a younger car buying market. A review of the advantages and disadvantages of various media types will lead you to decide that to reach the Scion market, you would most likely rely on targeted magazine advertising and internet. Magazine advertising boasts high geographic and demographic selectivity, along with high credibility and prestige. Likewise, the internet delivers a demographically skewed audience—skewed towards younger clientele, just the type interested in products such as Scion.

8.   Alternative media formats have grown rapidly in recent years, as advertising clutter continues to rise. Marketers are looking for any way to allow information about their product to "pop" through the advertising clutter. Here, you are looking for alternative media formats that fit with the intended target market. It may be something as wild as placing the Scion name and logo on streets in the SoHo district of New York or as unusual as skydivers at a sporting event with parachutes embellished with the Scion logo.

9.   Through press releases and press relations, the singer provides her audience with positive information regarding her actions and activities. Further, through public affairs, attention is given to her efforts to give back to communities.

10.   A quick review of the NRA website will let you know that lobbying of government officials is a central component of their overall public relations campaign.

Marketing ADventure Exercises

1.   Ad Interpretation Challenge: Advertising
       Ad: Apparel—Levi's New Collection Diamond Jean

This ad is designed to show a side of Levi's that many consumers had not seen and were not aware of—Levi's as a fashion-forward apparel company. As such, this ad does a good job of capturing the viewer's attention and informing them of the "new" Levi's.

2.   Ad Interpretation Challenge: Reminder Advertising
       Ad: Student Choice

There are several ads here that will fulfill the requirements of this exercise. Remember, you are looking for an ad for a product in the mature stage of the product life cycle. That narrows the list down somewhat. You might consider either the ad for Snickers candy bars (Food and Beverage—Snickers) or the ad for Aim toothpaste (Cosmetics and Pharmaceuticals—Aim). Both of these ads are for products in the mature phase of the product life cycle. Also, the main purpose of these two ads is simply to keep the name of the product in the mind of the consumer.

3.   Ad Interpretation Challenge: Informative Advertising
       Ad: Auto—Hyundai Lean Burn

Informative advertising is used to tell the market about a new product or to communicate customer value. Informative advertising may also be used to assist in building a brand or company image. This ad for Hyundai does all of these things.

4.   Ad Interpretation Challenge: Persuasive Advertising
      Ad: Electronics—LG

Yes. This ad has at its heart persuasion. The ad is designed to encourage brand switching.

5.   Ad Interpretation Challenge: Advertising Budget
      Ad: Apparel—Levi's New Collection Diamond Jean

This product would be in the early stages of the product life cycle. As a result of this, it would be wise to provide a relatively large advertising budget. New products typically need large advertising budgets to build awareness and to gain consumer trial.

6.   Ad Interpretation Challenge: Breaking Through the Clutter
      Ad: Student Choice

What you are looking for is an ad that just simply stands out far and above its competition. This is certainly not an easy feat to accomplish. One example you may consider is the advertisement for Leisure Entertainment (Travel & Tourism—Leisure Entertainment). This ad does a good job of being unique. The use of a scantily clad dancer helps draw attention to an ad that otherwise may have gone unnoticed.

7.   Ad Interpretation Challenge: Madison & Vine
      Ad: General Retail—Hallmark

Hoops&yoyo were created as just another card character. However, their growing popularity caused the characters to be used as a method of communicating with the consumer. Their ads are so lively and unique they easily cut through the clutter and are noticeable. They entertain as they inform.

8.   Ad Interpretation Challenge: Execution Style
      Ad: Auto—Honda Motorcycles

Honda is making use of the lifestyle execution style in all of these motorcycle ads. The ads indicate that users of these products typically have a certain lifestyle and that lifestyle is depicted in the ads.

9.   Ad Interpretation Challenge: Advertising Media
      Ad: Autos—Audi

This ad for the Audi A2 would work best in a magazine. Magazine advertising has high geographic and demographic selectively. It has high credibility and prestige and high-quality reproduction (important for the detail in the pictures).

10.   Ad Interpretation Challenge: Advertising Media
        Ad: Newspapers and TV—MTV Masters

Look at the target market for this product. MTV appeals most heavily to younger adults and teens. By reviewing the advantages and limitations of the various forms of media, you can see that magazines, radio, and the Internet do the best jobs of segmenting the market on demographic factors.

Chapter 16

Student Exercises

1.   By spending just a minimal amount of time on the website for the Journal of Personal Selling and Sales Management you may well be surprised at the level of professionalism displayed. No longer are salespeople just someone you pull off the street to hawk items to unsuspecting consumers. Today's salesforce is highly trained and professional.

2.   Many times, salespeople in department stores are little more than "order takers." You will find them often standing behind a cash terminal waiting for you to approach them with your merchandise ready to check out. This function of a salesperson is pretty much at the lower end of the spectrum.

3.   When you go to Limited Brands website, click on Career Opportunities. Here, you will find various links directing you to Campus and Career Coaching. Both of these areas provide the reader with valuable information useful in considering a career with Limited Brands. In this way, Limited Brands is working to recruit talented individuals to its company. Recruitment is one of the early stages of sales force management.

4.   IMS provides services to clients to assist them is properly setting up and controlling a territorial sales force. Their website provides the reader with basic information on when it is appropriate to utilize a territorial sales force structure and a basic understanding of sales force deployment.

5.   You will want to look for a company with a wide product line composed of technically sophisticated or complex products. Pharmaceutical companies are one possibility, particularly if you divide their products into those taken by mouth (pills) and those injected (shots). These are two very different product lines which may require different types of expertise on the part of the sales force. For an example, take a look at the products offered by Merck Pharmaceuticals (www.merck.com).

6.   Many vendors have devoted special sales teams to interact solely with Wal-Mart. Some have gone so far as to locate offices close by the Bentonville, Arkansas home of the company in an effort to build and maintain the closest of relationships.

7.   Outside sales forces are particularly important for companies that market highly complex products. The face-to-face interaction allows for potentially greater understanding between the parties. Additionally, face-to-face interaction many times better facilitates the transfer of knowledge and understanding – important factors to consider when marketing technical and complex products. Companies such as Boeing (www.boeing.com) and AstraZeneca (www.astrazeneca.com) come readily to mind.

8.   Office Depot has sales specialists on call to answer and assist educational customers in fulfilling the needs of their organizations. A review of the Office Depot website reveals contact information for specialists dealing with different parts of the educational system so that, as a customer, you may be connected with the appropriate salesperson for your needs. In this manner, Office Depot does away with the necessity of an outside sales force.

9.   You are looking to add new retailers to your list. The first step of this process is prospecting. You would probably want to consider the merchants financial ability, volume of business, any special needs they may have, their location, and possibilities for growth.

10.   Sales promotions are everywhere. Pick up a local Sunday newspaper and take a look at the freestanding insert for Best Buy. (You can also see the local insert at www.bestbuy.com) No doubt, this advertising insert will be filled with offers on products that are only valid during the current week. This is a great example of sales promotion.

Marketing ADventure Exercises

1.   Ad Interpretation Challenge: Personal Selling
        Ad: Student Choice

There are many possibilities you can select to fulfill the requirements of this question. Two that come to mind are Mercedes (Auto—Mercedes) and Royal Bank (Financial—Royal Bank). Automobiles need personal selling due to the complex nature of the product. Similarly, Royal Bank is promoting financing for businesses. Financial services have typically needed personal selling to explain the intricacies of the product.

2.   Ad Interpretation Challenge: Salesperson
        Ad: General Retail—Target

Target stores would employ salespeople for the general purpose of order taking. Target, like most discount stores and many department stores, is primarily a self-service establishment. The role of the salesperson is reduced to nothing more than acting as a checkout person.

3.   Ad Interpretation Challenge: Territorial Sales Force Structure
        Ad: Food and Beverage—Heinz

Heinz products are typically low-cost, high-volume products. With a territorial sales force structure, each salesperson is responsible for a geographic region and sells the entire line of company products. Such a structure is best suited to low cost, convenience goods products.

4.   Ad Interpretation Challenge: Product Sales Force Structure
      Ad: Electronics—Sony

Sony offers a very wide range of products and product lines, some with seemingly little connection to others. Some of the lines Sony offers are highly specialized, technical, and diverse. With such a wide range of highly complex and diverse product lines, Sony would be wise to use a product sales force structure.

5.   Ad Interpretation Challenge: Customer Sales Force Structure
      Ad: Apparel—Levi's

Levi Strauss would likely use a customer sales force structure to differentiate between major clients (such as Sears) and typical small merchants. By structuring their sales force in such a manner, Levi Strauss is better able to provide its primary clients with the level of service necessary.

6.   Ad Interpretation Challenge: Inside Sales Force
      Ad: Financial—H&R Block

Typically, H&R Block does not go out actively soliciting business (using an outside sales force). Rather, they wait for potential business to seek them out. When prospective buyers enter and H&R Block establishment, it becomes the responsibility of the inside sales force to provide them with the information they need and (hopefully) sell them the products and services that are correct for their needs.

7.   Ad Interpretation Challenge: Team Selling
      Ad: Student Choice

You need to be looking for companies that represent potentially large and complicated accounts. These are the type of accounts that would typically need more servicing than the traditional salesperson could provide. One possible example is Chevrolet (Autos—Chevy). For example, if you were a company responsible for providing Chevrolet with computers, you would likely choose to use a team selling approach. The size and complexity of the account would be daunting for one salesperson to have total responsibility for; multiple areas of expertise would be needed.

8.   Ad Interpretation Challenge: Prospecting
      Ad: Services and B2B—EMS

In addition to all of the qualities already mentioned in the question, you would be very interested to determine the potential volume of business you could derive from EMS. This would be of vital importance later in the selling process as you were preparing to negotiate prices.

9.   Ad Interpretation Challenge: Presentation
       Ad: Autos—Mercedes Keys

This ad is presenting the product to the consumer. The ad is highlighting the long history of Mercedes. The ad is saying, in essence, this is a car company that has been around for a long time and has a long proud history.

10.   Ad Interpretation Challenge: Sales Promotion
       Ad: Food and Beverage—Snickers

Remember, a sales promotion is a short-term incentive. There are many possibilities that Snickers could employ to boost sales of their candy bar. For example, they could run an ad with a coupon for "Buy 1, Get 1." Or, they might consider a special display in the candy aisle at your local grocery store. These are only two of a multitude of possible sales promotion ideas that could be employed.

Chapter 17

Student Exercises

1.   On the Gateway site you have the option of designing and purchasing a computer system but together just for you (direct marketing) or of being directed to a merchant where you can find a pre-packaged system (traditional in-store marketing). Gateway is one of a growing number of companies that are reaching out to consumers through multiple marketing avenues.

2.   Schools collect a wealth of data about their students, all of which may be "mined" for use later on. Some of the typical types of information collected include basic demographics (age, gender, ethnicity, home town, etc.), majors and specific classes taken.

3.   Columbia House sends out thousands of pieces of direct-mail yearly. While some of these mailing are targeted to past customers of the mail-order music and DVD site, many of the mailing are "cold calls" – mailing to consumers who have shown no prior interest in the company. By targeting their mailings only to those individuals who have shown interest in the products and services they offer, Columbia House could reduce their junk mail image somewhat.

4.   After visiting a Victoria's Secret store and perusing one of their catalogs, you will notice a dramatic difference in merchandise offered. While the stores have concentrated primarily on undergarments and lingerie, the catalog offering is a more varied. In the catalog, you will see, along with those items, a comprehensive line of clothing, shoes, and accessories. It is not possible for the retail stores to carry the wide array of merchandise available in the catalogs.

5.   A review of their website gives you some details on their customer help line. This line is available to consumers who have questions about turkey preparation and storage. You call the number and can be connected to an individual with specialized knowledge on turkeys. This is a form of telephone marketing. By providing the customer with needed information through an easy to use format, you increase the likelihood of repeat purchase.

6.   After watching HSNtv live on your PC for a few minutes, you can begin to understand just how they build product excitement. Every product is individually showcased and shown in its best possible form. Knowledgeable "hosts" provide on-air excitement and details about the product. Also, all products are marked down from their "list prices," further generating buyer excitement.

7.   Delta's online kiosks allow customers to perform many of the tasks themselves that were previously assigned to airline employees. Through a kiosk, customers can now check themselves in for a flight, change seats, make new reservations, even check in luggage.

8.	T-Mobile is currently making numerous services available to their customers. A quick tour of their website shows that you can purchase (from your cell phone handset) services such as ring-tones and wallpapers or access to the internet. All of this and more is available for purchase from your cell phone handset.

9.	Amazon offers a seemingly endless variety of product categories from which to choose. One of the best comparisons of Amazon's selection is to compare it to a very large mall. However, even that form of comparison is inadequate as the product selection available through Amazon is so much vaster.

10.	Sears uses its online presence in two ways to effectively compete with the click-only companies. First, the online version of Sears allows the customer to shop at anytime of the day or night. Therefore, they are not bounded by the traditional store operating hours. Second, by allowing its customers to shop from the convenience of their home (or office or school), Sears is providing a level of customer convenience they can not match with their stores. No longer does the typical Sears customer have to travel to visit a Sears store.

Marketing ADventure Exercises

1.	Ad Interpretation Challenge: Direct Marketing
	Ad: Advertising—Studio Funk

One thing that Studio Funk could do with their radio ads is to provide the listener with a Web address or toll-free number that could be used to directly communicate with the ad sponsor. In this way, the advertiser would be directly linked to the individual consumer.

2.	Ad Interpretation Challenge: Customer Database
	Ad: Internet—El Sitio

El Sitio boasts an online dating service (among other things). Knowledge of your customer is paramount to the success of any online dating venture. As a result, El Sitio would need a comprehensive database of member information from which to draw matches.

3.	Ad Interpretation Challenge: Direct-Mail Marketing
	Ad: Auto—Audi A3

Audi would not have to do much to make this a good direct-mail piece. However, to be effective as a direct-mail piece, this ad would have to be directed to someone in particular. It is important with direct-mail marketing that the effort be directed to a particular person at a particular address to assist in overcoming the "junk mail" image of so much direct-mail marketing.

4.   Ad Interpretation Challenge: Catalog Marketing
      Ad: Travel and Tourism—Travel Price

Go to their website (www.travelprice.es) and take a look around. You will see that they offer a multitude of travel and tourism options. The potential traveler only has to enter basic information, such as destination, to be presented with a wide range of options from their virtual catalog.

5.   Ad Interpretation Challenge: Telephone Marketing
      Ad: Travel and Tourism—Imperial Hotel

Yes. If you will look at the ads, you will realize the basic purpose of them is to generate telephone calls, which can then be turned into reservations. This is a great example of using a print advertisement to generate business through the telephone.

6.   Ad Interpretation Challenge: Direct-Response Television Marketing
      Ad: Newspaper and TV—MTV

Anytime that MTV asks viewers to text or call in to the network they are practicing direct-response television marketing.

7.   Ad Interpretation Challenge: Kiosk Marketing
      Ad: Travel and Tourism—American Airlines

The primary manner in which American Airlines is currently using kiosks is in allowing customers to check in for flights and check baggage. American also uses kiosks to allow customers to purchase tickets for future flights and change seating assignments.

8.   Ad Interpretation Challenge: Mobile Phone Marketing
      Ad: Electronics—Axiom

There are several services Axiom could make available to its customers by way of mobile phone marketing. Axiom could use mobile phone marketing to make available ring tones to its customers. Also, Axiom could sell wallpapers and Internet services.

9.   Ad Interpretation Challenge: Marketing Website
      Ad: Electronics—Polaroid

Yes this is a marketing website. The Polaroid site provides detailed information about Polaroid products. However, the site does more than just provide the consumer with information. Interested consumers have the opportunity to buy directly from the company, via their website, making this a marketing website.

10.   Ad Interpretation Challenge: Spam
       Ad: Travel and Transportation—Aeromexico

The easiest thing Aeromexico can do so as to not be viewed as "spamming" the consumer is simply to ask for permission to e-mail marketing information. By doing this, Aeromexico will have alerted its customers to its intention and will have received their permission to deliver marketing information to their e-mailbox.

Chapter 18

Student Exercises

1.   The "new" AT&T, formed by a merging of Cingular and BellSouth, enjoy advantages its competitors currently do not have. Name recognition is the biggest competitive advantage AT&T holds over its competition. The AT&T name has been an American icon for about a century. It boasts name recognition among the highest of any brand name in the country.

2.   Lenovo is a manufacturer of desktop and laptop computers geared primarily for business and industry. Their primary competitors are Dell (www.dell.com), Hewlett-Packard (www.hp.com), and Gateway (www.gateway.com).

3.   Palm belongs to a strategic group that produces handheld organizers and communications devices. Other members of the group include Blackberry (www.blackberry.com) and Nokia (www.nokia.com), and Dell (www.dell.com).

4.   You always want to look to the industry leader to benchmark. In this industry, Adobe Systems is the market leader for photo editing software. Other industry competitors include Apple (www.apple.com) and Microsoft (www.microsoft.com).

5.   One example that may come to mind is Southwest Airlines. Long an industry outsider, Southwest refuses to play by some of the basic industry rules, such as allowing its flights to be listed on the reservation systems of other airlines or third-party sellers such as Expedia (www.expedia.com).

6.   Apple has always been viewed as somewhat of a quirky company, different and unique from its competition. Apple perpetuates this image and earned a cult-like following among technophiles. Additionally, Apple has made a name by introducing products that are incredibly stylish as well as functional.

7.   Cathay Pacific Airways is one such company. You can view their website at www.cathaypacific.com. Cathay Pacific has chosen a focus strategy and concentrates their efforts on the top tier of business travelers. This segment of the market values comfort and convenience over cost.

8.   Wyndham Hotels and Resorts has created a program known as Wyndham ByRequest. Members of this program provide the company with some basic customer information. The company is then in a position to provide to that customer a level of service significantly above the average in the industry. Such high-level service keeps the well-paying customer coming back again and again.

9.   The market leaders in this industry are Kellogg's and Post. Quaker Oats Company, while no doubt a powerful competitor, is seldom seen to rock the boat in this slow growing industry. Quaker Oats Company would be considered a market follower.

10. A market nicher only goes after a small subset of the overall market. When you examine the companies that are competing in the breakfast cereal market, Healthy Choice (makers of Healthy Choice Apple & Almond Crunch Mueslix) stands out. This is a company that is only competing for breakfast customers who are health-conscious and willing to pay a premium for a healthy alternative breakfast cereal.

Marketing ADventure Exercises

1. Ad Interpretation Challenge: Competitive Advantage
    Ad: Financial—MBNA

MBNA has an affinity card deal with Clemson University. Alumni and diehard fans of Clemson may be drawn to this credit card. The card allows them to show school spirit, while at the same time actually benefiting the school. For every purchase made on the card, a percentage of the purchase is rebated to the university.

2. Ad Interpretation Challenge: Identifying Competitors
    Ad: Electronics—LG

LG (the world's largest manufacturer of flat panel televisions) does not operate without some major strong competitors. Principal among those competitors is Sony (www.sony.com) and Sharp (www.sharpusa.com), two of the largest marketers of flat panel televisions.

3. Ad Interpretation Challenge: Strategic Groups
    Ad: Auto—Porsche

Porsche is an automobile manufacturer. However, more specifically, Porsche is the manufacturer of high-performance, high-price luxury automobiles. This strategic group is made up of similar manufacturers. This could possibly include BMW (www.bmwusa.com) and Mercedes (www.mbusa.com).

4. Ad Interpretation Challenge: Benchmarking
    Ad: Cosmetics and Pharmaceuticals—Mentadent

You would want to benchmark against the largest players in the field, namely Crest (http://crest.com) and Colgate (www.colgate.com). You would want to closely examine their products and marketing strategies to see what they do best and how you might more effectively compete.

5. Ad Interpretation Challenge: Close Competitors
    Ad: Financial—Ameritrade

Ameritrade (www.tdameritrade.com) is an online stock trading company. Close competitors would be other online trading companies, such as ETrade Financial (https://us.etrade.com). Companies such as this are most similar to Ameritrade. Traditional trading companies, such as Merrill Lynch (Financial—Merrill Lynch), while certainly competitors, are not as close.

6.   Ad Interpretation Challenge: Entrepreneurial Marketing Strategy
        Ad: Student Choice

One example that may stand out is for the University of Toronto (Services and B2B—University of Toronto). These ads are unique. They stand out in a crowded competitive landscape. They are edgy and risk takers.

7.   Ad Interpretation Challenge: Differentiation
        Ad: Services and B2B—24 Hour Fitness

The simplest answer to this question is that 24 Hour Fitness differentiates itself through it hours of operation. The company is open 24 hours a day, making itself very convenient to its customers.

8.   Ad Interpretation Challenge: Focus
        Ad: Apparel—Polartec

Polartec (http://polartec.com) has made the conscious decision to concentrate their efforts on a small segment of the overall clothing market. Polartec focuses on what they term "performance fabrics."

9.   Ad Interpretation Challenge: Product Leadership
        Ad: Student Choice

One possible answer to this exercise is Motorola (Electronics—Motorola). Motorola is a leader in cell phone production. Motorola is constantly innovating, changing the form, functions, and features of its cell phones. Its goal is to stay ahead of the competition and render its current phones obsolete.

10.   Ad Interpretation Challenge: Market Leader Strategies
        Ad: General Retail—Hallmark

Hallmark must maintain a constant watch on its competitors. Additionally, they must also watch for subtle changes or trends in the marketplace. Small trends, if not realized and capitalized on quickly, can become big trends that a competitor controls. Finally, Hallmark must work constantly to remain relevant in today's market. They cannot afford to be viewed as old fashioned or out of touch.

Chapter 19

Student Exercises

1.   Yes. Saab is a global company. The company (a wholly owned unit of General Motors) manufactures automobiles for the global community. By examining their global home page, you can see that they have a presence in many countries. They offer the same product in every country in which they operate, with only minimal variation to meet local requirement.

2.   By reading of the most recent developments in the latest round of GATT negotiations, the one thing that should stand out most vividly to you is the difficulty and complexity of these negotiations. All members have their own special interests to think about; yet, there does seem to be an overall desire to accomplish something worthwhile. Only time will tell.

3.   The European Union has achieved more in a shorter period of time than most outsiders thought to be possible. The elimination of tariffs and other barriers to trade has opened their markets, not only to each other, but to those outside of the Union to a degree previously unobtainable. By reviewing the information on foreign students studying in the EU, you will see that a multitude of study options exist. You should consider spending a semester abroad!

4.   Under the NAFTA treaty, all non-tariff barriers to agricultural trade between the United States and Mexico were eliminated. Because of this, it should be much more economical for you to export to Mexico.

5.   Even the poorest of countries need basic goods and services. Economies such as these may offer limited markets for clean drinking water and basic agricultural assistance.

6.   In Mexico, the top 10 percent of the population is responsible for about 33 percent of the income. Also, about 60 percent of the population can be classified as belonging to the lowest socioeconomic groups. When looking at the U.S., you will notice that the income is more evenly distributed throughout society, with the top 10 percent of the population responsible for 17 percent of the income. This more evenly distributed income would lead you to believe that the overall market in the U.S. is considerably larger as a wider range of the population has access to monetary resources.

7.   Companies typically begin with indirect exporting. Indirect exporting is working through independent international marketing intermediaries. Indirect exporting involves less investment because the firm does not require an overseas marketing organization or network. It involves less risk.

8.   While licensing is the least risky method of entering a foreign market, it is not without risk. The company has less control over the licensee than it would over its own

302

operations. Also, if the licensee is very successful, the firm has given up these profits, and if and when the contract ends, it may find it has created a competitor.

9.   You are looking for a company that basically offers the same products and uses the same marketing strategy everywhere it operates, with only minimal variation. Take a look again at Saab automobiles (www.saab.com) as one example.

10.   The U.K. site contains a bit more partial nudity than is typically acceptable, by U.S. standards. Vaseline would want to tone this down a bit before launching this site in the U.S.

Marketing ADventure Exercises

1.   Ad Interpretation Challenge: Global Firm
         Ad: Auto—Audi

Yes, Audi is a true global firm. Audi manufactures a line of automobiles that are available in many countries throughout the world. Audi makes these products globally available; however, product adaptation does occur due to local custom, preference, or regulation.

2.   Ad Interpretation Challenge: Tariffs
         Ad: Auto—Audi

By placing a tariff—or tax—on the importation of these cars, the U.S. government is effectively raising the price of these products to consumers. Consumers will end up spending more to purchase one of these products, or will have to turn to another product of less expense. Either way, the consumer loses.

3.   Ad Interpretation Challenge: GATT
         Ad: Student Choice

Almost anything you come up with here would work. GATT has worked to reduce tariffs and other barriers to a vast variety of international goods and services—manufactured goods, agricultural goods, intellectual property, and others.

4.   Ad Interpretation Challenge: European Union
         Ad: Auto—Fiat

One of the primary barriers reduced or eliminated by the EU has been on the migration of labor forces. If Fiat was having difficulty with labor shortages in Italy, being a member of the EU makes it much simpler to recruit labor from other EU countries with minimal restrictions.

5.   Ad Interpretation Challenge: FTAA
       Ad: Food and Beverage—Brazilian Fruit

Currently, Brazil is not a member of an economic community with the United States. By both countries belonging to one community whose goal it is to positively impact trade, possible tariffs on the importation of Brazilian fruit would be reduced or eliminated.

6.   Ad Interpretation Challenge: Raw Material Exporting Economies
       Ad: Auto—Jaguar

If a raw material exporting economy has many foreigners or a wealthy upper class, there is a market for luxury items. Saudi Arabia is one such example.

7.   Ad Interpretation Challenge: Industrializing Economies
       Ad: Student Choice

Conspicuous products are in great demand in these emerging classes, as they "announce" to others that their owners have "made it." Such products as Mercedes (Autos—Mercedes) and expensive, showy clothing, such as Levi's New Collection Diamond Jeans (Apparel—Levi's) are example of products that would be successful.

8.   Ad Interpretation Challenge: Cultural Environment
       Ad: Apparel—Levi's New Collection Diamond Jeans

Muslim societies are very conservative, when it comes to the role of women and their dress. An advertisement such as this may be considered unacceptable due to the amount of uncovered female body shown. Companies must be aware and respond accordingly to such cultural variations.

9.   Ad Interpretation Challenge: "Americanizing" the World
       Ad: Student Choice

One product that you may consider here is Levi's. Levi's are viewed in many parts of the world as a "true American product." It probably would not take too much for them to become a true iconic symbol. Also, take a look at the ads for Cadillac (Auto-Cadillac) and MTV (Newspapers & TV-MTV). These ads represent two more products that have such potential.

10.   Ad Interpretation Challenge: Adapted Marketing Mix
       Ad: Apparel—Levi's New Collection Diamond Jeans

The easiest thing you can do is to vary the advertising part of the marketing mix. Alter the ads to place emphasis on the jeans, not on the female form.

Chapter 20

Student Exercises

1.   Advertising does add to the product cost, but it also provides information to the consumer. Branded products may cost more. Typically, unbranded or store brands of products are available at less cost to the consumer. However, branding gives buyers assurance of consistent quality. Many consumers want and are willing to pay more for branded products that also provide psychological benefits – they may make them feel special in some way.

2.   Yes. BCBG (like much of the fashion industry) is engaging in planned obsolescence. However, consumers like style changes. They get tired of the old look and want a new look in fashion. No one has to buy the new look, and if not too many people like it, it will fail (consider ponchos from a couple of fashion seasons back).

3.   By looking up the Better Business Bureau report on some of your favorite merchants you are able to get a better understanding of these businesses and how they treat their customers. Hopefully, you will not be faced with any unwelcome surprises!

4.   The primary benefit from Green Globe certification (or that of a number of other environmental certification programs) is through recognition. As travelers become more educated, their concern form the environment continues to rise. Green Globe certification indicates to these travelers that the property they are considering also shares this concern for the environment.

5.   According to Patagonia's mission statement, they are committed to using business to inspire solutions to the growing environmental crisis. The more you read about the company, the more you realize Patagonia easily fits into all parts of the Environmental Sustainability Grid.

6.   You are looking for a company that has made a practice of staying on the cutting edge of its industry and that has consistently turned that cutting edge position into new innovative products and product improvements. One such company you might take a look at is Apple (www.apple.com).

7.   Starbucks takes very seriously its role as a good corporate citizen. You will find evidence of Starbucks view of social responsibility in all of their stores and on their website. Starbucks wants its customers to know where they stand. They believe it is not only the right thing to do, but good for business.

8.   A societal marketing-oriented company wants to design products that are both pleasing AND beneficial to the consumer. One example of such a company is Herman Miller (www.hermanmiller.com). Herman Miller is a company long dedicated to the creation of office furniture that is ascetically pleasing AND ergonomically sound.

9.   Based strictly on the definitions given, you could easily place alcohol into this category; however, as with many other items, you can not always go simply by the strictest of definitions. In this instance, it become somewhat of a personal decision.

10.   This is an interesting question. While there is no doubt that casinos (and gaming in general) generate millions of dollars in tax revenue, some have questions about the social impacts. While the majority of casino patrons may view an evening out at a casino as just that, an entertaining evening out, there is a small percentage that ends up with a gaming addiction. Thus, whether the Hard Rock Casinos are a desirable product or not, tends to become somewhat of a personal assessment.

Marketing ADventure Exercises

1.   Ad Interpretation Challenge: Planned Obsolescence
        Ad: Apparel—Levi's New Collection Diamond Jeans

Levi's Diamond Jeans are a fashion forward product, designed to be on the edge of the fashion front. Such products typically do not stay at the forefront of fashion for long, thus encouraging their owners to move on to the next fashion item.

2.   Ad Interpretation Challenge: "Shop Till You Drop"
        Ad: Apparel—Johnsons

This ad is promoting a 50 percent off sale. Such sales are designed to draw consumers in with special pricing enticements to encourage them to shop and spend more than they would under normal circumstances.

3.   Ad Interpretation Challenge: "Congestion Toll"
        Ad: Auto—Porsche

Congestion tolls are tolls levied on drivers in some heavily congested areas in an effort to encourage them to ditch the car and utilize public transportation. Likewise, HOV (high-occupancy vehicle) and HOT (high-occupancy toll) lanes are being instituted in some areas to encourage greater carpooling.

4.   Ad Interpretation Challenge: Consumerism
        Ad: Food and Beverage—McDonald's

McDonald's (along with other fast-food restaurants) has already begun to take some flake for the food they serve to millions of customers a day. Many critics are saying that fast-food restaurants are partly to blame for America's overweight problem. Many say the foods they serve contain too much fat and too many calories to be healthy.

5.   Ad Interpretation Challenge: Environmental Sustainability
       Ad: Apparel—Timberland

Timberland is a big believer in supporting environmental sustainability efforts. For specific examples, take a look at their annual corporate social responsibility report.

6.   Ad Interpretation Challenge: Consumer-Oriented Marketing
       Ad: Student Choice

This is the type marketing that all good marketing companies want to practice. In essence, they are practicing the marketing concept. Only by viewing the world through their consumers' eyes can a company build long and lasting customer relationships. Just about any of the companies whose ads appear here would fit into this category.

7.   Ad Interpretation Challenge: Innovative Marketing
       Ad: Apparel—Polartec

Yes. Polartec could easily be viewed as a company that practices innovative marketing. A review of its history (found on its website) details the continuous innovations that have helped to make this company one of the most respected in the outdoor clothing market.

8.   Ad Interpretation Challenge: Sense-of-Mission Marketing
       Ad: Travel and Tourism—Wild Drift

Wild Drift adventures believe in immersing its clients in the environment for the dual purposes of excitement and education. By educating its cliental in a manner that is also stimulating and invigorating, the company is not only making money but also instilling a long-term appreciation for the environment in their guests.

9.   Ad Interpretation Challenge: Pleasing Products
       Ad: Student Choice

Remember that pleasing products are products that consumers like; however, they may not actually be good for them in the long run. Two possible solutions to this exercise are Snickers (Food and Beverage—Snickers) and Burger King (Food and Beverage—Burger King). Both of these ads are promoting products that have high fat content and calorie counts. But they are both tasty.

10.   Ad Interpretation Challenge: Marketing Ethics
       Ad: Auto—Jeep

Jeep should adhere to its corporate marketing ethics policies. This takes away the ambiguity that may exist in different cultural settings. Corporate marketing ethics policies are established for just this type of situation. Because different cultures have different ethical standards, it is important that U.S.–based companies have and adhere to their own established corporate ethics policies.